Video Games and Social Competence

"Our focus on video games has often been on moral issues, such as gaming and addiction. To date we know little about how games interact with players' social space. Dr. Kowert's book is an important investigation of how gaming impacts the socialization of players. This seminal work provides critical insights into this new medium and how it influences the way we interact on-line and in real-life."

—*Christopher J. Ferguson, Stetson University, USA*

Despite their popularity, online video games have been met with suspicion by the popular media and academic community. In particular, there is a growing concern that online video game play may be associated with deficits in social functioning. Due to a lack of empirical consistency, the debate surrounding the potential impact of online video game play on a user's sociability remains an active one. This book contributes to this debate by exploring the potential impact of online video game involvement on social competence outcomes, theoretically and empirically. Through empirical research, Kowert examines the relationships between online video game involvement, social goals, and social skills and discusses the underlying mechanisms of these effects.

Rachel Kowert is an associate researcher at the University of Münster. She has published numerous articles and book chapters on the social impact of online gaming and serves on the board of DiGRA (Digital Games Research Association) and the Game Studies SIG of the International Communication Association (ICA).

Routledge Advances in Game Studies

1 Video Games and Social Competence
Rachel Kowert

Video Games and Social Competence

Rachel Kowert

Routledge
Taylor & Francis Group

LONDON AND NEW YORK

First published 2015 by Routledge

2 Park Square, Milton Park, Abingdon, Oxfordshire OX14 4RN
711 Third Avenue, New York, NY 10017

Routledge is an imprint of the Taylor & Francis Group,
an informa business

First issued in paperback 2018

Library of Congress Cataloging-in-Publication Data

Kowert, Rachel.
  Video games and social competence / Rachel Kowert.
    pages cm — (Routledge advances in game studies ; 1)
  Includes bibliographical references and index.
  1. Video games—Social aspects.   2. Video games—Psychological aspects.
3. Social psychology.   4. Social skills.   I. Title.
  GV1469.17.S63K68 2014
  794.8—dc23
  2014030110

ISBN: 978-1-138-80426-5 (hbk)
ISBN: 978-1-138-54897-8 (pbk)

Typeset in Sabon
by Apex CoVantage, LLC

Contents

Tables

Figures

Acknowledgments

Selected content from chapter 5 is reprinted from *Computers in Human Behavior*, Volume 29 (Issue 4), R. Kowert and J. A. Oldmeadow, (A)Social reputation: Exploring the relationship between online video game involvement and social competence, pp. 1872–1878. Copyright 2013, with permission from Elsevier.

Table 6.7 in chapter 6 is reprinted from *Computer in Human Behavior*, R. Kowert and J. A. Oldmeadow, Playing for social comfort: Online video game play as a social accommodator for the insecurely attached, online ahead of print. Copyright 2014, with permission from Elsevier.

There are many individuals who deserve acknowledgment for their support throughout the process of constructing this monograph. Firstly, I would like to thank my PhD supervisor from the University of York, Julian A. Oldmeadow, for his willingness to delve into unfamiliar territory in support of my research interests. I would also like to thank Jane Clarbour, for her support, guidance, and enthusiasm throughout my PhD journey. Thank you for all of the time, energy, and resources you so willingly devoted to my personal development as a researcher.

There are also many friends and colleagues, in particular my fellow games scholars, whose welcoming spirit and constant encouragement helped guide me through the writing process. I would like to especially thank Richard Bartle, Jon Fanning, Mark Griffiths, James D. Ivory, Esther MacCallum-Stewart, Thorsten Quandt, and Sally Quinn. An extra special thanks to Gina Humphries and Katya Krieger-Redwood for their unyielding encouragement and support.

I would also like to thank my virtual family, the members of *Outlandish Fortune* and *Fruit of Elune*, for their unparalleled generosity and innumerable nights of dragon slaying. A special thanks to my dear Avi, Greg Lewis, whose support did not go unnoticed. Khronakai Khristor!

My greatest gratitude goes to my family. I must thank my parents, Valerie and John, and my brother, Joshua. None of this would have been possible without your support.

And, last but not least, I would like to thank my husband, Rex McConnell. Thank you for the late night pep talks and the early morning coffees. My sanity would not be possible without you.

1 Rising Social Concerns of Online Gaming

1.1 THE PROBLEM AREA

While video game play was once considered a niche activity, today, it is a global, multibillion-dollar, worldwide enterprise (Bacon, 2011; Cuçuel, 2011; Hinkle, 2011; Johns, 2005). From a reported $200 million dollar industry in 1978 (Aoyama & Izushi, 2003), to a value of $74 billion in 2011 (Hinkle, 2011), the video game industry will likely remain the fastest growing current form of media, with projected sales figures expected to rise to $82 billion by 2015 (Bacon, 2011). This market has experienced incredible growth, particularly in comparison to other media markets (Zimmerman, 2002). By 2008, the global video game industry had overtaken the combined worldwide music and movie industry in sales (Global Industry Analysts, Inc. 2009). This new form of media is also highly engaging, as representative data of American players acquired by the Pew Internet and American Life Project survey reports that 21% of all users engage in video game play daily (Lenhart, Jones, & Macgill, 2008).

The proliferation of affordable and accessible Internet has widened this medium's scope by incorporating 'real-time' social services within a shared interactive environment, providing shared gaming spaces in which millions of individuals across the globe regularly participate. This new, interactive medium is being consumed at a staggering rate. In 2008, there were a reported 1.5 billion unique registered accounts of online games worldwide (TMachine. org, 2008). This market continues to grow; in the U.S. alone, the online gaming community is reportedly growing at 10 times the rate of the total U.S. Internet population (Alvarez, 2009). By the end of 2013, over 700 million people, 44% of the world's population, were reportedly engaging in online game play (Spil Games, 2013). While the exact number of hours dedicated to online game play has not been assessed among representative samples (such as in the Pew Internet and American Life Project survey), opportunity samples of dedicated game players have found that users often devote 10 to 20 hours a week to online game play (Griffiths, 2010; Lemmens, Valkenburg, & Peter, 2011).

Due to its popularity and intensity of play, researchers have grown concerned as to whether or not engagement within online video gaming environments is physically, socially, and psychologically healthy. These concerns have reinvigorated old debates, such as video games' potential to incite violence and aggression, as well as spawned new concerns about the potential negative influences of online games on users' sociability. In particular, there is a growing concern that online video game (OVG) play may be associated with deficits in social functioning, such as hindering one's ability to form and maintain reciprocal offline relationships (Cole & Griffiths, 2007; Shen & Williams, 2010) or to develop effective social and emotional skills (Chiu, Lee, & Huang, 2004; Kim, Namkoong, Ku, & Kim, 2008; Peters & Malesky, 2008; Shen & Williams, 2010). While the validity of these claims remains tenuous (the rise of online gaming and its corresponding concerns is discussed in more detail in the following section), the theoretical ways in which OVG play may be associated with poorer social outcomes for players has been widely discussed.

There are two ways in which OVG play may be associated with social (in)competence. The first is that engaging in OVG play offsets social development because players are spending less time than non-players socially interacting in offline contexts. This is referred to as the social displacement hypothesis, which assumes that online and offline social interactions are zero-sum. That is, that there is a substantial trade-off between online and offline friendships, relationships, and interactions and that offline interactions are more 'socially valuable' than online ones in terms of promoting the development and maintenance of social skills (Cole & Griffiths, 2007; Hussain & Griffiths, 2009; Lo, Wang, & Fang, 2005; Morahan-Martin & Schumacher, 2003; Shen & Williams, 2010). From this perspective, online gaming does not directly cause social deficits, but rather, social deficits are an indirect consequence of play caused by the displacement of offline social interaction. In this sense, the potential negative social impact of OVG play would be no different than the effects of other activities that 'displace' offline interactions, such as online gambling or offline gaming. However, there is a sub-type of the displacement hypothesis that argues gaming does directly affect social competence by influencing cognitive development. For example, Sigman (2009) has hypothesized that a lack of 'real' social networking (i.e., socialization that involves face-to-face interaction) may alter the way genes work and negatively influence mental performance. However, the research in this area remains largely exploratory.

The other way OVG play may be associated with social competence is if people with lower levels of social resources (e.g., poor social skills, greater social anxiety, lower quality or quantity of offline friendship circles, etc.) are drawn to this activity. This is referred to as the social compensation hypothesis. From this perceptive, online gaming spaces hold particular qualities (e.g., visual anonymity, few non-verbal cues, etc.) that are attractive to individuals who are lacking in social competence or social opportunity. Again, there is no sense in which playing games is directly detrimental to social competence. While displacement effects could exacerbate the pre-existing disposition (e.g., lead to increased rates of loneliness, depression, and social anxiety), a certain degree of social inadequacy is believed to pre-exist among those who are motivated to engage within online gaming spaces (a more detailed discussion of the theoretical constructs underpinning the social displacement and compensation hypotheses is presented in chapter 3).

However, it has also been suggested that OVG play may not contribute to poorer social outcomes, but rather increase social competence through training social skills, increasing social self-esteem, and developing online friendships. For example, it has been suggested that online gaming spaces may be ideal for cognitive-social learning (Bandura, 1962, 1977, 1986), a framework that is often employed in social-skill training programs (Evers-Pasquale & Sherman, 1975; Gresham & Nagel, 1980; Keller & Carlson, 1974; Ladd & Mize, 1983), as they can provide a venue for social observation, rehearsal, and feedback. Steinkuehler and Williams (2006) have also postulated that the social immersion provided by online games could even contribute to an increase in one's overall sociability by expanding and diversifying one's world views (the potential role of social learning through OVG play is discussed in more detail in section 3.2.4.1).

While the social displacement and compensation hypotheses differ in the proposed origin of social differences among the online game playing community, they both contend that social differences do exist and either originate from or are exacerbated by an increase in time spent within online gaming environments. However, empirical evidence in support of these hypotheses has been mixed. For example, Griffiths (2010) found that high-frequency game players achieved poorer outcomes than low-frequency players on the Social Situations Questionnaire (SSQ) (Bryant & Trower, 1974), indicating that more frequent players exhibit greater social inadequacies. Framed in the context of the social displacement hypothesis, these results are presented as evidence that displacement effects due to OVG play exist and are negatively influencing players' social skills. This is in contrast to a 2009 investigation by Barnett and colleagues, which concluded that video game players exhibit no social skill differences as compared to non-players as both groups chose assertive, rather than aggressive, responses when administered the Novaco Provocation Inventory (Novaco, 1994), indicating socially competent behavior. Empirical support for social compensation processes has been more straightforward, as researchers have consistently found that more involved OVG players display higher rates of the symptoms associated with loneliness, depression, and social anxiety (Caplan, Williams, & Yee, 2009; Kim et al., 2008; Lemmens et al., 2011; Lo et al., 2005; Shen & Williams, 2010; Williams, Yee, & Caplan, 2008). However, the majority of this work has focused on the relationships between psychosocial outcomes and problematic video game playing and/or video game addiction (Caplan et al., 2009; Kim et al., 2008; Lemmens et al., 2011). As problematic/addicted play is associated with a range of other psychosocial components (e.g., tolerance, mood modification, conflict and problems, etc.), it is difficult to determine if the relationships uncovered within this research are related to OVG play specifically or would be evident among media-addicted populations regardless of the nature of the activity. Additionally, a lack of longitudinal research in this area has made it difficult to determine if these particular psychosocial dispositions are a cause (i.e., compensation motivation) or consequence (i.e., displacement effect) of play (the empirical links between social displacement and compensation processes and video game involvement are overviewed in more detail in chapter 3).

The variability of findings in support of, or disputing, the underlying role of social displacement and compensation processes in the relationship between OVG involvement and social outcomes is partially attributable to inconsistencies in research design (i.e., employed outcome measures, sample selection and assessment focus, and assessment strategy) and the conceptualization of the two primary variables of interest: video game involvement and social competence. For example, while play frequency has been the most commonly employed characteristic to differentiate between varying levels of video game involvement (M. Barnett et al., 1997; Colwell & Kato, 2003; Griffiths, 2010; Kolo & Baur, 2004; Lo et al., 2005; Senlow, 1984; Shen & Williams, 2010; Smyth, 2007), there has been a lack of standardization within these categorizations. For example, Barnett et al. (1997) identified frequent video game players as those who played at least 1 hour per week of video games, Kolo and Baur (2004) identified frequent video game players as those who played between 5 and 15 hours a week, and Griffiths's (2010) criteria for a frequent player was more than 7 hours a week of video game play. In lieu of play frequency categories, other researchers have conceptualized play frequency on a spectrum (Colwell & Kato, 2003; Lo et al., 2005; Shen & Williams, 2010). Similar inconsistencies have been evident in the conceptualization of social competence. While some researchers have taken a relationship approach and assessed variability in the size and quality of players' social circles (Cole & Griffiths, 2007; Hussain & Griffiths, 2009; Kim et al., 2008; Shen & Williams, 2010; Smyth, 2007; Williams, 2006), others have adopted a more psychosocial approach by examining the relationships between OVG play and social anxiety (Lo et al., 2005), loneliness (Caplan et al., 2009; Lemmens et al., 2011; Morahan-Martin & Schumacher, 2003; Shen & Williams, 2010; Visser, Antheunis, & Schouten, 2013), and depression (Caplan et al., 2009; Williams et al., 2008). Additionally, some researchers have taken a social skill approach to conceptualizing social competence (J. Barnett, Coulson, & Foreman, 2009; Chiu et al., 2004; Griffiths, 2010; Lemmens et al., 2011; Liu & Peng, 2009). While this variability is not inherently problematic, as social competence is a broad concept that can, and does, incorporate a wide variety of variables (Rose-Kransor, 1997), the inconsistency in quantifying this variable has made it difficult to establish the exact nature of the relationship between social outcomes and OVG involvement (see chapter 3, section 3.3 for a more detailed discussion of these limitations).

Due to a lack of empirical consistency, the debate as to whether or not OVG play has detrimental effects (either direct or indirect) on users' social resources remains an active one. The aim of this monograph is to contribute to this debate by providing further evidence for the effects of OVG involvement on social competence by addressing the following research questions:

RQ1: Are there significant associations between video game involvement and social competence?

RQ2: If so, are these relationships more attributable to social displacement or social compensation phenomena?

1.2   RISING CONCERNS OF ONLINE GAMING

Since the advent of the telegraph, popular media has approached new forms of technology with suspicion (Williams, 2005). Video games are no exception, as controversial debates about them have been evident since their introduction in the 1970s (Williams, 2005). However, OVGs have incited a new range of concerns, as parents and researchers alike have expressed their apprehension over the potential negative consequences of prolonged use of online games.

This section will outline the rising concerns surrounding online video games. It will begin with an evaluation of the cultural perceptions of online gamers, examining the comical, and more serious, depictions of them in Western popular culture and news media. The validity of these generalizations will be also evaluated through a comparison with demographic data. Following this, an overview of the rising academic interest in online video gaming and online gamers will be presented, with a focus on the potential negative influence of OVGs on a user's social competence.

1.2.1   Social Perceptions of Online Gamers

For numerous reasons, perhaps in part because of its rapid growth, online gaming is an activity that has become highly stereotyped. That is, it is an activity that has come to be associated in popular culture with a highly specific, caricatured, and often negative image (Kowert, Griffiths, & Oldmeadow, 2012; Kowert & Oldmeadow, 2012; Williams et al., 2008). The 'stereotypical online gamer' has been portrayed in numerous television shows, news reports, current affairs programs, and other sources of popular culture. As Williams et al. (2008) states, "[online] game players are stereotypically male and young, pale from too much time spent indoors and socially inept. As a new generation of isolated and lonely 'couch potatoes,' young male game players are far from aspirational figures" (p. 995).

Within popular culture, this 'stereotype' has become widely disseminated, through print media, television, as well as Web-based programs. A classic example comes from the popular U.S. animated series *South Park*. In an episode devoted to the massively multiplayer online role-playing game (MMORPG) *World of Warcraft*, the stereotypical gamer was portrayed as overweight, lazy, isolated, and aggressive. Additionally, the four main characters of the series became increasingly overweight and lazy and developed acne as their immersion into the game deepened (Parker & Stone, 2006). In an episode of the U.S. television series *The Big Bang Theory*, a primary character in the series also conforms to stereotypic expectations as she becomes obsessive, reclusive, and unkempt upon playing a fantasy-based online game (Lorre, Molaro, & Kaplan, 2008).

The highly successful Web series *The Guild* took a more comical approach with a plot that followed a group of online gamers who decided to meet each other in the offline world after many months of regular online interaction. In the opening scene of the first episode, the main character was told by her therapist that her online friends did not constitute a genuine support system and that immersion in an imaginary social environment was stunting her personal growth. Within the first few minutes of this episode, themes of obsession, addiction, reclusiveness, and loneliness arose (Day & Morgan, 2007).

The stereotypical portrayal of an online gamer has also taken forms that are more serious. In an episode of *Law and Order: SVU*, a popular U.S. television series, two individuals are arrested and accused of neglecting their child due to their immersion in an online gaming world (Truly, 2010). In addition to the depiction of the more physical aspects of the stereotype (both suspects are overweight and have poor personal hygiene), the obsessive and addictive qualities of online gaming are implicated in a much more serious context of child neglect.

The negative characterization of online gamers has been further sensationalized by news reports focusing on the potential consequences of this activity, as reflected in the following headlines:

- "Addicted: Suicide over *EverQuest*" (Kohn, 2002)
- "Chinese man drops dead after 3-day gaming binge" (Associated Press, 2007)
- "Chinese gamer sentenced to life" (BBC News, 2005)

Popular news media often highlight the problematic and addictive nature of OVGs, and a variety of Internet websites, magazine articles, and news articles dispense advice for individuals with problematic playing behaviors (it is worth noting that problematic video game behavior has not been officially designated as an addiction by the American Medical Association but is listed in the appendix of the *DSM-V* as a topic for further research).

1.2.1.1   Empirical Evaluations

Current empirical evidence confirms that online gamers are perceived as incompetent and undesirable, with a stereotype centering on themes of unpopularity, unattractiveness, idleness, and social incompetence (Kowert et al., 2012). Online gamers are perceived as being competitive, addicted loners who are obsessive, socially inept, isolated, immature, and young. The image of an individual playing alone and for long periods of time seems to be at the heart of this representation, as multiple traits refer to the idea of being engrossed in the activity (addicted, obsessive), and doing so without the company of others (loner, isolated). The addition of the quality of social ineptness hints at the inability of online gamers to interact with others even if desired (Kowert et al., 2012). These representations are also largely limited to online players, as individuals who engage in offline gaming environments are perceived quite differently. In a recent study investigating the stereotypical perceptions of various gaming groups (e.g., online, arcade, MMORPG, console), console gamers were perceived as skillful and fun loving, emerging with a significantly less negative stereotypical profile than online gamers and their subgroups (e.g., MMORPG gamers) (Kowert & Oldmeadow, 2012).

1.2.1.2   Social Perceptions: Summary

Taken together, these media portrayals, news reports, and Internet forums present a consistent and negative image of online gaming and its participants. Online gaming is presented as a dangerous activity that may lead to social withdrawal, physical and mental ill health, and even suicide. These concerns are reflected in stereotypical portrayals of online gamers as socially anxious and incompetent, mentally stunted and withdrawn, and physically unhealthy (e.g., overweight, pale). Furthermore, offline and online gamers seem to be perceived very differently, particularly in regards to the social aspect of the stereotype (e.g., loner, isolated, socially inept) (Kowert & Oldmeadow, 2012).

1.2.1.3   Demographic Assessments: Online Game Players

The demographic profile of online game players provides little empirical evidence to support these stereotypical characterizations (Griffiths, Davies, & Chappell, 2004; Kowert, Festl, & Quandt, 2013). While there is a disproportionate ratio of male to female game players within the online gaming community (Axelsson & Regan, 2002; Cole & Griffiths, 2007; Griffiths, Davies, & Chappell, 2003; Williams, Ducheneaut, Xiong, Yee, & Nickell, 2006; Yee, 2006, 2007), there is no evidence to suggest that these individuals are particularly young or overweight (Kowert et al., 2013; Williams et al., 2008). Players' ages have also been found to span more than 60 years, with as little as one-quarter of gamers being teenagers (Ghuman & Griffiths, 2012; Williams et al., 2008; Yee, 2006). There are actually more online players in their thirties than in their twenties (Yee, 2006), indicating that online gaming is an activity enjoyed by a wide range of age groups (Williams et al., 2008). Williams et al. (2008) and Kowert et al. (2013) provide the only empirical evidence in regards to game players' physical health. Williams et al. (2008) evaluated the BMI (body mass index) of American players of *EverQuest II*, a popular MMORPG, as compared to the national average. Game players reported having an average BMI of 25.19, which, while qualifying as slightly overweight, is substantially lower than the average BMI of an American adult (i.e., 28). Kowert and colleagues (2013) also found little evidence to support the notion that online game players are overweight. Within a representative sample, the researchers found that online players, offline players, and non-players reported no difference in their average frequency of exercise. Although these findings are subject to scrutiny due to being based on self-reports from the players, they do suggest individuals who play online games do not necessarily lead sedentary and unhealthy lives.

The social aspects of the stereotype have received substantial attention in recent years. Links between loneliness, depression, social anxiety, and online game play have been found, with online gamers frequently displaying high rates of symptoms associated with these diagnoses (M. Barnett et al., 1997; Caplan et al., 2009; Chak & Leung, 2004; Kim et al., 2008; Peters & Malesky, 2008; Williams et al., 2008; Yee, 2002). A cross-sectional study by Lo and colleagues (2005) found that increased time spent playing online games coincided with higher levels of social anxiety among Taiwanese adolescents. Williams et al. (2008) uncovered similar patterns among players of *EverQuest II*, as players reported higher rates of depression than found in the general population. Similarly, Shen and Williams (2010) found increased OVG play to be associated with higher levels of loneliness. While these inquiries provide preliminary evidence to suggest that there may be social differences between the online game playing community and the non-online game playing community, the nature of these links remains unclear. The potential relationships between loneliness, depression, social anxiety, and OVG play are further discussed in section 3.2.2.

1.3   ACADEMIC INTEREST IN ONLINE GAMING: SOCIAL COMPETENCE

Since the popularization of e-mail and online chat rooms, researchers have noted concern over the potential consequences of utilizing the Internet for social purposes (Beniger, 1987; Kraut et al., 1998; Slouka, 1995; Young, 1996). The rising popularity of online gaming, online dating services, and social networks such as Facebook and Twitter has revived these concerns. Branded as 'pseudo communities,' these Internet-based, social spaces are believed to provide a superficial sense of social support and displace the time that could be spent fostering meaningful offline relationships (Beniger, 1987; Slouka, 1995).

Much of the concern stems from the supposition that relationships that are formed online are weaker than offline face-to-face relationships due to a lack of situational cues (Slouka, 1995) and the ability to freely engage, or disengage, without repercussions in one's physical lives (Galston, 2000; Roberts &

Strayer, 1996). However, a considerable amount of research is inconsistent with these assertions, indicating instead that the Internet provides the ability to foster meaningful social relationships (Lea & Spears, 1995; Parks & Floyd, 1996; Steinkuehler & Williams, 2006; Wellman & Gulia, 1999; Williams, 2006, 2007). Supporting these claims, researchers have found that players perceive their online contacts to be as 'real' as any 'real-life' friendship (Yee, 2007), and they provide social capital (Williams, 2007), satisfy social needs that have not been met in offline contexts (Hussain & Griffiths, 2008), and promote greater social and psychological well-being, such as reduced depression (Bessière, Kiesler, Kraut, & Boneva, 2004).

While concerns regarding the utilization of online social services in general remain actively debated, greater attention has been given to OVGs as they not only provide a social space, but one that is characterized by shared, playful, and often novel activities. This difference is key, as these shared activities contribute to the formation of long-lasting, highly intimate friendship bonds with sustainable levels of self-disclosure and intimacy not traditionally found in other mediated spaces (Cole & Griffiths, 2007; Hsu, Wen, & Wu, 2009; Iacono & Weisband, 1997; Williams, 2006; Yee, 2002). The formation of such bonds could contribute to a preference for online interaction that is potentially greater than other mediated outlets. This could lead to a variety of negative consequences for the player, as the sustained displacement of offline for online socialization has been found to negatively influence users in a number of ways.

For example, in a one-month panel study of online gamers, Williams (2006) found that the more social online players began to isolate themselves over time, leading to an erosion of pre-existing friendships. Additionally, players began to place a higher value on their in-game social contacts at the expense of pre-existing relationships and displayed several drops in physical social contact by reporting declines in how often friends came over to visit their home, the frequency at which they visited their friends' homes, and how often they visited relatives. Similarly, Shen and Williams (2010) found the social use of OVGs to be related to declines in family communication and increased loneliness. Lemmens at al. (2011) also found increases in loneliness and diminished self-esteem among OVG players over a six-month period.

The displacement of offline for online contacts is generally regarded as troublesome and is believed to contribute to a variety of negative social outcomes, as it is a disproportional exchange. Due to the reduced sense of social presence online (Rice & Love, 1987; Rice, 1993; Slouka, 1995) and the production of bridging, rather than bonding, social capital among online contacts (Bargh & McKenna, 2004; Putnam, 2000; Williams, 2007), online friendships are believed to be more limited in their capability to provide feelings of social support and closeness. Thus, rather than replacing one's offline friends with a virtual substitute, users are supplanting valuable sources of social and emotional support for less intimate and more diffuse online relationships. Consequently, over time, this displacement may have a negative impact on a player's sociability, as evidenced by the various inverse relationships between increased OVG involvement and social outcome measures as discussed earlier (e.g., Lemmens et al., 2011; Shen & Williams, 2010; Williams, 2006).

While findings such as these continue to bolster rising concerns over the potential for OVG involvement to negatively influence socialization, some researchers argue that online gaming spaces have the potential to be socially beneficial for those who may have social difficulties in their offline lives, by providing an alternative social space that can grant access to new friendships or supplement pre-existing ones (Griffiths et al., 2003; Hussain & Griffiths, 2009; Kolo & Baur, 2004; Steinkuehler & Williams, 2006). With a history of poor interpersonal relationships, individuals may become motivated to engage in OVG environments for access to an alternative social space that provides easily accessible and less risky friendships (Cole & Griffiths, 2007; Jakobsson & Taylor, 2003; Kowert, Domahidi, & Quandt, 2014; Suler, 2004; Taylor, 2003; Yee, 2002). Particularly for those with low social resources, such as less perceived social support, lower interpersonal activity, and fewer group memberships, using the Internet for social purposes can reduce negative feelings and bolster one's social network. Evidence for this has been found among lonely (Caplan et al., 2009; Lemmens et al., 2011; Morahan-Martin & Schumacher, 2003), depressed (Bessière et al., 2004), and socially anxious (Kim et al., 2008; Lo et al., 2005; Peters & Malesky, 2008) individuals, who have been found to utilize mediated social spaces to modulate their negative moods and gain companionship. For instance, Morahan-Martin and Schumacher (2003) found lonely individuals reported that they go online when they feel down, anxious, or isolated and that they feel totally absorbed online, as compared to non-lonely people.

OVGs could be particularly suited to accommodate individuals with social difficulties, as the visual anonymity provided by them could decrease feelings of social self-consciousness, while the shared experiences facilitate friendship formation. Thus, rather than OVG involvement leading to negative social consequences, OVG involvement may be socially beneficial for those with low offline social resources. Additionally, pre-existing friendship bonds could also be augmented through play, as online games provide an easily accessible shared, social activity, where the ability to participate is not limited to one's current geographical location (Shen & Williams, 2010; Williams et al., 2006). This seems likely, as researchers have not only noted that a large proportion of players play with pre-existing contacts (Cole & Griffiths, 2007), but also that individuals who play with their pre-existing social ties report less loneliness, and greater social engagement, and of a higher quality, with their friends and family than those who played with strangers (Shen & Williams, 2010). A full discussion of the potential social implications of prolonged OVG engagement is presented in more detail in chapter 3.

While considerable amounts of research are underpinned by the mounting concerns surrounding the negative social influence of OVG involvement on its users, researchers have yet to establish consistent relationships between social competence and OVG involvement or develop a comprehensive understanding of the relationships that have been uncovered. Today the field remains divided, with some researchers suggesting inverse relationships between OVG involvement and social competence are attributable to displacement effects (Brightman, 2006; Colwell & Kato, 2003; Hussain & Griffiths, 2008, 2009; Shen & Williams, 2010; Steinkuehler & Williams, 2006; Williams, 2006; Yee, 2006), while others attribute them to social compensation phenomena (Griffiths et al., 2003; Hussain & Griffiths, 2009; Kolo & Baur, 2004; Steinkuehler & Williams, 2006). There is also a third perspective, which contends there are no substantial social differences between online game players and non-players and that engagement within these spaces does not considerably affect sociability (J. Barnett et al., 2009; Visser, Antheunis, & Schouten, 2013). Additional research is needed to clarify the potential social consequences or benefits of OVG involvement as well as further elucidate the potential basis of these relationships.

1.4 CONCLUSION

The video game industry is a multibillion-dollar, worldwide enterprise. The incorporation of 'real-time' social services within a shared interactive environment has furthered this medium's scope, providing an Internet-based, shared gaming space in which millions of individuals across the globe regularly participate. Despite their popularity, OVGs have been met with suspicion by the popular media and the academic community as the potential consequences of engagement within these spaces continue to be given considerable attention. In particular, researchers are concerned about the potential social consequences of online game play, as fear about the medium's ability to produce a generation of socially inept, reclusive individuals continues to rise. While preliminary evidence suggests that there are inverse relationships between OVG play and social competence, some researchers contend that engagement within online gaming spaces may be socially beneficial. Following a general discussion of social competence (i.e., what it is, how it can be conceptualized, and what influences social competencies) in chapter 2, a closer examination of the research evaluating the social implications of OVG involvement will be presented in chapter 3.

REFERENCES

Alvarez, M. (2009). *ComScore: Game sites growing 10-times faster than Internet.* Retrieved from http://www.atelier-us.com/consumers-and-ecommerce/article/comscore-game-sites-growing-10-times-faster-than-internet

Aoyama, Y., & Izushi, H. (2003). Hardware gimmick or cultural innovation? Technological, cultural, and social foundations of Japanese video game industry. *Research Policy, 32*(3), 423–444.

Associated Press. (2007). Chinese man drops dead after 3-day gaming binge. *Fox News*. Retrieved from http://www.foxnews.com/story/0,2933,297059,00.html?sPage=fnc/scitech/videogaming

Axelsson, A., & Regan, T. (2002). *How belonging to an online group affects social behaviour—a case study of Asheron's Call*. Redmond, WA: Microsoft Research.

Bacon, D. (2011). All the world's a game. *Economist*. Retrieved from http://www.economist.com/node/21541164

Bandura, A. (1962). Social learning through imitation. In M. R. Jones (Ed.), *Nebraska Symposium on Motivation*. Lincoln: University of Nebraska Press.

Bandura, A. (1977). *Social learning theory*. Englewood Cliffs, NJ: Prentice-Hall.

Bandura, A. (1986). *Social foundations of thought and action: A social cognitive theory*. Englewood Cliffs, NJ: Prentice-Hall.

Bargh, J., & McKenna, K. (2004). The Internet and social life. *Annual Review of Psychology, 55*(1), 573–590.

Barnett, J., Coulson, M., & Foreman, N. (2009). *The WoW! factor: Reduced levels of anger after violent on-line play*. London: Middlesex University.

Barnett, M., Vitaglione, G., Harper, K., Quackenbush, S., Steadman, L., & Valdez, B. (1997). Late adolescents' experiences with and attitudes towards videogames. *Journal of Applied Social Psychology, 27*(15), 1316–1334.

BBC News. (2005). South Korean dies after games session. *BBC News*. Retrieved from http://news.bbc.co.uk/1/hi/technology/4137782.stm

Beniger, J. (1987). Personalization of mass media and the growth of pseudo-community. *Communication Research, 14*(3), 352–371.

Bessière, K., Kiesler, S., Kraut, R., & Boneva, B. (2012). Longitudinal effects of Internet uses on depressive affect: A social resources approach. Unpublished manuscript, Carnegie Mellon University, Philadelphia, PA.

Brightman, J. (2006). Study: Video games can promote sociability. *Game Daily*. Retrieved from http://www.gamedaily.com/articles/features/study-video-games-can-promote-sociability/69323/?biz=1

Bryant, B., & Trower, P. E. (1974). Social difficulty in a student sample. *British Journal of Educational Psychology, 44*, 13–21.

Caplan, S., Williams, D., & Yee, N. (2009). Problematic Internet use and psychosocial well-being among MMO players. *Computers in Human Behavior, 25*(6), 1312–1319. doi:10.1016/j.chb.2009.06.006

Chak, K., & Leung, L. (2004). Shyness and locus of control as predictors of Internet addiction and Internet use. *Cyberpsychology and Behavior, 7*(5), 559–570. doi:10.1089/cpb.2004.7.559

Chiu, S., Lee, J., & Huang, D. (2004). Video game addiction in children and teenagers in Taiwan. *Cyberpsychology and Behavior, 7*(5), 571–581.

Cole, H., & Griffiths, M. D. (2007). Social interactions in massively multiplayer online role-playing games. *Cyberpsychology and Behavior, 10*(4), 575–583. doi:10.1089/cpb.2007.9988

Colwell, J., & Kato, M. (2003). Investigation of the relationship between social isolation, self-esteem, aggression and computer game play in Japanese adolescents. *Asian Journal of Social Psychology, 6*, 149–158.

Cucuel, Q. (2011). The video game industry: Explaining the emergence of new markets (pp. 1–23). Otago: University of Otago.

Day, F. (Writer), & Morgan, J. S. (Director) (2007). *Wake-up call* [Television series episode]. In F. Day, K. Evey, & J. S. Morgan (Producers), *The Guild*.

Evers-Pasquale, W., & Sherman, M. (1975). The reward value of peers. *Journal of Abnormal Child Psychology, 3*(3), 179–189.

Galston, W. A. (2000). Does the Internet strenghten community? *National Civic Review, 89*(3), 193–202.

Ghuman, D., & Griffiths, M. D. (2012). A cross-genre study of online gaming: Player demographics, motivation for play, and social interactions among players. *International Journal of Cyber Behavior, Psychology, and Learning, 2*(1), 13–29.

Global Industry Analysts, Inc. (2009). *Global strategic business report.* Retrieved from http://www.strategyr.com/Video_Games_Market_Report.asp

Gresham, F., & Nagel, R. J. (1980). Social skills traning with children: Responsiveness to modeling and coaching as a function of peer orientation. *Journal of Consulting and Clinical Psychology, 48,* 718–729.

Griffiths, M. D. (2010). Computer game playing and social skills: A pilot study. *Aloma, 27,* 301–310.

Griffiths, M. D., Davies, M., & Chappell, D. (2003). Breaking the stereotype: The case of online gaming. *Cyberpsychology and Behavior, 6*(1), 81–91.

Griffiths, M. D., Davies, M., & Chappell, D. (2004). Demographic factors and playing variables in online computer gaming. *Cyberpsychology and Behavior, 7,* 479–487.

Hinkle, D. (2011). Report: Game industry worth $74 billion in 2011. *Joystiq.* Retrieved from http://www.joystiq.com/2011/07/05/report-game-industry-worth-74-billion-in-2011/

Hsu, S., Wen, M., & Wu, M. (2009). Exploring user experiences as predictors of MMORPG addiction. *Computers and Education, 53*(3), 990–999.

Hussain, Z., & Griffiths, M. (2008). Gender swapping and socializing in cyberspace: An exploratory study. *Cyberpsychology and Behavior, 11*(1), 47–53.

Hussain, Z., & Griffiths, M. (2009). The attitudes, feelings, and experiences of online gamers: A qualitative analysis. *Cyberpsychology and Behavior, 12*(6), 747–753.

Iacono, C. S., & Weisband, S. (1997). Developing trust in virtual teams. In *Hawaii International Conference on System Sciences.* Hawaii.

Jakobsson, M., & Taylor, T. L. (2003). *The Sopranos* meets *EverQuest*: Social networking in massively multiplayer online games. In *Proceedings of the 2003 Digital Arts and Culture (DAC) conference, Melbourne, Australia* (pp. 81–90).

Johns, J. (2005). Video games production networks: Value capture, power relations and embeddedness. *Journal of Economic Geography, 6,* 151–180.

Keller, M., & Carlson, P. (1974). The use of symbolic modeling to promote social skills in preschool children with low levels of social responsiveness. *Child Development, 45,* 912–919.

Kim, E., Namkoong, K., Ku, T., & Kim, S. (2008). The relationship between online game addiction and aggression, self-control, and narcissistic personality traits. *European Psychiatry, 23*(3), 212–218. doi:10.1016/j.eurpsy.2007.10.010

Kohn, D. (2002). Addicted: Suicide over *Everquest*? *CBS News.* Retrieved from http://www.cbsnews.com/stories/2002/10/17/48hours/main525965.shtml

Kolo, C., & Baur, T. (2004). Living a virtual life: Social dynamics of online gaming. *International Journal of Computer Game Research, 4*(1).

Kowert, R., Domahidi, E., & Quandt, T. (2014). The relationship between online video game involvement and gaming-related friendships among emotionally sensitive individuals. *Cyberpsychology, Behavior, and Social Networking, 17*(7), 447–453. doi:10.1089/cyber.2013.0656

Kowert, R., Festl, R., & Quandt, T. (2013). Unpopular, overweight, and socially inept: Reconsidering the stereotype of online gamers. *Cyberpsychology, Behavior, and Social Networking, 17*(3), 141–146. doi:10.1089/cyber.2013.0118

Kowert, R., Griffiths, M. D., & Oldmeadow, J. A. (2012). Geek or chic? Emerging stereotypes of online gamers. *Bulletin of Science, Technology & Society, 32*(6), 471–479. doi:10.1177/0270467612469078

Kowert, R., & Oldmeadow, J. A. (2012). The stereotype of online gamers: New characterization or recycled prototype. In *Nordic DiGRA: Games in Culture and Society conference proceedings.* Tampere, Finland: DiGRA.

Kraut, R., Patterson, M., Lundmark, V., Kiesler, S., Mukopadhyay, T., & Scherlis, W. (1998). Internet paradox: A social technology that reduces social involvement and psychological well-being? *American Psychologist, 53*(9), 1017–1031.

Ladd, G. W., & Mize, J. (1983). A cognitive-social learning model of social-skill training. *Psychologial Review, 90*(2), 127–157.

Lea, M., & Spears, R. (1995). Love at first byte? Building personal relationships over computer networks. In J. T. Wood & S. W. Duck (Eds.), *Understudied relationships: Off the beaten track* (pp. 197–233). Newbury Park, CA: Sage.

Lemmens, J., Valkenburg, P., & Peter, J. (2011). Psychological causes and consequences of pathological gaming. *Computers in Human Behavior, 27*(1), 144–152. doi:10.1016/j.chb.2010.07.015

Lenhart, A., Jones, S., & Macgill, A. (2008). *Adults and video games.* Pew Internet and American Life Project. Retrieved from http://www.pewinternet.org/2008/12/07/adults-and-video-games/

Liu, M., & Peng, W. (2009). Cognitive and psychological predictors of the negative outcomes associated with playing MMOGs (massively multiplayer online games). *Computers in Human Behavior, 25*(6), 1306–1311. doi:10.1016/j.chb.2009.06.002

Lo, S., Wang, C., & Fang, W. (2005). Physical interpersonal relationships and social anxiety among online game players. *Cyberpsychology and Behavior, 8*(1), 15–20. doi:10.1089/cpb.2005.8.15

Lorre, C., Molaro, S., & Kaplan, M. (Writer) (2008). *Barbarian sublimation* [Television series episode]. In F. Belyeu (Producer), *The Big Bang Theory.* Warner Brothers Studios.

Milton, M. (Producer). (2010). *Homo Interneticus* [Television special]. UK: BBC.

Morahan-Martin, J., & Schumacher, P. (2003). Loneliness and social uses of the Internet. *Computers in Human Behavior, 19*, 659–671.

Novaco, R. W. (1994). *Novaco Anger Scale and Provocation Inventory (NAS-PI).* Los Angeles, CA: Western Psychological Services.

Parker, T., & Stone, M. (2006). *Make love, not* Warcraft [Television series episode]. In T. Parker & M. Stone, Eds., *South Park.* South Park Studios.

Parks, M. R., & Floyd, K. (1996). Making friends in cyberspace. *Journal of Communication, 46*, 80–97.

Peters, C., & Malesky, A. (2008). Problematic usage among highly-engaged players of massively multiplayer online role playing games. *Cyberpsychology and Behavior, 11*(4), 481–484.

Putnam, R. (2000). *Bowling alone: The collapse and revival of American community.* New York: Simon & Schuster.

Rice, R. E. (1993). Media appropriateness: Using social presence theory to compare traditional and new organization media. *Human Communication Research, 19*(4), 451–484.

Rice, R. E., & Love, G. (1987). Electronic emotion. *Communication Research, 14*(1), 85–108.

Roberts, W., & Strayer, J. (1996). Empathy, emotional expressiveness, and prosocial behavior. *Child Development, 67*, 449–470.

Rose-Kransor, L. (1997). Nature of social competence: A theoretical review. *Social Developmental Psychology, 6*(1), 111–135.

Senlow, G. (1984). Playing videogames: The electronic friend. *Journal of Communication, 34*(2), 148–156.

Shen, C., & Williams, D. (2010). Unpacking time online: Connecting Internet and massively multiplayer online game use with psychological well-being. *Communication Research, 20*(10), 1–27. doi:10.1177/0093650210377196

Sigman, A. (2009). Well-connected? *Biologist, 56*(1), 14–20.

Slouka, M. (1995). *War of the worlds: Cyberspace and the high-tech assault on reality.* New York: Basic Books.

Smyth, J. (2007). Beyond self-selection in video game play. *Cyberpsychology and Behavior, 10*(5), 717–721.

Spil Games. (2013). *State of online gaming report*. Retrieved from http://auth-83051f68-ec6c-44e0-afe5-bd8902acff57.cdn.spilcloud.com/v1/archives/1384952861.25_State_of_Gaming_2013_US_FINAL.pdf

Steinkuehler, C., & Williams, D. (2006). Where everybody knows your (screen) name: Online games as "third places." *Journal of Computer-Mediated Communication, 11*(4), 885–909.

Suler, J. (2004). The online disinhibition effect. *Cyberpsychology and Behavior, 7*(3), 321–326.

Taylor, T. L. (2003). Multiple pleasures: Women and online gaming. *Convergence: The International Journal of Research into New Media Technologies, 9*(1), 21–46.

TMachine.org. (2008). *More than 1 billion people play online games in 2008*. Retrieved from http://t-machine.org/index.php/2008/11/18/more-than-1-billion-people-play-online-games-in-2008/

Truly, M. (Writer) (2010). *Bullseye* [Television series episode]. *Law and Order: Special Victims Unit*. NBC Studios.

Visser, M., Antheunis, M. L., & Schouten, A. P. (2013). Online communication and social well-being: How playing *World of Warcraft* affects players' social competence and loneliness. *Journal of Applied Social Psychology, 43*, 1508–1517. doi:10.1111/jasp.12144

Wellman, B., & Gulia, M. (1999). Net surfers don't ride alone: Virtual communities as communities. In B. Wellman (Ed.), *Networks in the Global Village* (pp. 331–366). Boulder, CO: Westview.

Williams, D. (2005). A brief social history of game play. In *DiGRA 2005 Conference: Changing Views—Worlds in Play*. Vancouver, British Columbia, Canada.

Williams, D. (2006). Groups and goblins: The social and civic impact of online games. *Journal of Broadcasting and Electronic Media, 50*, 651–681. doi:10.1207/s15506878jobem5004_5

Williams, D. (2007). The impact of time online: Social capital and cyberbalkanization. *Cyberpsychology and Behavior, 10*(3), 398–406.

Williams, D., Ducheneaut, N., Xiong, L., Yee, N., & Nickell, E. (2006). From tree house to barracks. *Games and Culture, 1*(4), 338–361.

Williams, D., Yee, N., & Caplan, S. (2008). Who plays, how much, and why? Debunking the stereotypical gamer profile. *Journal of Computer-Mediated Communication Monographs, 13*(4), 993–1018. doi:10.1111/j.1083–6101.2008.00428.x

Yee, N. (2002). Befriending ogres and wood-elves—Understanding relationship formation in MMORPGs. *Nickyee*. Retrieved from http://www.nickyee.com/hub/relationships/home.html

Yee, N. (2006). The demographics, motivations, and derived experiences of users of massively-multi-user online graphical environments. *Teleoperators and Virtual Environments, 15*(3), 309–329.

Yee, N. (2007). Motivations of play in online games. *Journal of CyberPsychology and Behavior, 9*(6), 772–775.

Young, K. (1996). Internet addiction: The emergence of a new clinical disorder. *Cyberpsychology and Behavior, 1*, 237–244.

Zimmerman, E. (2002). Do independent games exist? In L. King (Ed.), *Game on: The history and culture of video games*. New York: Universe Publishing.

2　What Is Social Competence?

To unravel the potential associations between social competence and OVG involvement, one must first explore social competence. The current chapter will provide an overview of social competence and examine the four principal conceptualizations of this concept (i.e., sociometric, relationship quality and quantity, functional outcomes, and social skills), the ways it can be operationalized, external influences, and established correlates.

The primary focus will be placed on the social skills approach as social skills represent the foundation of social competence upon which all other facets of sociability develop, as evidenced theoretically (Cavell, 1990; DuBois & Felner, 1996; Rose-Kransor, 1997) and empirically (Baron & Markman, 2003; Ladd & Mize, 1983; Ladd, 1981; Oden & Asher, 1977). Furthermore, adopting a social skills approach in the current research will provide the unique opportunity to clarify the relationship between social competence and involvement by pinpointing the precise social abilities that may hold a relationship with OVG involvement. The social skills approach is discussed in more detail in section 2.1.2.4.

2.1　WHAT IS SOCIAL COMPETENCE?

2.1.1　Historical Overview

Social intelligence, or social competence, was first identified as an important facet of development in the early 20th century. Thorndike (1920) is often credited as being among the first to suggest that the ability to understand and manage people was a unique form of intelligence, separate from other forms of intelligences, such as abstract (i.e., the ability to understand and manage ideas) or mechanical (i.e., the ability to understand and manage concrete objects) (E. Thorndike, 1920).

Initial assessments of social competence were inspired by general intelligence measures (e.g., Moss, Hunt, Omwake, & Ronning, 1927; Pinter & Upshall, 1928; R. Thorndike & Steinfield, 1937). For example, Gilliand and Burke (1926) quantified social intelligence through a correlation between the accuracy with which a participant could identify faces that had previously been seen within an array and peer ratings of the sub-jects' sociability. While peer ratings of sociability are a valid assessment of popularity, it could be argued that the facial recognition task is more an assessment of recognition ability or short-term memory than social competence.

It was not until the late 20th century that an empirical distinction between social and academic intelligence was firmly established (Ford & Tisak, 1983; Marlowe, 1986; Riggio, Messamer, & Throckmorton, 1991) and specific social competence assessments were developed. The conceptualization of social intelligence as a separate form of competency was largely driven by the work of Ford and Tisak (1983), who found social competence variables (i.e., personality test, two self-rating measures, teacher ratings, and peer nominations) to account for 31% of the variance in the behavioral observa-tions of social competence recorded in an interview, whereas less than 1% was accounted for by academic variables (i.e., three standardized test scores and grade point average). These findings motivated a surge of interest in social competence and its links to social development and spurred a wide range of research examining the associations between social competence and mental health. For example, researchers uncovered significant links between social competence and loneliness (DiTommaso, Brannen-McNulty, Ross, & Burgess, 2003; Segrin & Kinney, 1995; Wittenberg & Reis, 1986), depression (Segrin & Flora, 2000; Segrin, 1998), and social anxiety (Leary & Kowalski, 1995), indicating that social development plays a key role in one's overall psychosocial adjustment. For instance, in a cross-sectional survey study, Segrin and Kinney (1995) found self-rated and peer-rated social com-petence to be negatively correlated with loneliness. Similarly, DiTommaso et al. (2003) found social loneliness to be negatively correlated with social skills, as indicated by the total outcome score from the Social Skills Inven-tory (SSI; see Riggio, 1989). Today, social competence is commonly regarded as being central to one's psychological development and plays a critical role in diagnosing those with mental difficulties (American Psychiatric Associa-tion, 2000; Grossman, 1983). While exceptional individuals often display socially competent behavior (e.g., social effectiveness), those on the other side of the spectrum often display few pro-social behaviors, are less socially initiative, and are less liked by their peers (Coie, 1985; Gresham & Elliot, 1989; Gresham, 1981).

Despite the vast growth in understanding social competence over the last century, including the development of Vygotsky's (1978) Social Development Theory and Bandura's (1977) Social Learning Theory, which center on the role of social competence in development, numerous definitions remain for this concept. They range from the very broad "social success" (Atteli, 1990, p. 241) to the more narrow ". . . attainment of relevant social goals in speci-fied social contexts" (Ford, 1982, p. 323). Despite the varied definitions of this concept, it is generally agreed upon that social competence requires some element of being effective in social interaction (Dodge, 1985; Rose-Kransor,

1997). To assess this 'social effectiveness,' social competence can be broken down into more specific levels of classification (Anderson & Messick, 1974). Most commonly, this has been done through operationalizing social competence as a measure of sociometric status (popularity), relationship quality and quantity, functional outcomes, and/or social skills. These four conceptualizations of this social competence, and established external influences and correlates, are discussed in more detail in the following.

2.1.2   Conceptualization Approaches

2.1.2.1   *Sociometric (Peer Status)*

Sociometric approaches combine behavioral and affective components of social competence and quantify one's social ability through measures of popularity among one's peers (Denham, McKinley, Couchard, & Holt, 1990; Dodge, 1985; Gottman, Gonso, & Rasmussen, 1975). Sociometric status is typically assessed through an evaluation of popularity for a single group member by other members, or through direct researcher observations of social interactions within a group. Due to its reliance upon others' perceptions (i.e., ratings from other group members), the sociometric approach is not typically enlisted without the support of other measures, as it could lead to inaccurate conclusions. For instance, individuals who are well liked by a deviant peer group (e.g., gang members) could be judged more socially competent than those who are only moderately liked by a non-deviant peer group (e.g., sports team), even though popularity among a deviant peer group is often associated with social and academic difficulties later in life (Cairns & Cairns, 1994; Luthar, 1995).

The work of Gottman et al. (1975) provides an example of this approach, as they enlisted measures of popularity as one component of a social competence assessment among elementary school children. Popularity ratings were generated by asking participants to list their best friends (any number), three children they would go to for help, three children that "really listen to you," three children that "really like you," and three children that they most like playing with. However, following a principle components analysis, the researchers decided only to utilize the first variable, best friends, as the measure of popularity. A median split on the number of times an individual was listed as a best friend was used to subdivide the children into "high-friends" and "low-friends" groups. The results showed that more popular children (i.e., the high-friends groups) performed significantly better than the low-friends groups on six of the eight other social skills measures included in the study (e.g., labeling emotions, word pair tasks, perspective taking tasks, ability to make friends, etc.). The researchers concluded that popular children are more socially skillful than unpopular children and interact differently with their peers.

While this method is able to identify an outcome linked to social competence (e.g., whether or not an individual is well liked by his or her peers), it is unable to determine the source of the outcomes without the support of other assessments (Dodge, 1985; Rose-Kransor, 1997). Thus, one could conclude that an individual is not well received by his or her peers but would not be able to pinpoint the source of the problem or suggest particular programs to improve the individual's social effectiveness without additional assessments.

2.1.2.2 *Relationship Quality and Quantity*

The relationship approach operationalizes social competence as one's ability to form and maintain reciprocal relationships (Hartup, 1989; Rose-Kransor, 1997). The importance of interpersonal relationships for social and psychological development has been widely recognized (see Newcomb & Bagwell, 1995 for a review of the literature). Interpersonal relationships provide valuable sources of information, emotional support, companionship, and opportunities for social learning, including social skills such as conflict resolution (Rose-Kransor, 1997).

To evaluate relationship quality, measures of the positive and negative aspects of relationships are often assessed (which can include measures of intimacy, conflict, and friendship satisfaction, among others), with the presence of more positive than negative factors indicating a higher friendship quality (Berndt, 1996). This approach differs from the sociometric approach, as the number and quality of reciprocal, interpersonal relationships determines one's competence regardless of the individual's relational status among his or her peers or general peer acceptance. Despite this key difference, few empirical studies have investigated the unique contributions of friendship independent of sociometric status (Hartup, 1993; J. G. Parker & Asher, 1993).

For example, in a 1993 study by Parker and Asher, the researchers aimed to examine the prevalence of friendships among children in general, as well as across popularity categories (i.e., high-, average-, and low-accepted children). The results revealed that non-popular children were significantly less likely to have a friend, as only 45.3% of low-accepted children, 82.3% of average-accepted, and 93.8% of high-accepted children reported having at least one friend. No differences were found across popularity categories in terms of how much companionship and recreation they believed their friendships provided them. However, the low-popularity children did report that their friendships provided less validation, caring, help, and guidance, as well as reported a greater difficulty resolving conflicts within their friendship group, than average- and high-accepted children, who did not differ between each other. Furthermore, low-accepted children reported less self-disclosure with their friends than their high-accepted counterparts.

This intertwining of the relationship and sociometric approaches has led to an inability to distinguish outcomes from their sources (Rose-Kransor, 1997). For example, while Parker and Asher (1993) found that low-accepted children had fewer friends, and of a lower quality, it is unclear whether these findings are driven by the unique contributions of friendship to development (i.e., the lack of friends has perpetuated poorer relationship outcomes) independent of peer acceptance. There are a few exceptions, however, where researchers have examined differences between children who have friends and those who have none (e.g., Dishion, Andrews, & Crosby, 1995; J. G. Parker & Asher, 1993; Vandell & Hembree, 1994). For example, in post hoc analyses, Parker and Asher (1993) found a significant main effect of popularity (i.e., low, average, high) and friendship status (i.e., friends or no friends) on loneliness, but no interaction. The researchers also found relationship quality to be negatively related to loneliness independent of popularity and relationship quantity.

While many researchers have found links between relationship variables and adaptive outcomes (e.g., loneliness, popularity, social skill development, etc.), considerable variation in the definition of friendship, and what constitutes a high-quality friendship, has limited this area of research in terms of its consistency and generalizability. While some researchers operationalized friendships through their ability to provide status, power, and intimacy (Candy, Troll, & Levy, 1981), others have focused on the ability of friendships to provide more tangible resources, such as affection, information, and services (Shea, Thompson, & Blieszner, 1988) or the exchange of a single element, such as self-disclosure (Hacker, 1981), to determine the existence, and quality, of a friendship. Other researchers have enlisted compressive assessments, such as Parker and de Vries (1993), who assessed a wide range of affective (e.g., self-disclosure, appreciation, trust, authenticity, etc.) and more tangible (e.g., assistance, empathetic understanding, shared activities, empowerment, etc.) dimensions of friendship. This variation has led to considerable variability in the literature in terms of assessments, findings, and conclusions and has made it difficult to determine the causal direction of the findings. For example, while many researchers have found links between relationship variables and adaptive outcomes (e.g., loneliness, popularity, social skill development), it is unclear whether individuals with more high-quality friendships acquired them due to less psychosocial difficulties, higher popularity, and high social ability (all of which could be influenced by extraneous variables, such as attractiveness, socioeconomic status, etc.), or if these characteristics developed through interaction within their particular friendship group.

2.1.2.3 *Functional Outcomes*

Largely built upon social problem-solving research (D'Zurilla & Goldfried, 1971; Rubin & Rose-Krasnor, 1992), functional approaches assess the outcomes, and the processes leading up to the outcomes, of social interactions (Connolly & Doyle, 1984; Dodge, 1986; Goldfried & D'Zurilla, 1969; McFall, 1982). An assessment of this kind can focus solely on the specific outcome of an interaction (e.g., successful or unsuccessful) or can evaluate one's ability to perform each step required for effective social communication (i.e., goal selection, environment monitoring, strategy selection, strategy implementation, outcome evaluation, and determining a subsequent action) and the ability to integrate these steps into a continuous, fluid interaction (Dodge, 1986; Rose-Kransor, 1997).

As this method evaluates context-specific social goals, tasks, and outcomes, observational methods are commonly utilized. For instance, role-play scenarios are often employed via a structured interview or a videotaped interaction with a confederate (Bellack, Morrison, Wixted, & Mueser, 1990; Glasgow & Arkowitz, 1975; Mueser et al., 1996). These recorded interactions are then coded by researchers to rate an individual's overall social skills, fluency and clarity of speech, affect, gaze, and ability to stay on topic, among other things (Mueser et al., 1996). While this approach assesses one's capacity to integrate a variety of abilities and generate successful outcomes in a transactional interaction, it is only able to do so within a specific context, therefore limiting the generalizability of the findings. For instance, an individual who is found to successfully engage another through a telephone conversation may not necessarily be exhibiting global social competence, but simply the ability to effectively communicate in the absence of physical cues.

2.1.2.4 *Social Skills Approach*
The social skills approach conceptualizes social competence in terms of either having or not having certain desirable skills (Baron & Markman, 2003; Bellack et al., 1990; Ford, 1982; Glasgow & Arkowitz, 1975; Rose-Kransor, 1997; Waters & Sroufe, 1983). Social skills are the specific abilities that motivate, and contribute to, effective communication, such as perspective taking, communication, empathy, affect regulation, and problem solving (Rubin, Bukowski, & Parker, 2007). Determining if an individual possesses 'effective' social skills can be a binary distinction, such as whether or not one achieves a particular score on an assessment, or conceptualized as existing on a continuum, rather than in terms of a deficit or surplus.

Numerous social competence models (Cavell, 1990; DuBois & Felner, 1996; Rose-Kransor, 1997) have identified social skills as the foundation upon which other facets of competence build upon. For instance, according to Cavell's (1990) tri-component model of social competence, an operational set of social skills must be acquired before social performance and adjustment can develop. Similarly, in Rose-Kransor's (1997) Prism Model of social competence, social skills comprise the foundation upon which the index and theoretical level of social competence are based. Thus, without the successful attainment of effective social skills, one is likely to experience substantial difficulties in acquiring and demonstrating any higher-level social processes and may fail to demonstrate 'effectiveness' in social interactions. These theoretical relationships between social skills and other facets of social competence have gained empirical support through experimental research.

For example, Oden and Asher (1977) trained unpopular children in social skills that had been previously identified as correlates of peer acceptance (i.e., participation, cooperation, communication, validation and support).

After five training sessions, the trained children made substantial gains in peer acceptance as compared to control groups. The main effects of time and condition (trained by experimenter, peer parings, or control) were not significant; however, the condition by time interaction was. Coached children increased significantly from pre- to post-test, while the controls remained the same. Planned a priori comparisons revealed that the coaching group's change was significantly greater than the other two groups taken together. Similarly, Ladd (1981) trained unpopular children in asking questions and leading others. The participants were selected on the basis of low popularity (from peer ratings of likeability) and low social activity, as based upon behavioral observations by the researchers. After training, peer ratings of likeability and behavioral observations were repeated. The children who received training showed significant gains in their classroom sociability, with increases in all three of their trained skills: asking questions, leading others, and "social other," which was defined as any other untrained positive social behavior. The children also showed significant gains in sociometric status. No significant effects were found for the non-treatment control group for any measure. These findings indicate that children trained in social skills, as compared to untrained peers, exhibit greater social knowledge and greater social proficiency post training (for a review of this literature see Ladd & Mize, 1983) and suggests that social skills underwrite peer acceptance and other positive functional outcomes (e.g., making friends, achieving social goals, etc.). Similar directional relationships between social skills and functional outcomes have also been evidenced among adult samples, as Baron and Markman (2003) found the ability to accurately perceive others significantly predicted entrepreneurial success.

While the aforementioned research demonstrates the foundational nature of social skills, researchers continue to debate what qualifies as a skill as one that 'facilitates effective interpersonal communication.' Several selection criteria have been proposed, ranging from values approaches (Dodge & Murphy, 1984; Hughes, 1990), which suggest that fundamental social skills should be identified by teachers, peers, or experts, to normative approaches, whereby relevant social skills are based upon normative data, such as age-appropriate social skills or skills associated with a particular IQ level (Anderson & Messick, 1974; Koning & Magill-Evans, 2001). Due to the relative strengths and weaknesses of each approach, one has not been universally endorsed over the others. For instance, values approaches have largely fallen out of favor due to criticisms of their arbitrary, and culturally biased, selection processes (Dodge, 1985; Lee, 1979; Ogbu, 1981). Enlisting this 'bag of virtues' approach (Kohlberg & Mayer, 1972) can lead to contextually dependent results as the same individual who is deemed competent for his or her ability to cooperate with others could be deemed incompetent for his or her inability to be self-reliant in a group task. Similarly, normative approaches have not been universally enlisted, as the normative behaviors of some dysfunctional peer groups may be ones that lead to long-term, adverse consequences (e.g., using violence or aggression to obtain social goals) (Cairns & Cairns, 1994; Dishion, McCord, & Poulin, 1999; Sussman, Unger, & Dent, 2004). This lack of consistency in selection approaches has contributed to the use of a wide variety of social, cognitive, and emotional skill assessments in social competence evaluations. This has included, but has not been limited to, measures of empathy and means-end thinking (Ford, 1982), social adjustment (Bellack et al., 1990), emotion identification, and perspective taking (Gottman et al., 1975). However, most of these measures only examine a single dimension of social skill. In an attempt to account for some of this incongruity, some broad, overarching measures of social skills, such as the Social Performance Survey Schedule (Lowe & Cautela, 1978) or the Social Skills Inventory (Riggio, 1989), have also been developed to assess a wide range of skill assessments within a single self-report questionnaire.

A wide variety of assessment methods have also been employed, including behavior checklists (Mize & Ladd, 1990), surveys (Dodge, McClaskey, & Feldman, 1985; Riggio, Throckmorton, & DePaola, 1990; Riggio, Watring, & Throckmorton, 1993), and direct observation (Barlow, Abel, Blanchard, Bristow, & Young, 1977). Combination approaches have also been enlisted (Connolly & Doyle, 1984; Glasgow & Arkowitz, 1975). For instance, Glasgow and Arkowitz (1975) enlisted surveys and observational methods when assessing social skill differences between high- and low-frequency daters. While the survey assessed social skills and social anxiety, the role-plays assessed the participants' ability to apply social skills within a real-world scenario. The researchers found a significant main effect of dating frequency (i.e., high or low frequency) on self-ratings of social skill and social anxiety, with lower-frequency daters rating themselves as significantly less skilled and more anxious than higher-frequency daters. However, post-tests from the role-plays revealed that lower-frequency daters were not perceived differently from high-frequency daters in terms of social skill or social anxiety by their communication partners, suggesting that lower-frequency daters may be overly critical of their social performance rather than socially inept. In this instance, the utilization of a combination approach was critical to uncover the relationships between low- and high-frequency dating, (perceived) social skills, and functional outcomes. Without the use of multiple methods, the researchers may have concluded that significant social skill differences exist between low- and high-frequency daters rather than uncovering that the main difference lies in the perception of their social abilities. However, due to financial and time constraints, it is not always possible to enlist combination approaches such as these.

While the social skills approach has been the most commonly utilized throughout the literature (for a review see Rose-Kransor, 1997), its limitations need to be considered. While combination approaches can, and have, been utilized to assess social skills, self-report methodologies are the most commonly enlisted. Heavy reliance on self-report methodologies can be disadvantageous, as they can be prone to social desirability biases. However, recent research suggests the potential for skewed results may not be as problematic for self-report measures of social skills. For example, Baron and Markman (2003) found self-report ratings of social skills to closely align with third-party ratings of participants' social abilities. Gifford and O'Connor (1987) and Moskowitz (1990) uncovered similar relationships between subjective self-reported evaluations of interpersonal behaviors (i.e., conversation participation) and objective standardized assessments of social personality characteristics (e.g., friendliness, dominance, agreeableness, etc.). While this cannot dismiss the possibility of social desirability biases completely, these results suggest that self-report measures of social skills show significant correspondence with more objective measures of competency.

A second potential limitation of the social skills approach is its inability to assess the more transactional elements of social communication. For instance, one may have the skill components that would classify one as being 'socially effective' but may lack the ability to integrate them in a functional way to achieve short- and long-term social goals, such as developing and maintaining friendships or gaining popularity among one's peers. This is made evident in the results of Glasgow and Arkowitz (1975) discussed earlier, who, without the confirmation of the role-plays, would have erroneously concluded that the social differences between low- and high-frequency daters lie in their social abilities rather than the perception of them. However, research suggests that this is the exception rather than the rule, as self-report social skills measures have been found to significantly correspond with other social competence assessments, including sociometric status (Eisenberg, Fabes, Bernzweig, Poulin, & Hanish, 1993; Watson, Nixon, Wilson, & Capage, 1999), relationship quality (Carton, Kessler, & Pape, 1999; Grisset & Norvell, 1992), and functional outcomes, such as psychosocial adjustment (Riggio et al., 1993), financial success (Baron & Markman, 2003), and social adaptability (Gresham & Elliot, 1987). This suggests that the social skills approach is a valid measurement of both social skills and performance.

For example, Gottman and Graziano (1983) found that the possession of specific conversational skills (i.e., communication clarity, information exchange, and common ground) increased the likelihood that children would establish peer friendships. Similar relationships were found within the school-based sample of Eisenberg and colleagues (1993), where negative correlational relationships between emotional intensity (i.e., a lack of emotional control) and functional outcomes for male and female children were found. Among adults, relationships between social skills and functional outcomes have also been demonstrated, as Baron and Markman (2003) found the ability to accurately perceive others significantly predicted entrepreneurial success.

Riggio et al. (1993) uncovered similar relationships between social skills and psychosocial adjustment. Riggio and colleagues were among the first to examine these links within a normal population using standardized measures of both social skills and psychosocial adjustment. Correlational analyses uncovered a significant negative relationship between social skills and loneliness and positive relationships between social skills and self-esteem, life satisfaction, and participation in extracurricular activities. Furthermore, regression analyses found that social skill outcomes accounted for a significant proportion of variance in loneliness, self-esteem, life satisfaction, and participation in extracurricular activities, supporting the postulation that the possession of social skills is directly linked to functional outcomes (e.g., psychosocial adjustment) in college students. Gresham and Elliot (1987) demonstrated similar relationships in their examination of social skills and social adaptability by uncovering significant correlational links between these variables. For example, the Adaptive Behavioral Inventory for Children showed significant positive relationships with parental ratings of social skills spanning the environmental, interpersonal, self-related, and task-related behavioral domains. A variety of other adaptability measures (i.e., Weschler Intelligence Scale for Children, Peabody Individual Achievement Test, and Children's Adaptive Behavior Scale) showed similar correlations with parent- and teacher-based ratings of social skills.

Social skill deficits have also shown significant links with psychosocial dispositions, leading some researchers to believe that they may be underlying their behavioral symptoms. According to the social skills deficit vulnerability hypothesis, an individual's psychosocial well-being can be threatened by a lack of social competence (Lewinsohn, Chaplin, & Barton, 1980; Segrin, 1990, 1993, 1998, 2000). As ineffective social skills "enhance the likelihood of eliciting punishment from the social environment" (Segrin, 1990, p. 293), including interpersonal rejection, embarrassment, and relationship failure, they can contribute to the development of loneliness, depression, or social anxiety. Substantial support has been generated for this hypothesis as loneliness (DiTommaso et al., 2003; Riggio et al., 1990, 1993; Wittenberg & Reis, 1986), depression (Segrin & Flora, 2000; Segrin, 1996, 1998; Tse & Bond, 2004), and social anxiety (Leary & Kowalski, 1995; Riggio et al., 1990; Segrin, 1996) have been empirically linked to social skills deficits. For example, DiTomasso et al. (2003) and Riggio et al. (1993) identified inverse relationships between total SSI outcome scores and loneliness, indicating that those who are less socially skilled are also less socially satisfied. Segrin (1996, 1998, 2000) has widely examined the links between social skills and depression, uncovering consistent inverse links between these variables. Furthermore, the work of Segrin and Flora (2000) demonstrated linear associations between social skills and loneliness, depression, and social anxiety.

The work of Gottman et al. (1975) provides the only known example where all four approaches to social competence were included within a single assessment (i.e., relationship, sociometric, functional, and self-reported social skills). While the intercorrelations between the outcomes were not specifically reported, significant associations between the attainment of interpersonal relationships, social skills, and functional outcomes were found, as the more popular children were also more socially skillful, were more knowledgeable about how to make friends, and performed better on a functional task.

2.1.2.5   *Summary of Approaches*

The social skills, sociometric status, relationship, and functional approaches each represent an independent, yet interdependent, facet of social competence. While the social skills approach appraises the individual abilities that can contribute to successful social interactions, the functional, relationship, and sociometric approaches examine the proficiency with which one can utilize these skills to attain social goals within specific social contexts. As each approach evaluates different aspects of 'social effectiveness' (i.e., the one agreed upon element of social competence), they can be separately enlisted to assess different components of social competence. However, regardless of one's approach, the results from one assessment are likely to be reflective of outcomes on other competency evaluations, as moderate relationships have been found between all four approaches (Baron & Markman, 2003; Bukowski & Hoza, 1989; Eisenberg et al., 1993; Gottman et al., 1975; J. G. Parker & Asher, 1987). The emergence of significant relationships across social competence assessments highlights the wide variety of skills and abilities contained within this multifaceted concept. While it is best to utilize varied assessments, across approaches, this is not always feasible due to financial and time constraints.

2.1.3   External Influences on Social Competence

Outcomes on social competence assessments can be influenced by a variety of extraneous factors. Gender and age are two of the most influential, with substantial social differences being consistently uncovered across these dimensions.

2.1.3.1   *Gender*

Differences in social skills and relationship development across gender have been well documented (Adler & Kless, 1992; Anastasi, 1984; Block, 1983; Crick & Dodge, 1994; DiPrete & Jennings, 2012; Eder & Hallinan, 1978; Eisenberg, Miller, Shell, McNalley, & Al, 1991; Friedman, Prince, Riggio, & DiMatteo, 1980; Nemeth, 1999; Riggio, 1986; Roberts, Gotlib, & Kassel, 1996; Rosenthal, 1979). These differences are discernible from early childhood, as males and females begin to diverge in their interpersonal orientations. Females exhibit strong interpersonal orientations, displaying a preference for pro-social and cooperative behaviors, and a greater concern for social disapproval, than their male counterparts, who tend to be instrumentally oriented, caring less about their popularity among peers and more about dominance over them (Anastasi, 1984; Block, 1983; Crick & Dodge, 1994; Eisenberg, Shell, Pasternack, Lennon, & Al, 1987; Nemeth, 1999). These differences likely contribute to the structural variance found among male and female friendship groups, as females tend to develop more exclusive, dyadic relationships characterized by self-disclosure, while males tend to form larger friendship groups oriented around mutual interests (Benenson, 1990; Eder & Hallinan, 1978; Erwin, 1985). While social skills are not specifically dyadic, greater interaction within dyadic relationships has been implicated as a significant contributor to the development of social skills and emotional intimacy, at a quicker rate, for females (Adler & Kless, 1992; Benenson, 1990). These social differences appear to remain stable over time, as males regularly achieve lower outcomes on a variety of social skills measures as compared to their female counterparts (DiPrete & Jennings, 2009; Friedman et al., 1980; Riggio, 1986; Rosenthal, 1979).

For example, research indicates that adult females are better communicators of emotion than adult males. During the development of the Social Skills Inventory, Riggio (1986) found women to score higher on the expressivity and sensitivity subscales, whereas males scored higher on the emotional control subscale. Friedman et al. (1980) uncovered similar patterns during the development of the Affective Communication Test (an assessment of individual differences in non-verbal emotional expressiveness, commonly referred to as charisma), as males obtained lower scores than females. Evidence from DiPrete and Jennings (2009) suggests that these gender differences are evident from an early age. Employing a large sample of elementary school children, DiPrete and Jennings (2009) conducted a longitudinal study assessing a wide range of social and behavioral variables of students from kindergarten to fifth grade. In the initial assessment, girls scored higher than boys on the social skills assessments (e.g., measures of attentiveness, emotional control, forming and maintaining friendships, comforting and helping behaviors, etc.) for both teacher and parent reports. Over time, the gap between males and females widened, and by fifth grade, boys were .53 standard deviations behind females on social and behavioral skills, up from .40 in kindergarten.

These particular social differences are often attributed to the gender-based socialization processes. For example, young boys are typically given greater social independence than young girls (for a review of this literature see Cross & Madson, 1997). This greater independence could lead to greater time with their peers, where males can learn new socialization strategies. Similarly, female gender roles specify that they are the nurturing caregivers. Through the socialization processes and group norms women may become more skilled in abilities such as encoding and decoding emotional communication, whereas males become better able to control their expressive behavior.

It should be noted that these gender differences do not reflect an invalidity of these particular social skill assessments, but rather suggest that potential gender differences should be controlled for when evaluating skill differences within a population. Further discussion of gender differences is beyond the scope of this monograph.

2.1.3.2   *Age*

Regardless of gender, social competencies continue to develop and change over time. With time comes physical and mental development and exposure to new social situations, which contribute to the cultivation of one's ability to effectively navigate and adapt to a variety of social situations and environments (Ladd, 1999). While some facets of sociability are established in infancy, such as the set of expectations about how to effectively interact with others (Sroufe & Fleeson, 1986), others are not acquired, or fully established, until early childhood, adolescence, or adulthood. Through increased social experience, individuals refine their social abilities (Bartholomew & Horowitz, 1991; Cassidy, Kirsh, Scolton, & Parke, 1996; Engles, Finkenauer, Meeus, & Dekovic, 2001) and develop more effective social strategies (Berndt, 1996).

For example, schoolchildren quickly develop interpersonal problem solving skills (Rubin & Rose-Krasnor, 1992), such as negotiation (Laursen, Finkelstein, & Townsend-Betts, 2001) and conflict resolution (Newcomb & Bagwell, 1995), as they begin to navigate the social worlds of their classrooms. During adolescence, when one's priorities shift away from relationships based on common activities and toward emotional intimacy (Hartup, 1993), additional social proficiencies are acquired. For instance, the ability to cultivate emotional closeness with others (Field, Lang, Yando, & Bendell, 1995; Hansen, Christopher, & Nangle, 1992) and social control (Murphy, Shepard, Eisenberg, & Guthrie, 1999) become established during this time, while empathy skills (Pecukonis, 1990) and pro-social behaviors, such as perspective taking and cooperation (Wentzel & Caldwell, 1997), continue to develop.

While some social skills are associated with particular developmental periods, such as emotional intimacy (Hartup, 1993), other social skills, such as emotion regulation, are established from a very early age and continue to develop throughout one's life (Carstensen, 1995; Gross et al., 1997; Lawton, Kleban, Rajagopal, & Dean, 1992). In early childhood, moments of fleeting frustration, anger, or even tiredness can often be expressed on the most extreme ends of the spectrum (e.g., screaming, crying). However, as individuals get older, they begin to exhibit greater self-regulatory capacities and demonstrate higher levels of emotional control (Carstensen, 1995; Gross et al., 1997; Lawton et al., 1992). While the mechanisms underlying these increases in emotional regulation are not entirely clear, researchers have postulated that it is due to the adaptation of more effective coping strategies over time (Carstensen, 1995; Folkman, Lazarus, Pimley, & Novacek, 1987).

When assessing social competence, one not only needs to remain aware of the potential enhanced outcomes among older, more socially experienced, participants, but also mindful that different competence assessments may be more appropriate than others at different stages of development (Waters & Sroufe, 1983). For instance, while friendship initiation is relevant in elementary age, it is not until adolescence that peer relationships take precedence and romantic relationships begin to gain significance (Erikson, 1959;

Ruble, 1983; Waters & Sroufe, 1983). Thus, a competence assessment based on the quality and quantity of relationships may not be as appropriate when evaluating young children, as it would be for an adolescent sample. Additionally, different social skills are pertinent for different developmental periods. For instance, assessments among young children may involve an appraisal of negotiation (Laursen et al., 2001) and conflict resolution (Newcomb & Bagwell, 1995), whereas an adolescent assessment may focus on higher-order skills, such as forming and maintaining intimate emotional bonds (Field et al., 1995; Hansen et al., 1992). Age-appropriate methodology should also be considered. For instance, teacher-based competence ratings may be appropriate assessments for young children; however, their validity among an adult population would be questionable.

2.1.3.3 Other Correlates

A variety of other factors have also been shown to have significant relationships with social competence outcomes. For instance, attachment has shown significant relationships with various aspects of social competence. A secure attachment provides individuals with a set of expectations about how to effectively interact with others (Sroufe & Fleeson, 1986), and the ability to develop the skills necessary for establishing and maintaining reciprocal interpersonal relationships (Bartholomew & Horowitz, 1991; Cassidy et al., 1996; Engles et al., 2001), making it a fundamental component for the development of skills associated with social competence (Gutstein & Whitney, 2002). It has been identified as an important component in social support-seeking behavior (Blain, Thompson, & Whiffen, 1993; Cutrona, Cole, Colangelo, Assouline, & Russell, 1994), social adjustment and self-efficacy (Rice, Cunningham, & Young, 1997), and the development of effective skills (DiTommaso et al., 2003). Increased levels of loneliness (DiTommaso et al., 2003; Jones, Hobbs, & Hockenbury, 1982; Riggio et al., 1990; Wittenberg & Reis, 1986), depression (Segrin, 1998, 2000; Tse & Bond, 2004), and social anxiety (Leary & Kowalski, 1995; Riggio et al., 1990; Segrin, 1996) have also shown significant inverse relationships with social skill outcomes.

2.1.4 Social Competence: Overview

Social competence is difficult to operationalize. Researchers have evaluated this concept in a wide variety of ways, ranging from skills approaches that quantify social competence as the possession of a range of particular social abilities, to functional approaches that assess the cognitive, affective, and behavioral components of effective socialization. Even though moderate relationships between approaches are evident, utilizing varied assessments, across approaches, is ideal and will produce the most comprehensive and accurate appraisals. When it is not possible to employ multiple evaluations within a single assessment, due to time or financial constraints, researchers often utilize the social skills approach (Rose-Kransor, 1997), due to its foundational nature (Cavell, 1990; DuBois & Felner, 1996; Rose-Kransor, 1997), ease of administration, and significant relationships with sociometric (Eisenberg et al., 1993; Watson et al., 1999), relationship (Carton et al., 1999; Grisset & Norvell, 1992), and functional (Baron & Markman, 2003; Riggio et al., 1993) assessments. As a valid measure of social skill and social performance, the social skills approach will be ideal for assessing the associations between social competence and OVG involvement as well as pinpointing the precise social abilities that may hold a relationship with OVG play.

REFERENCES

Adler, P., & Kless, S. (1992). Socialziation to gender roles: Popularity among elementary school boys and girls. *Sociology of Education, 65*(3), 169–187.

American Psychiatric Association. (2000). *Diagnositc and statistical manual of mental disorders.* Washington, DC: American Psychiatric Association.

Anastasi, A. (1984). Reciprocal relations between cogntivie and affective development with implciations for sex differences. In T. B. Sonderegger (Ed.), *Psychology and gender: Nebraska Symposium on Motivation* (pp. 1–35). Lincoln: University of Nebraska Press.

Anderson, S., & Messick, S. (1974). Social competency in young children. *Developmental Psychology, 10*, 282–293.

Atteli, G. (1990). Successful and disconfirmed children in the peer group: Indices of social competence within an evolutionary perspective. *Human Development, 33*, 238–249.

Bandura, A. (1977). *Social learning theory.* Englewood Cliffs, NJ: Prentice-Hall.

Barlow, D., Abel, G., Blanchard, E., Bristow, A., & Young, L. (1977). A heterosexual skills behavior checklist for males. *Behavior Therapy, 8*(2), 229–239.

Baron, R., & Markman, G. (2003). Beyond social capital: The role of entrepreneurs' social competence in their financial success. *Journal of Business Venturing, 18*(1), 41–60.

Bartholomew, K., & Horowitz, L. M. (1991). Attachment styles among young adults. *Journal of Personality and Social Psychology, 61*(2), 226–244.

Bellack, A., Morrison, R., Wixted, J., & Mueser, K. (1990). An analysis of social competence in schizophrenia. *British Journal of Psychiatry, 156*(6), 809–818.

Benenson, J. (1990). Gender differences in social networks. *Journal of Early Adolescence, 10*, 472–495.

Berndt, T. J. (1996). Exploring the effects of friendship quality on social development. In W. M. Bukowski, A. F. F. Newcomb, & W. W. Hartup (Eds.), *The company they keep: Friendship in childhood and adolescence* (pp. 346–365). Cambridge: CambridgeUniversity Press.

Blain, M. D., Thompson, J. M., & Whiffen, V. E. (1993). Attachment and perceived social support in late adolescence. *Journal of Adolescent Research, 8*(2), 226–241.

Block, J. H. (1983). Differential premises arising from differential socialization of the sexes: Some conjectures. *Child Development, 54*, 1335–1354.

Bukowski, W. M., & Hoza, B. (1989). Popularity and friendship: Issues in theory, measurement, and outcome. In T. J. Berndt & G. W. Ladd (Eds.), *Peer relationships in child development* (pp. 15–45). New York: Wiley.

Cairns, R. B., & Cairns, B. D. (1994). *Lifelines and risks: Pathways of youths in our time.* Cambridge: Cambridge University Press.

Candy, S., Troll, L., & Levy, S. (1981). A developmental exploration of friendship functions in women. *Psychology of Women Quarterly, 5*, 456–471.

Carstensen, L. L. (1995). Evidence for a life-span theory of socioemotional selectivity. *Current Directions in Psychologial Science, 4*(5), 151–162.

Carton, J., Kessler, E., & Pape, C. (1999). Nonverbal decoding skills and relationship well-being in adults. *Journal of Nonverbal Behavior, 23*(1), 91–100.

Cassidy, J., Kirsh, S., Scolton, K., & Parke, R. (1996). Attachment and representations of peer relationships. *Developmental Psychology, 32*(5), 892–904.

Cavell, T. A. (1990). Social adjustment, social performance, and social skills: A tricomponent model of social competence. *Journal of Clinical Child Psychology, 19,* 111–122.

Coie, J. D. (1985). Fitting social skills intervention to the target group. In B. H. Schneider, K. H. Rubin, & J. E. Ledingham (Eds.), *Children's peer realtions: Issues in assessment and intervention* (pp. 141–156). New York: Springer-Verlag.

Connolly, J., & Doyle, A. (1984). Relation of social fantasy play to social competence in preschoolers. *Developmental Psychology, 20*(5), 797–806.

Crick, N., & Dodge, K. A. (1994). A review and reformulation of social information-processing mechanisms in children's social adjustment. *Psychologial Bulletin, 115*(1), 74–101.

Cross, S. E., & Madson, L. (1997). Models of the self: Self-construals and gender. *Psychologial Bulletin, 122*(1), 5–37.

Cutrona, C. E., Cole, V., Colangelo, N., Assouline, S. G., & Russell, D. W. (1994). Perceived parental support and academic achievement: An attachment theory perspective. *Personality and Social Psychology, 66*(2), 369–378.

D'Zurilla, T. J., & Goldfried, M. R. (1971). Problem solving and behavior modification. *Journal of Abnormal Psychology, 78,* 107–126.

Denham, S. A., McKinley, M., Couchard, E., & Holt, R. (1990). Emotional and behavioral predictors of preschool peer ratings. *Child Development, 61,* 1145–1152.

DiPrete, T. A., & Jennings, J. L. (2012). Social and behavioral skills and the gender gap in early educational achievement. *Social Science Research, 41*(1), 1–15.

Dishion, T., Andrews, D., & Crosby, L. (1995). Antisocial boys and their friends in early adolescence: Relationship characteristic, quality, and interactional process. *Child Development, 66*(1), 139–151.

Dishion, T., McCord, J., & Poulin, F. (1999). When interventions harm. *American Psychologist, 54,* 755–764.

DiTommaso, E., Brannen-McNulty, C., Ross, L., & Burgess, M. (2003). Attachment styles, social skills and loneliness in young adults. *Personality and Indivdiual Differences, 35*(2), 303–312.

Dodge, K. A. (1985). Facets of social interaction and the assessment of social competence in children. In B. H. Schneider, K. H. Rubin, & J. Ledingham (Eds.), *Children's peer relations: Issues in assessment and intervention* (pp. 3–22). New York: Springer-Verlag.

Dodge, K. A. (1986). A social information processing model of social competence in children. In M. Perlmutter (Ed.), *Cognitive perspectives on children's social and behavioral development* (Vol. 18). Hillsdale, NJ: Lawrence Erlbaum.

Dodge, K. A., McClaskey, C., & Feldman, E. (1985). Situational approach to the assessment of social competence in children. *Journal of Consulting and Clinical Psychology, 53*(3), 344–353.

Dodge, K. A., & Murphy, R. R. (1984). The assessment of social compentece in adolescents. In P. Karoly & J. J. Steffan (Eds.), *Adolescent behavior disorders: Current perspectives* (pp. 61–96). Lexington, MA: D C Heath.

DuBois, D. L., & Felner, R. D. (1996). The quadripartite model of social competence: Theory and applications to clinical intervention. In M. A. Reinecke (Ed.), *Cognitive therapy with children and adolescents: A casebook for clinical practice.* New York: Guilford Press.

Eder, D., & Hallinan, M. (1978). Sex differences in children's friendships. *American Sociologial Review, 43,* 237–250.

Eisenberg, N., Fabes, R., Bernzweig, M. K., Poulin, R., & Hanish, L. (1993). The relations of emotionality and regulation to preschoolers' social skills and sociometric status. *Child Development, 64*(5), 1418–1438.

Eisenberg, N., Miller, P. A., Shell, R., McNalley, S., & Al, E. (1991). Prosocial development in adolescence: A longitudinal study. *Developmental Psychology, 27,* 849–857.

Eisenberg, N., Shell, R., Pasternack, J., Lennon, R., & Al, E. (1987). Prosocial development in middle childhood: A longitudinal study. *Developmental Psychology, 23,* 712–718.

Engles, R., Finkenauer, C., Meeus, W., & Dekovic, M. (2001). Parental attachment and adolescents' emotional adjustment: The associations with social skills and relational competence. *Journal of Counseling Psychology, 48*(4), 428–439.

Erikson, E. (1959). *Identity and the life cycle.* New York: International Universities Press.

Erwin, P. (1985). Similarity of attitudes and constructs in children's friendships. *Journal of Experimental Child Psychology, 40*(3), 470–485.

Field, T., Lang, C., Yando, R., & Bendell, D. (1995). Adolescents' intimacy with parents and friends. *Adolescence, 30*(117), 113–140.

Folkman, S., Lazarus, R. S., Pimley, S., & Novacek, J. (1987). Age differences in stress and coping processes. *Psychology and Aging, 2*(2), 171–184.

Ford, M. (1982). Social cognition and social competence in adolescence. *Developmental Psychology, 18*(3), 323–340.

Ford, M., & Tisak, M. (1983). A further search for social intelligence. *Journal of Educational and Psychologial Consulation, 75*(2), 196–206.

Friedman, H. S., Prince, L. M., Riggio, R. E., & DiMatteo, M. R. (1980). Understanding and assessing nonverbal expressiveness: The Affective Communication Test. *Journal of Personality and Social Psychology, 39,* 333–351.

Gifford, R., & O'Connor, B. (1987). The interpersonal circumplex as a behavior map. *Journal of Personality and Social Psychology, 52*(5), 1019–1026.

Gilliland, A., & Burke, R. (1926). A measure of sociability. *Journal of Applied Psychology, 10,* 315–326.

Glasgow, R., & Arkowitz, H. (1975). The behavioral assessment of male and female social competence in dyadic heterosexual interactions. *Behavior Therapy, 6*(4), 488–498.

Goldfried, M., & D'Zurilla, T. (1969). A behavioral-analytic model for assessing competence. In C. Spielberger (Ed.), *Current topics in clinical and community psychology* (Vol. 1, pp. 151–196). New York: Academic Press.

Gottman, J., Gonso, J., & Rasmussen, B. (1975). Social interaction, social competence, and friendship in children. *Child Development, 46*(3), 709–718.

Gottman, J., & Graziano, W. (1983). How children become friends. *Monographs of the Society for Research in Child Development, 48*(3), 1–86.

Gresham, F. (1981). Assessment of children's social skills. *Journal of School Psychology, 19*(2), 120–133.

Gresham, F., & Elliot, S. (1987). The relationship between adaptive behavior and social skills. Issues in definition and assessment. *Journal of Special Education, 21*(1), 167–181.

Gresham, F., & Elliot, S. (1989). Social skills deficits as a primary learning disability. *Journal of Learning Disabilities, 22*(2), 120–124.

Grisset, N., & Norvell, N. (1992). Perceived social support, social skills, and quality of relationships in bulimic women. *Journal of Consulting and Clinical Psychology, 60*(2), 293–299.

Gross, J., Carstensen, L., Pasupathi, M., Tsai, J., Skorpen, C., & Hsu, A.Y.C. (1997). Emotion and aging: Experience, expression, and control. *Psychology and Aging, 12,* 590–599.

Grossman, H. (1983). *Classification in mental retardation*. Washington, DC: American Assoication on Mental Deficiency.

Gutstein, S., & Whitney, T. (2002). Asperger syndrome and the development of social competence. *Focus on Autism and Other Development Disabilities, 17*(3), 161–171.

Hacker, H. (1981). Blabbermouths and clams: Sex differences in self-disclosure in same-sex and cross-sex friendship dyads. *Psychology of Women Quarterly, 5*, 385–401.

Hansen, D. J., Christopher, J. S., & Nangle, D. W. (1992). Adolescent heterosocial interactions and dating. In V. B. van Hasselt & M. Hersen (Eds.), *Handbook of social development: A lifespan perspective* (pp. 371–394). New York: Plenum Press.

Hartup, W. (1989). Social relationships and their developmental significance. *American Psychologist, 44*(2), 120–126.

Hartup, W. (1993). Adolescents and their friends. *New Directions for Child Development, 1993*(60), 3–22.

Hughes, J. (1990). Assessment of children's social competence. In C. R. Reynolds & R. Kamphaus (Eds.), *Handbook of psychologial and educational assessment of children* (pp. 423–444). New York: Guilford Press.

Jones, W., Hobbs, S., & Hockenbury, D. (1982). Loneliness and social skill deficits. *Journal of Personality and Social Psychology, 42*(4), 682–689.

Kohlberg, L., & Mayer, R. (1972). Development as the aim of education. *Harvard Educational Review, 42*(4), 449–496.

Koning, C., & Magill-Evans, J. (2001). Social and language skills in adolescent boys with Asperger syndrome. *Autism, 5*(1), 23–26.

Ladd, G. W. (1981). Effectiveness of a social learning method for enhancing children's social interaction and peer acceptance. *Child Development, 52*(1), 171–178.

Ladd, G. W. (1999). Peer relationships and social competence during early and middle childhood. *Annual Review of Psychology, 50*, 333–359.

Ladd, G. W., & Mize, J. (1983). A cognitive-social learning model of social-skill tranining. *Psychologial Review, 90*(2), 127–157.

Laursen, B., Finkelstein, B. D., & Betts, N. T. (2001). A developmental meta-analysis of peer conflict resolution. *Developmental Review, 21*(4), 423–449.

Lawton, M. P., Kleban, M. H., Rajagopal, D., & Dean, J. (1992). Dimensions of affective experience in three age groups. *Psychology and Aging, 7*(2), 171–184.

Leary, M., & Kowalski, R. (1995). *Social anxiety*. New York: Guilford Press.

Lee, L. (1979). Is social competence indepdent of cultural context? *American Psychologist, 34*(9), 795–796.

Lewinsohn, P. M., Mischel, W., Chaplin, W., & Barton, R. (1980). Social competence and depression: The role of illusory self-perceptions. *Journal of Abnormal Psychology, 89*(2), 203–212.

Lowe, M. R., & Cautela, J. R. (1978). A self-report measure of social skill. *Behavior Therapy, 9*(4), 535–544.

Luthar, S. (1995). Social competence in the school setting: Prospective cross-domain associations among inner-city teens. *Child Development, 66*(2), 416–429.

Marlowe, H. (1986). Social intelligence: Evidence for multidimensionality and construct indepedence. *Journal of Educational and Psychologial Consulation, 78*(1), 52–58.

McFall, R. (1982). A review and reformulation of the concept of social skills. *Behavioral Assessment, 4*(1), 1–33.

Mize, J., & Ladd, G. W. (1990). Toward the development of successful social skills training for preschool children. In S. R. Asher & J. D. Coie (Eds.), *Peer rejection in childhood* (pp. 338–364). Cambridge: Cambridge University Press.

Moskowitz, D. S. (1990). Convergence of self-reports and independent observers: Dominance and friendliness. *Journal of Personality and Social Psychology, 58*(6), 1096–1106.

Moss, F., Hunt, T., Omwake, K., & Ronning, M. (1927). Social Intelligence Test. Washington, DC: Center for Psychologial Science.

Mueser, K. T., Doonan, R., Penn, D., Blanchard, J., Bellack, A., Nishith, P., & DeLeon, J. (1996). Emotion recognition and social competence in chronic schizophrenia. *Journal of Abnormal Psychology, 105*(2), 271–275.

Murphy, B.C., Shepard, S. A., Eisenberg, N., & Guthrie, I. K. (1999). Contemporaneous and longitudinal relations of dispositional sympathy to emotionality, regulation, and social functioning. *Journal of Early Adolescence, 19*, 66–97.

Nemeth, E. (1999). Gender differences in reaction to publich achievement feedback. *Educational Studies, 25*, 297–310.

Newcomb, A., & Bagwell, C. L. (1995). Children's friendship relations: A meta-analytic review. *Psychologial Bulletin, 117*(2), 306–347.

Oden, S., & Asher, S. R. (1977). Coaching children in social skills for friendship making. *Child Development, 48*(2), 495–506.

Ogbu, J. (1981). Origins of human competence: A cultural ecologial perspective. *Child Development, 52*, 413–429.

Parker, J. G., & Asher, S. R. (1987). Peer relations and later personal adjustment: Are low-accepted children at risk? *Psychologial Bulletin, 102*(3), 357–389.

Parker, J. G., & Asher, S. R. (1993). Friendship and friendship quality in middle childhood: Links with peer group acceptance and feelings of loneliness and social dissatisfaction. *Developmental Psychology, 29*(4), 611–621.

Parker, S., & DeVries, B. (1993). Patterns of friendship for women and men in same and cross-sex relationships. *Journal of Social and Personal Relationships, 10*, 617–626.

Pecukonis, E. V. (1990). A cognitive/affective empathy training program as a function of ego development in aggressive adolescent females. *Adolescence, 25*(97), 59–76.

Pinter, R., & Upshall, C. (1928). Some results of social intelligence tests. *School and Society, 27*, 369–370.

Rice, K. G., Cunningham, T. J., & Young, M. B. (1997). Attachment to parents, social competence, and emotional well-being. *Journal of Counseling Psychology, 44*(1), 89–101.

Riggio, R. (1986). Assessment of basic social skills. *Journal of Personality and Social Psychology, 51*(3), 649–660.

Riggio, R. (1989). *Manual for the Social Skills Inventory.* Palo Alto, CA: Consulting Psychologists Press.

Riggio, R., Messamer, J., & Throckmorton, B. (1991). Social and academic intelligence: Conceptually distinct but overlapping constructs. *Personality and Indivdiual Differences, 12*(7), 695–702.

Riggio, R., Throckmorton, B., & DePaola, S. (1990). Social skills and self-esteem. *Personality and Indivdiual Differences, 11*(8), 799–804.

Riggio, R., Watring, K., & Throckmorton, B. (1993). Social skills, support, and psychosocial adjustment. *Personality and Individual Differences, 15*(3), 275–280.

Roberts, J., Gotlib, I., & Kassel, J. (1996). Adult attachment security and symptoms of depression: The mediating roles of dysfunctional attitudes and low self-esteem. *Journal of Personality and Social Psychology, 70*(2), 310–320.

Rose-Kransor, L. (1997). Nature of social competence: A theoretical review. *Social Developmental Psychology, 6*(1), 111–135.

Rosenthal, R. (1979). *Skill in nonverbal communication.* Cambridge, MA: Oelgeschlager, Gunn, & Hain.

Rubin, K. H., Bukowski, W. M., & Parker, J. C. (2007). Peer interactions, relationsihps, and groups. In W. Damon & N. Eisenberg (Eds.), *Handbook of child psychology: Social, emotional, and personality development.* New York: Wiley.

Rubin, K. H., & Rose-Krasnor, L. (1992). Interpersonal problem-solving and social competence in children. In V. B. van Hasselt & M. Hersen (Eds.), *Handbook of social development: A lifespan perspective*. New York: Plenum.

Ruble, D. N. (1983). The development of social-comparison processes and their role in acheivement-related self-socialization. In E. T. Higgins, D. N. Ruble, & W. Hartup (Eds.), *Social cogntion and social development* (pp. 134–157). Cambridge: Cambridge University Press.

Segrin, C. (1990). A meta-analytic review of social skill deficits in depression. *Communication Monographs*, 57(4), 292–308.

Segrin, C. (1993). Social skills deficits and psychosocial problems: Antecedent, concomitant, or consequent? *Journal of Social and Clinical Psychology*, 12, 336–353.

Segrin, C. (1996). The relationship between social skills deficits and psychosocial problems. A test of a vulnerability model. *Communication Research*, 23, 425–450.

Segrin, C. (1998). Interpersonal communication problems associated with depression and loneliness. In P. Andersen & L. Guerrero (Eds.), *Handbook of communication and emotion: Research, theory, applications, and contexts* (pp. 215–242). San Diego, CA: Academic Press.

Segrin, C. (2000). Social skills deficits associated with depression. *Clinical Psychology Review*, 20(3), 379–403.

Segrin, C., & Flora, J. (2000). Poor social skills are a vulnerability factor in the development of psychosocial problems. *Human Commuication Research*, 26(3), 489–514.

Segrin, C., & Kinney, T. (1995). Social skills deficits among the socially anxious: Loneliness and rejection from others. *Motivation and Emotion*, 19(1), 1–24.

Shea, L., Thompson, L., & Blieszner, R. (1988). Resources in older adults' old and new friendships. *Journal of Social and Personal Relationships*, 5, 83–96.

Sroufe, L. A., & Fleeson, J. (1986). Attachment and the construction of relationships. In W. Hartup & Z. Rubin (Eds.), *Relationships and development* (pp. 51–57). Hillsdale, NJ: Erlbaum.

Sussman, S., Unger, J. B., & Dent, C. W. (2004). Peer group self-identification among alternative high school youth: A predictor of their psychosocial functioning five years later. *International Journal of Clinical and Health Psychology*, 4(1), 9–25.

Thorndike, E. (1920). Intelligence and its use. *Harper's Magazine*, 140(January), 227–235.

Thorndike, R., & Steinfield, C. (1937). An evaluation of the attempts to measure social intelligence. *Psychologial Bulletin*, 34(5), 275–285.

Tse, W., & Bond, A. (2004). The impact of depression on social skills: A review. *Journal of Nervous and Mental Disease*, 192(4), 260–268.

Vandell, D., & Hembree, S. (1994). Peer social status and friendship: Independent contributors to childen's social and academic adjustment. *Merrill-Palmer Quarterly*, 40(4), 461–477.

Vygotsky, L. (1978). Interaction between learning and development. In M. Cole (Ed.), *Mind and society* (pp. 79–91). Cambridge, MA: Harvard University Press.

Waters, E., & Sroufe, L. (1983). Social competence as a developmental construct. *Developmental Review*, 3, 79–97.

Watson, A., Nixon, C. L., Wilson, A., & Capage, L. (1999). Social interaction skills and theory of mind in young children. *Developmental Psychology*, 35(2), 386–391.

Wentzel, K. R., & Caldwell, K. (1997). Friendships, peer acceptance, and group membership: Relations to academic achievement in middle school. *Child Development*, 68(6), 1198–1209.

Wittenberg, M., & Reis, H. (1986). Lonliness, social skills, and social perception. *Personality and Social Psychology Bulletin*, 12(1), 121–130.

3 Social Implications of Online Video Game Involvement

The proliferation of affordable and accessible Internet connectivity has changed the way video games are played by allowing individuals to connect worldwide in shared gaming spaces. These highly social environments allow players to connect, interact with, and learn from each other. However, there is a growing concern that these social environments also have the potential to displace real-world connections and interactions, contributing to a variety of losses in 'offline' sociability (Chiu, Lee, & Huang, 2004; Cole & Griffiths, 2007; Kim, Namkoong, Ku, & Kim, 2008; Peters & Malesky, 2008; Shen & Williams, 2010). While the belief in the association between OVG play and social incompetence remains widespread, so much so that it has evolved into a core component of the cultural perceptions of those who participate within these spaces (Kowert, Griffiths, & Oldmeadow, 2012; Kowert & Oldmeadow, 2012), empirical evidence illustrating this relationship has been conflicting, and the potential mechanisms underlying these associations remain unclear.

To clarify the associations between social competence and OVG involvement, as well as provide insight into the potential mechanisms underlying them, the current chapter will overview the relationships between these two variables theoretically and empirically. The chapter will begin with a discussion of the theoretical links between social competence and OVG involvement, focusing on social displacement and social compensation perspectives. While the proponents of these theories both contend that inverse relationships exist between social competence and OVG involvement, they differ in the proposed foundation of social differences among online players. Displacement theorists highlight the potential for social atrophy over time due to OVG engagement (Hussain & Griffiths, 2009; Kim et al., 2008; Liu & Peng, 2009; Lo, Wang, & Fang, 2005; Morahan-Martin & Schumacher, 2003; Shen & Williams, 2010), while compensation theorists focus on the role of pre-existing social dispositions (e.g., loneliness, depression, social anxiety) and their motivational role in OVG involvement (Cole & Griffiths, 2007; Hsu, Wen, & Wu, 2009; Iacono & Weisband, 1997; D. Williams, 2006; Yee, 2002). While displacement effects may exacerbate these dispositions, a certain degree of social inadequacy is believed to pre-exist amongst those who are motivated to engage within online gaming spaces.

After an overview of the theoretical links, an examination of the empirical links between social competence and OVG involvement will be presented, focusing on the three primary facets of sociability that have shown significant relationships with involvement: relationship quality/quantity, psychosocial dispositions, and social skills. The small, but noteworthy, amount of literature challenging the contention that OVG players are somehow socially deficient will also be examined. This new wave of research not only suggests that there are no significant social differences between online players and non-online players, but also that engagement within online video gaming environments may actually be socially beneficial by expanding one's social network and providing an easily accessible social space where individuals can learn, practice, and perfect a variety of social skills (Ducheneaut & Moore, 2005; Steinkuehler & Williams, 2006; Visser, Antheunis, & Schouten, 2013).

The chapter will conclude with an examination of the methodological limitations of the work in this area. Variability in outcome measures, sample selection, assessment focus, and the conceptualization of video game involvement and social competence, as well as genre-specific approaches, has made it difficult to determine the magnitude, consistency, and origin of the relationships between OVG involvement and social competence. Suggestions as to how to overcome these limitations in future work will also be presented.

3.1 THEORETICAL LINKS

Social displacement and compensation theories (originally developed for research on excessive use of the Internet, see Davis, 2001; Segrin, 1993) are commonly enlisted to explain the inverse relationships between OVG involvement and social outcomes. While these two theories differ in the proposed origin of social differences among the online game playing community, they both contend that social differences do exist and either originate from or are exacerbated by a general increase in time spent within online gaming environments. An examination of these two theoretical perspectives is presented in more detail in the following.

3.1.1 Social Displacement

Interaction within Internet-based social spaces can be "a socially liberating experience" (Davis, Flett, & Besser, 2002, p. 332). Freed from the rules and pressures of traditional socialization, users may begin to perceive themselves as "safer, more efficacious, more confident, and more comfortable with online interpersonal interactions and relationships than traditional face-to-face social activities" (Caplan, 2003, p. 629). However, largely because of the "inelasticity of time" (Nie & Hillygus, 2001, p. 420) (e.g., there are a finite number of hours that one can dedicate to socialization), one's online social community may begin to thrive at the expense of face-to-face interactions (Caplan, Williams, & Yee, 2009; Chiu et al., 2004; Kraut et al., 1998; Morahan-Martin & Schumacher, 2003; Nie & Erbring, 2002; D. Williams, 2006), which can lead to the displacement, or exchange, of offline social contacts for online ones (Bessière, Kiesler, Kraut, & Boneva, 2004; Blais, Craig, Pepler, & Connolly, 2008; Davis, 2001; Kraut et al., 1998).

The exchange of offline contacts for online ones is believed to be socially problematic due to a reduced sense of social presence online as well as the production of bridging, rather than bonding, social capital among online contacts. These differences in social presence and social capital are believed to limit the capability of Internet-based relationships to provide feelings of social support and closeness, thereby making the displacement of offline for online social contacts a disproportionate exchange. Rather than replacing one's offline friends with a virtual substitute, users are supplanting valuable sources of social and emotional support for less intimate and more diffuse online relationships (Galston, 2000; Slouka, 1995; D. Williams, 2007). An examination of these arguments, as supported by social presence and social capital theorists, is presented in the following sections.

3.1.1.1 *Social Presence*

The relative weakness of online interpersonal contacts, as compared to their offline counterparts, is often discussed in relation to differences in social presence across contexts. Social presence refers to the degree of awareness of the other person in a communication interaction (Short, Williams, & Christie, 1976). This idea developed from Mehrabian's (1969b) concept of "Immediacy," which refers to the mutual exchange of specific "communication behaviors that enhance closeness to, and nonverbal interaction with, another" (p. 77). Typically, Immediacy is promoted through the mutual exchange of non-verbal cues such as facial expressions, gestures, and eye contact. When these cues are present, more intense and affective social interactions ensue (see E. Williams, 1977 for a review of the research). The impact of these cues was first documented in Mehrabian's (1969a, 1969b) work, where communicators who displayed more immediacy cues (e.g., close physical proximity, eye contact, orientation toward the communication partner, etc.) were rated as being more liked than disliked. The general social impact of immediacy cues can also be seen in Milgram's (1965) classic obedience study. The rate of obedience for the experimenter's request to continue the administration of more painful shocks to a confederate participant declined from 66% when the confederate could not be seen to 40% when the participants were face-to-face. The reverse effect was observed when the proximity of the experimenter varied. Three times as many subjects were obedient to the authorities' instructions in the face-to-face condition than when clues were given only auditorily (i.e., by telephone). Reductions in the experimenter's physical proximity, and, consequently, immediacy cues, reduced the overall sense of social presence, the intimacy of the interaction, and the sense of realism, all of which led to greater dissention.

However, Social Presence Theory (Short et al., 1976) was not developed to explain differences in individual social interactions but across social systems. The fewer immediacy cues that are available within a particular social system (e.g., face-to-face communication, telephone, computer-mediated communication, etc.), the less attention one will give to the presence of other social participants and the less likely the other participants will be perceived as "real" (Short, 1976). Consequently, social interactions become less intimate as the rate of social presence decreases.

While some offline, non-verbal norms, such as interpersonal distance, have transferred into online gaming communities (Yee & Bailenson, 2008), online gaming environments generally provide few non-verbal cues. As such, they are believed to be particularly low in social presence (Rice & Love, 1987; Rice, 1993; Slouka, 1995) and, therefore, are believed to generate more impersonal, and less intimate, communication than those supported by immediacy cues (Slouka, 1995; Sproull & Kiesler, 1986). Some game developers have attempted to increase the sense of social presence by integrating in-game gesturing systems and adopting a variety of text-based 'emoticons,' both of which can be used in games to express emotional cues that are typically only expressed non-verbally in face-to-face interactions (Wilkins, 1991). While research suggests that the adoption of emoticons in text-based communications does accommodate for a substantial proportion of non-verbal cues that are missing in text-based communication (Gunawardena & Zittle, 1997), in order to provide these cues, players must explicitly communicate the information through in-game commands or text-based messages. Thus, rather than simulating face-to-face interactions, this non-verbal cue system simulates a world in which verbal and non-verbal cues are disjointed (Moore, Ducheneaut, & Nickell, 2007). This is in stark contrast to face-to-face socialization, whereby one emanates a plethora of information even when they are not intending to communicate (Goffman, 1959). For instance, a study by Naumann and colleagues (2009) found that both static (e.g., clothing) and dynamic (e.g., posture, facial expressions) cues provide information about an individual and that this information is used to form judgments about a person's personality, such as their level of agreeableness or self-esteem.

However, some researchers are beginning to consider the possibility that the absence of social cues found online may actually be beneficial by providing a level of social accommodation not found in traditional interpersonal interactions (Kiesler & Sproull, 1992; Lea & Spears, 1995; McKenna & Bargh, 2000; Parks & Floyd, 1996; Whitty & Gavin, 2001; Yee & Bailenson, 2007). For instance, the lack of non-verbal cues can promote both dissociative anonymity (i.e., "*You don't know me*") and invisibility (i.e., "*You can't see me*"). Together, this generates a unique combination of trust and anonymity, often referred to as the Online Disinhibition Effect (Suler, 2004), which can stimulate open and intimate conversations as it removes the fear of any social repercussions (Morahan-Martin & Schumacher, 2003; Suler, 2004; Walther, 1996). Consequently, individuals become inclined to self-disclose at a quicker rate than is found in non-visually anonymous relationships (Joinson, 2001; McKenna & Bargh, 2000; Parks & Floyd, 1996; Parks & Roberts, 1998; Suler, 2004) and to be more honest and open (Whitty & Gavin, 2001). This link between anonymity and self-disclosure is not a new association. In the classic study by Gergen, Gergen, and Barton (1973), individuals who conversed in a darkened room were found to disclose more intimate information about themselves and their lives than individuals who conversed in a lighted room. Furthermore, the participants who interacted anonymously reported more positive feelings toward their communication partner than those who were not anonymous to their partners. Socialization within online environments is equivalent to the darkened room, but on a much larger scale.

Thus, while a lack of non-verbal cues was originally believed to limit the quality of communication within OVGs, researchers are now beginning to suggest that a lack of immediacy cues may be more socially beneficial than harmful. Due to a lack of non-verbal cues, mediated communication is able to provide a sense of anonymity and invisibility, which can positively influence the social perceptions and behaviors of others, including the promotion of greater self-disclosure (Joinson, 2001; McKenna & Bargh, 2000; Parks & Floyd, 1996; Parks & Roberts, 1998; Suler, 2004) than is found in offline communication.

Before moving forward, it should be noted that online games do not provide complete anonymity. While a game player's identity is typically not initially detectable within the gaming space, how one presents oneself online often provides clues to one's real-world identity (Whitty & Carr, 2006). Researchers have found that users unintentionally transmit a variety of personal information online through linguistic and behavioral cues, such as nationality, education level, gender, and other sociodemographic factors (Back, Schmukle, & Egloff, 2008; Kendall, 1998; Lam, Chen, & Chen, 2008; Martey, Stromer-Galleyb, Banks, Wu, & Consalvo, 2014; Schwartz et al., 2013; D. Williams, Yee, & Caplan, 2008). For example, the name one chooses to represent oneself in a mediated environment (e.g., screen name, avatar name, etc.) can give off clues to the player's personality, such as his or her level of openness, agreeableness, conscientiousness, and narcissism (Back, Schmukle, & Egloff, 2008). Personality characteristics and gender (Herring, 2001; Schwartz et al., 2013) can also be revealed through linguistic cues, as females have been found to use more emotion words (e.g., *excited*) than males (Schwartz et al., 2013), as well as express more politeness, and less assertiveness, in computer-mediated communication (Herring, 2001).

Linguistic and behavioral cues to a user's identity have also been noted in online gaming environments specifically (Martey et al., 2014; D. Williams et al., 2008). While engaged within the gaming space, male players have been found to express more incidences of action directive statements while females express more emotional and appreciation phrases (Martey et al.,

2014). Female players have also been found to express more non-verbal cues through emoticons than male players (Martey et al., 2014). Differences in behavior have also been noted, with male players tending to place their avatars further away from groups (Martey et al., 2014; D. Williams et al., 2008) as well as jump and move backward more than female players (Martey et al., 2014).

Thus, even when a player is attempting to actively conceal his or her identity, clues to the player's real-world persona can be disseminated through unintentional linguistic and behavioral cues. Due to this, complete anonymity cannot be guaranteed. However, online games provide partial anonymity by granting visual anonymity through physical isolation from other players (Joinson, 2001; Lea, Spears, & de Groot, 2001; McKenna & Bargh, 2000; Morahan-Martin & Schumacher, 2003; Morio & Buchholz, 2009; Suler, 2004) and a dissociation of real and online identities (Morio & Buchholz, 2009; Suler, 2004), particularly when engaging in an avatar-driven gaming environment.

3.1.1.2 Social Capital

While the impact of social presence on the quality of mediated communication remains debatable, face-to-face and Internet-based friendships remain significantly different in terms of the social capital they generate. Broadly speaking, social capital refers to the resources that are accumulated within interpersonal relationships (Coleman, 1988). As defined by Bourdieu and Wacquant (1992), social capital is "the sum of the resources, actual or virtual, that accrue to an individual or a group by virtue of possessing a durable network of more or less institutionalized relationships of mutual acquaintance and recognition" (p. 14). The particular resources that can be gained will vary across social relationships but can include intellectual resources (e.g., new information), social and emotional resources (e.g., social and emotional support), and/or physical resources (e.g., tangible favors). The successful accumulation of social capital has been linked to a range of positive outcomes, including career success (Gabbay & Zuckerman, 1998), increased life satisfaction (Bjornskov, 2003; Putnam, 2000; Winkelmann, 2009), enhanced self-esteem, and general physical and psychosocial well-being (Helliwell & Putnam, 2004; Helliwell, 2006).

The kind of social capital that is generated through interpersonal relationships can be further differentiated into two subtypes: bridging and bonding (Putnam, 2000). Individuals are believed to generate bridging social capital through their inclusive and diffuse networks, such as a community choir or bowling club. These kinds of social networks form from loose connections between individuals (often of different backgrounds) and are seen to be valuable tools in helping expand one's social and world views (Putnam, 2000) but typically do not provide substantial emotional support (Granovetter, 1982). Conversely, bonding social capital is generated among close interpersonal bonds that provide substantial emotional support for one another (Putnam,

2000). These friendship bonds are more exclusive and tend to form among individuals who are from similar backgrounds, such as close family members and friends.

While many researchers have questioned if and how mediated relationships support the production of bridging and/or bonding social capital (for a review see Bargh & McKenna, 2004), few have examined these links empirically. Perhaps the most comprehensive evaluation of social capital across offline and online contexts comes from Williams (2007). In a large-scale survey study, Williams (2007) asked members of an online gaming community to complete social capital scales for both offline and online social contexts. After controlling for demographics, time online was found to be negatively associated with offline bridging and bonding social capital. Additionally, significantly more bridging social capital and less bonding social capital was found to be generated online than offline. Williams (2007) concludes that the social connections that are established within OVGs are related to increases in bridging and decreases in bonding social capital, thus illustrating the lack of equivalency between online and offline interpersonal relationships. Similar trends have been noted in cross-sectional research examining the production of social capital within Internet-based social networking (e.g., Ellison, Steinfield, & Lampe, 2007; Steinfield, Ellison, & Lampe, 2008). The production of bridging, rather than bonding, social capital has been attributed to a combination of the low entry and exit costs of online communities (Galston, 2000), which encourages broad membership, and a diminished sense of social presence (Mehrabian, 1969a, 1969b; Walther, 1996).

3.1.1.3   Social Displacement: Summary

Displacement theorists contend that OVG players suffer significant social consequences due to the displacement of offline contacts. As the social freedoms granted by online video gaming spaces generate highly intimate and sustainable bonds with one's co-players, offline social contacts may quickly be replaced for online ones (Cole & Griffiths, 2007; Hussain & Griffiths, 2009; Lo et al., 2005; Morahan-Martin & Schumacher, 2003; Shen & Williams, 2010). Over time, this displacement may lead to severe social disengagement, substantially affecting one's ability to maintain real-world interpersonal relationships (Cole & Griffiths, 2007; Hussain & Griffiths, 2009; Lo et al., 2005; Morahan-Martin & Schumacher, 2003; Shen & Williams, 2010) and impeding social and emotional skill development (Chiu et al., 2004; Griffiths, 2010; Kim et al., 2008; Liu & Peng, 2009).

Due to differences in social presence and social capital, Internet-based friendships are believed to be unable to produce levels of social and emotional support equivalent to those of their offline counterparts. Thus, the displacement of offline for online contacts is thought to be a disproportionate exchange, whereby individuals lose valuable sources of social and emotional support provided by offline social ties and gain less intimate and more diffuse online relationships. These qualitative differences in online and offline friendships may help explain why Internet-based friendships have been found to rarely lead to sustained, committed offline relationships (Cornwell & Lundgren, 2001; Parks & Roberts, 1998; Wolak, Mitchell, & Finkelhor, 2003) and why, for the majority of users, online friendships do not adequately satisfy social needs and are not preferred to offline friendships (Cummings, Butler, & Kraut, 2002; Hussain & Griffiths, 2008). As OVGs are highly social activities, these inverse links are likely attributable to the qualitative, rather than quantitative, differences in socialization across contexts.

3.1.2   Social Compensation

Proponents of the social compensation theory suggest that the inverse relationships between sociability and increased OVG play are more reflective of inherent qualities of the game players than direct social consequences due to engagement. Researchers have long suggested that mediated social environments, particularly OVGs, appeal to those who are socially unskilled, have an unmet need for sociability in their lives, and feel anxious over establishing real-world relationships (Chak & Leung, 2004; McKenna & Bargh, 2000; Peters & Malesky, 2008; Whitty & Carr, 2003, 2006; Whitty, 2003). The distinctive characteristics of OVGs have generated a highly desirable, social space, as the combination of greater communicative flexibility, enhanced social presentation strategies, and shared experiences diminishes the possibility of social rejection while stimulating the formation of intimate friendships (D. Chan & Cheng, 2004; Joinson, 2001; Pena & Hancock, 2006; Suler, 2004; D. Williams, 2007; Yee, 2007). Thus, individuals who have experienced difficulties in forming interpersonal relationships in traditional contexts may be drawn to engage within OVGs as an alternative social outlet. While displacement effects may exacerbate these relationships, a certain degree of social inadequacy is believed to exist among those who are motivated to engage within online video gaming spaces. Supporting this contention, researchers have found that more involved OVG players display higher rates of the symptoms associated with loneliness, depression, and social anxiety (Caplan et al., 2009; Kim et al., 2008; Lemmens, Valkenburg, & Peter, 2011; Lo et al., 2005; Shen & Williams, 2010; D. Williams et al., 2008), all of which display significant inverse associations with social skills (DiTommaso, Brannen-McNulty, Ross, & Burgess, 2003; Leary & Kowalski, 1995; Riggio, Throckmorton, & DePaola, 1990; Segrin & Flora, 2000; Segrin, 1996, 1998; Tse & Bond, 2004). These empirical links are discussed in more detail in section 3.2.

3.1.3   Theoretical Links: Summary

The social displacement and compensation theories attempt to clarify why online game players may exhibit the qualities associated with social ineptitude. Even though these theories differ in the proposed origin of social differences among the online game playing community, both contend that a general increase in time spent in these environments detrimentally affects various aspects of social competence. While displacement theorists contend that social differences within the online gaming population are attributable to the direct displacement of offline social interactions due to increased participation within OVG environments due to the "inelasticity of time" (Nie & Hillygus, 2001, p. 420), social compensation theorists maintain that they are reflective of an exacerbation of an underlying disposition, such as loneliness, depression, or social anxiety.

However, these theories are not necessarily mutually exclusive. It is possible that certain psychosocial predispositions (e.g., loneliness, depression, and/or social anxiety) motivate the initial engagement within online video gaming environments; over time, these predispositions become exacerbated through the displacement of offline for online contacts, negatively influencing the development and maintenance of interpersonal relationships or certain social skills. Empirical links support this possibility, as increased OVG play has been found to be associated with a range of social outcomes indicative of both social displacement and compensation effects, including declines in the quantity and quality of offline communication and the size of one's social circle (Blais et al., 2008; Cole & Griffiths, 2007; Hussain & Griffiths, 2009; Kim et al., 2008; Lo et al., 2005; Shen & Williams, 2010; D. Williams, 2006), a failure to develop and maintain effective social and emotional skills (Chiu et al., 2004; Griffiths, 2010; Kim et al., 2008; Liu & Peng, 2009), and higher rates of the symptoms associated with loneliness, depression, and social anxiety (Caplan et al., 2009; Kim et al., 2008; Lemmens et al., 2011; Lo et al., 2005; Shen & Williams, 2010; D. Williams et al., 2008).

There is also a small, but notable, new wave of research that suggests that OVG involvement does not actively contribute to negative social outcomes, but is socially beneficial, as it provides an ideal space for social learning (Ducheneaut & Moore, 2005; Steinkuehler & Williams, 2006; Visser et al., 2013). An examination of the empirical relationships between OVG involvement and social competence, as supported by social displacement, compensation, and learning theorists, is presented in the following section.

3.2 EMPIRICAL LINKS

The empirical relationships between video game involvement and social competence were first explored in the 1980s when researchers found that high frequency arcade players displayed lower self-esteem (Dominick, 1984) than low frequency players and were more likely to report that arcade machines provided them with companionship that was preferable to interaction with their peers (Senlow, 1984). Coining the term "electronic friendship," Senlow (1984) believed that these findings suggested that arcade machines could be emerging as substitutes for social engagement. However, with the proliferation of affordable and accessible Internet access, Senlow's ideas have been expanded to propose that one's online, in-game friends have the potential to replace one's 'offline' friends (Brightman, 2006; Colwell & Kato, 2003; Steinkuehler & Williams, 2006). Preliminary evidence supports this possibility, with a large percentage of online game players reporting that their in-game friends are equivalent or superior to their offline ones (Yee, 2006) and that their online friends satisfy some social needs that are not satisfied by pre-existing offline relationships (Hussain & Griffiths, 2008, 2009). While causal links have not been established, increased OVG involvement has been implicated as an important contributor to a variety of social consequences for online players, such as a hindered ability to form and maintain reciprocal offline relationships (Cole & Griffiths, 2007; Shen & Williams, 2010) or develop and maintain effective social and emotional skills (Chiu et al., 2004; Kim et al., 2008; Peters & Malesky, 2008; Shen & Williams, 2010).

The following section will outline the empirical research that has examined the relationship between social competence and OVG involvement. Focus will be placed on relationship quality/quantity, psychosocial dispositions, and social skills outcomes as these are the three primary facets of sociability that are believed to be negatively influenced due to increased OVG play. Following this, the literature that proposes that online video gaming spaces could be ideal for cognitive-social learning will be presented.

3.2.1 Relationship Quality/Quantity

Kraut and colleagues (1998) were among the first to examine the potential impact of social Internet use on pre-existing interpersonal relationships. Utilizing a longitudinal design, the researchers evaluated the social displacement effects of social Internet use during individuals' first one to two years online. Supporting their hypotheses, greater Internet use was found to be associated with significant declines in social involvement, including decreased family communication, and the size of one's local and distant social networks. Similar results were uncovered in a large-scale survey study conducted by Bessière et al. (2004), whereby social uses of the Internet (e.g., to meet others) were found to significantly predict declines in community involvement and reduced participation in organized groups such as churches and clubs.

Parallel relationships have been uncovered when evaluating the specific social impact of OVG play. For example, when administering the Interpersonal Relationship Scale (Garthoeffner, Henry, & Robinson, 1993), Lo and colleagues (2005) found that heavier users of OVGs (i.e., 30+ hours a week of play) report a poorer quality of offline interpersonal relationships than light users (i.e., 2 to 7 hours a week of play) or non-playing participants. In a large-scale survey of OVG players, Shen and Williams (2010) uncovered a negative linear association between OVG play frequency and family communication quality, indicating poorer family communication quality for those who did not play online games with their family members. Meeting new people online was pinpointed as a particularly strong predictor of shorter family communication and of a worse quality. Furthermore, socially motivated online game players (rather than achievement or immersion) were the only group to retain a negative linear relationship between play frequency and family communication time when play motivations were accounted for in the regression model. When examining the relationship between online game addiction and a variety of psychological characteristics, Kim et al. (2008) uncovered a significant negative correlation between online game addiction scores and offline social relationship scores, suggesting that more involved OVG players experience social difficulties and stress in offline interpersonal relationships.

In the only known experimental study evaluating the potential social effects of engagement across gaming modalities, Smyth (2007) randomly assigned participants to play offline, single-player video games (e.g., arcade, console, or computer games) or a massively multiplayer online role-playing game (MMORPG). After one month of play, online game players reported a greater play frequency, a greater reduction in the time spent socializing with real-world friends, and a greater interest in continuing to play than players of single-player offline games. These results illustrate the desirability of online games in relation to more traditional video game playing activities. As players grew closer to their in-game contacts, offline activities were displaced and online game play became more desirable. Williams (2006) found a similar pattern of cocooning (i.e., retreating into the seclusion of one's home during leisure time) among online game players, as, over time, they began to place a higher value on their in-game social contacts at the expense of pre-existing relationships. Over a one-month period, online players displayed several drops in physical social contact by reporting declines in how often friends came over to visit their home, the frequency at which they visited their friends' homes, and how often they visited relatives. Similarly, Cole and Griffiths (2007) found that one-fifth of MMORPG players reported that participation within these gaming environments had a negative effect on their out-of-game relationships. In a follow-up study, a substantial proportion of online game players actively discussed the breakdown of friendships and relationships due to play and linked being social online to being anti-social offline (Hussain & Griffiths, 2009). Kolo and Baur (2004) noted a similar relationship, as 39% of their participants reported a mild decline in the quality of their offline friendships with whom they did not play the game. An additional 10% of their sample reported considerable social changes, stating a disconnection from friends who did not play the same online game.

While this research suggests that increased use of OVGs may directly contribute to negative social outcomes, a lack of longitudinal research makes it difficult to determine if this is the case. Furthermore, as the literature discussed earlier did not assess pre-existing social dispositions, in addition to relationship outcomes, it is not possible to determine whether these results are reflective of the direct influence of OVG involvement on social outcomes or are an exacerbation of pre-existing social dispositions. Regardless, these results indicate that there is a significant relationship between poorer social relationships and increased OVG play.

3.2.2 Psychosocial Dispositions

Researchers have long suggested that OVGs appeal to those who are socially unskilled, have an unmet need for sociability in their lives, and feel anxious over establishing real-world relationships (Chak & Leung, 2004; McKenna & Bargh, 2000; Peters & Malesky, 2008). The distinctive characteristics of OVGs have generated highly desirable social spaces, as the combination of greater communicative flexibility, enhanced social presentation strategies, and shared experiences can diminish the possibility of social rejection while stimulating the formation of friendships. Thus, individuals who have experienced difficulties in forming interpersonal relationships in traditional contexts may be drawn to engage within OVGs as an alternative social outlet. Supporting this contention, researchers have found that more involved OVG players display higher rates of the symptoms associated with loneliness, depression, and social anxiety (Caplan et al., 2009; Kim et al., 2008; Lemmens et al., 2011; Lo et al., 2005; Shen & Williams, 2010; D. Williams et al., 2008). This work is discussed in more detail in the following.

3.2.2.1 *Loneliness*
Morahan-Martin and Schumacher (2003) were among the first to note that lonely participants were more likely than non-lonely individuals to prefer online to offline communication. Lonely individuals were found to prefer the speed of communicating online, as compared to offline, as well as report that the sense of anonymity offered by online spaces was socially liberating. Lonely participants also reported that they felt "more themselves" online and had a greater propensity to self-disclose while online, making it easier to make friends and generate a social network.

Similar results have been found among online gaming populations. In one of the largest surveys in the field, Caplan and colleagues (2009) found loneliness to emerge as the single most influential psychosocial predictor of increased OVG use, with lonelier participants reporting increased involvement. Shen and Williams (2010) also found significant, positive linear relationships between loneliness and time spent in online gaming environments. Additionally, game players who reported a social motivation to play (i.e., to "socialize and develop supportive friendships"), rather than to achieve or immerse, reported higher levels of loneliness. Thus, more involved and socially motivated game players displayed higher rates of loneliness than less involved, or non-socially motivated, game players.

A 2013 investigation by Visser and colleagues challenges these findings, as the researchers uncovered no direct relationships between loneliness and online game playing among young players (aged 14–20), but rather an indirect relationship between play frequency, variety of online communication partners, and loneliness. The researchers conclude that it is not play time that directly influences players' perceived level of loneliness, but rather the richness of the social environment (i.e., number of communication partners) while engaged online. However, as magnitude of this indirect relationship was relatively low ($\beta = -0.17$), definitive findings cannot be drawn.

Perhaps the most convincing research comes from Lemmens and colleagues (2011), who conducted a longitudinal study and found loneliness to be both a cause and a consequence of increased problematic video game play. Loneliness emerged as a significant individual consequence of pathological OVG play six months later, and pathological OVG play predicted subsequent loneliness, indicating the potential reciprocal nature of the relationships between loneliness and increased game play.

Taken together, this collection of research suggests that lonely individuals are more drawn to Internet-based social spaces, including OVGs, than non-lonely individuals. More involved users report higher rates of loneliness, greater social motivations to play, and, once they are engaged within these online gaming spaces, a sense of social liberation. Despite somewhat conflicting findings from Visser and colleagues (2013), longitudinal work from Lemmens and colleagues (2011) demonstrates that loneliness can be both a cause (i.e., motivating force) and, over time, a consequence, of increased problematic video game play.

3.2.2.2   Depression

Research has also suggested that more involved online game players exhibit higher rates of depression than less involved players. For instance, while Caplan and colleagues (2009) found loneliness to be the single most influential psychosocial predictor of increased use, depression also emerged as a significant individual predictor of problematic Internet use among OVG players. In a large-scale survey study, Williams et al. (2008) also uncovered a greater incidence of depression among U.S. OVG players than the general U.S. population, as 36.52% of the female players and 19.38% of the male players reported having been diagnosed with depression. As noted by the authors, these figures are higher than the corresponding rates of depression found within the general population (23% for females and 11% for men).

3.2.2.3   Social Anxiety

Although the links between social anxiety and OVG involvement have not been extensively examined, a cross-sectional study by Lo et al. (2005) revealed that increased time spent playing online games coincided with higher levels of social anxiety among Taiwanese adolescents. Heavy users of OVGs (individuals who played an average of 4.70 hours per day, 7 days a week) reported significantly higher levels of social anxiety as compared to light users (2.45 hours a day, 1–3 days a week) and non-players. Kim et al. (2008) uncovered a positive, linear relationship between social anxiety and

OVG addiction, indicating a significant relationship between Internet addiction and social anxiety. However, a lack of comparison measures (such as an assessment of relationship quality or quantity) makes it difficult to determine the magnitude of these effects on users' everyday social life.

3.2.3 Social Skills

Researchers have become increasingly concerned about the potential long-term effects of increased OVG involvement on an individual's social skills. Because increased OVG involvement has been shown to negatively affect one's level of offline social engagement, and having and maintaining relationships is integral to developing effective social skills and learning socially appropriate behavior (Bartholomew & Horowitz, 1991; Cassidy, Kirsh, Scolton, & Parke, 1996; Engles, Finkenauer, Meeus, & Dekovic, 2001), becoming socially disengaged or isolated from one's offline contacts due to OVG play is feared to substantially hinder the development, or stimulate the deterioration, of effective 'offline' social skills, for instance the ability to verbally engage others (i.e., social expressivity) or manage one's social self-presentation (i.e., social control) in real time (Cole & Griffiths, 2007; Hussain & Griffiths, 2009; Lo et al., 2005; Morahan-Martin & Schumacher, 2003; Shen & Williams, 2010).

This concern has spurred numerous examinations into the associations between video game involvement and social skills (J. Barnett, Coulson, & Foreman, 2009; Chiu et al., 2004; Griffiths, 2010; Lemmens et al., 2011; Liu & Peng, 2009; see Table 3.1 for an overview). In one of the first investigations, Chiu et al. (2004) examined the relationship between video game addiction and social skills among child and teenage video game users. While social skills did not emerge as a significant predictor of video game addiction, lower rates of boredom and greater family functioning did emerge as significant predictors of effective social skills. The researchers suggested these results indicate the potential for video game playing to replace the development of immediate social relationships and, subsequently, negatively influence social skills, particularly among younger players.

Griffiths drew similar conclusions from a 2010 study evaluating the relationship between social skills and video game play frequency. Griffiths found that high-frequency players scored poorer outcomes than low-frequency players on the Social Situations Questionnaire (SSQ) (Bryant & Trower, 1974), indicating that more frequent players exhibit greater social inadequacies. A substantial proportion of the high-frequency players also fulfilled Bryant and Trower's (1974) criteria for exhibiting "psychosocial problems" (i.e., by answering six or more of the SSQ questions as "great difficulty" or "avoid if possible") and were more likely to report a greater preference for computer game playing than offline socializing compared to low-frequency players and that play conflicted with their offline social life. Taken together, these results suggest that in addition to psychosocial differences, high-frequency players exhibit less effective social skills than low-frequency players.

Liu and Peng (2009) uncovered similar results, as they found play frequency to be a positive predictor of psychological dependency on MMORPG playing, preference for a virtual life, and personal life problems, one of which was low social engagement. Lower social control also emerged as a significant individual predictor of an increased preference for a virtual life, which, in turn, was a significant individual predictor of psychological dependency on MMORPGs. While the link between social control and MMORPG dependency was not a direct one, these results indicate an indirect relationship between lower social control and problematic play in the form of preference for a virtual life.

In the only known longitudinal assessment, Lemmens et al. (2011) found a direct linear relationship between social skills and pathological gaming, with lower social skill outcomes predicting increased pathological gaming six months later. However, this relationship was not reciprocal, as pathological gaming did not predict social skill outcomes, suggesting that lower social skills are more likely to be a cause, rather than a consequence, of increased video game involvement.

As evidenced by this research, there are significant relationships between social skills, video game play frequency, and problematic play. In general, the social profile of more involved players indicates that they are overly concerned with social norms and their public appearance, perceive themselves as being less verbally fluent and able to engage others in conversation, as well as are unable to effectively express their emotions and adapt to social situations. Combined, these findings indicate that more involved players may have a social self-consciousness that could inhibit social participation and be indicative of a certain degree of social hesitancy (Riggio & Carney, 2003; Riggio et al., 1990; Riggio, 1989).

However, there are a variety of methodological limitations to that need to be considered before such conclusions can be drawn from this research. For instance, wide variation in outcome measures, sample selection, assessment focus, and the conceptualization of video game involvement and social competence within this research, as well as a reliance on genre-specific approaches, greatly limits its generalizability. These limitations are discussed in the more detail in section 3.3.

The mechanisms underlying these relationships also remain unclear. The most common interpretation of these findings has been a displacement perspective. As outlined by Kim et al. (2008), "*the [use of] online games is associated with a decline in participants' communication with family members in the household and a decline in the size of their social circles, and because of this they become socially isolated and are no longer able to socialize in a normal way*" (p. 215, italics added). While, on the surface, OVGs seem to be environments that may stimulate social learning (Bandura, 1962, 1977, 1986), as they are highly social spaces that actively facilitate social

Table 3.1 Overview of studies examining the links between social skills and video game involvement

Study	Sample Categorization	Social Skills Measure	Results	Limitations
Barnett et al., 2009	Player/Non-player	Novaco Provocation Inventory (Novaco, 1994)	• Online game players and non-players chose constructive (assertive), not destructive (aggressive), responses, suggesting socially competent behavior	• Ambiguous measure of social skill
Chiu et al., 2004	Levels of game addiction (self-designed scale)	Maston's evaluation of social skills (Maston et al., 1983)	• Game addiction did not significantly predict social skill outcomes	• Non-Western population • Non-adult sample • Focus on addicted players
Griffiths, 2010	Play frequency/duration	SSQ (Bryant & Trower, 1974)	• High frequency players (>7 h/wk) indicated greater social incompetence than low frequency players • "Heavy" players (>14 h/wk) indicated greater social incompetence than non-heavy players	• Ambiguous skills measure • Arbitrary categorization of game players
Lemmens et al., 2011	Problematic play (Lemmens et al., 2009)	4-item skills scale (self-designed)	• Lower social competence in Wave 1 predicted pathological gaming in Wave 2 • Pathological gaming in Wave 1 did not predict social skills outcomes in Wave 2	• Limited measure of social skills • Focus on problematic use
Liu and Peng, 2009	Weekly play time, life consequences due to play (Liu & Peng, 2009)	Social Control (SC) subscale of Social Skills Inventory (SSI) (Riggio, 1989)	• Lower SC predicted preference for a virtual life	• Focus on problematic use • No direct analysis between use and skills

interaction between players (Chen, 2009; Ducheneaut & Moore, 2005; Jakobsson & Taylor, 2003; Moore et al., 2007), the disparities between online and offline social communication (e.g., a lack of non-verbal cues, absence of time constraints in sending and receiving messages, the ability to carefully craft any communicative messages, etc.) may substantially reduce their viability as social learning spaces. For instance, the ability to verbally engage others (i.e., social expressivity) in real time is integral for initiating and guiding face-to-face conversation. Individuals need to be able to simultaneously interpret their message and formulate a response to maintain a fluid social interaction (Moore et al., 2007; Sacks, Schegloff, & Jefferson, 1974). However, in the text-based communication systems often found in online games, one cannot achieve these traditional pairs of actions (i.e., question-answer) (Garcia & Jacobs, 1999); an individual receives a message from his or her communication partner in its entirety, and they must read and interpret it prior to formulating a response (Halloran, 2011). This expectation of asynchronicity grants players communicative flexibility in regards to message constructing by providing considerable leeway in the immediacy of responses to any incoming communication. The game environment further accommodates this flexibility, as engagement within game-related tasks may further delay (or provide an excuse for delaying) communication. This absence of time constraints in sending and receiving messages within online gaming environments affords players the opportunity to carefully craft, edit, and re-edit any outgoing messages (E. Chan & Vorderer, 2006), providing a wide variety of self-presentation strategies not available in the offline world. Without the ability to observe, rehearse, or receive feedback on the use of this particular skill, one's proficiency in enlisting it may atrophy. Alternatively, if an individual had not yet mastered this ability, prolonged interaction within a space where it is not necessary for effective socialization may thwart its development. Taken together, the combination of prolonged engagement within a mediated social environment and the displacement of offline interpersonal relationships, which are integral to developing effective social skills and learning socially appropriate 'offline' behavior (Bartholomew & Horowitz, 1991; Cassidy et al., 1996; Engles et al., 2001), may substantially hinder the development, or stimulate the deterioration of, effective 'offline' social skills.

However, other researchers dispute this contention and instead suggest that OVG involvement is primarily driven by ineffective social skills (e.g., Lemmens et al., 2011). A pre-existing social skills deficit could explain the inverse links between social skills and involvement as well as the links between loneliness, depression, and social anxiety and OVG involvement. According to the social skills deficit vulnerability hypothesis, an individual's psychosocial well-being can be threatened by a lack of social competence (Lewinsohn, Chaplin, & Barton, 1980; Segrin, 1990, 1993, 1998, 2000). As ineffective social skills "enhance the likelihood of eliciting punishment from the social environment" (Segrin, 1990, p. 293), including interpersonal rejection, embarrassment, and relationship failure, they can contribute to the development of loneliness, depression, or social anxiety. Substantial support has been generated for this hypothesis as loneliness, depression, and social anxiety have been empirically linked to social skills deficits (DiTommaso et al., 2003; Leary & Kowalski, 1995; Riggio et al., 1990; Segrin, 1996, 1998, 2000; Tse & Bond, 2004; Wittenberg & Reis, 1986). For example, DiTommaso et al. (2003) found significant, negative correlations between emotional expressivity, emotional sensitivity, social expressivity, and social control with social loneliness. Segrin et al. (2000) uncovered similar correlations between social adjustment and depression, loneliness, and social anxiety.

3.2.4 Conflicting Evidence: Alternative Perspectives

There is a small, but noteworthy, amount of literature contending that OVG players are not somehow socially deficient. While some researchers have only hypothesized that the relationship between OVG involvement and social ineptitude may be misplaced (e.g., Ng & Wiemer-Hastings, 2005 contend OVG players may not be socially inept but socially apathetic), the only known empirical evidence comes from Barnett and colleagues. Barnett et al. (2009) administered the Novaco Provocation Inventory (Novaco, 1994) to MMORPG players and non-online game players. This inventory presents participants with a series of hypothetical real-life, anger-producing provocations, such as *"You are talking to someone and they are not listening to you."* The ability to choose an assertive, rather than aggressive, response indicates socially competent behavior. As the results indicated that the majority of both online game players and non-players chose constructive (assertive) rather than destructive (aggressive) responses, the researchers concluded that OVG players are not socially deficient as compared to non-players. While it is difficult to draw broad conclusions from this study, particularly due to methodological concerns, these results are among the first to suggest that OVG players may not exhibit a global level of social incompetency.

There has also been considerable support for the potential social benefits of OVG involvement in the form of social learning.

3.2.4.1 Social Learning Theory

Video games have been widely employed for educational purposes such as training doctors to perform complex surgeries (Rosser et al., 2004) and allowing military personnel to practice strategic, coordinated actions (Prensky, 2001). In addition to being direct mediums for instruction, unintentional learning can also occur. For instance, exposure to action-based games has been shown to improve visuospatial (Cherny, 2008; Dye, Green, & Bavelier, 2009a; Feng, Spence, & Pratt, 2007; Green & Bavelier, 2010) and attention skills (Dye, Green, & Bavelier, 2009b), as well as help prevent cognitive decline in older adults (Basak, Boot, Voss, & Kramer, 2008).

Although extensive research has not been conducted in this area, it has been suggested that online gaming spaces may be ideal for cognitive-social learning (Bandura, 1962, 1977, 1986), a framework that is often employed in social-skill training programs (Evers-Pasquale & Sherman, 1975; Gresham & Nagel, 1980; Keller & Carlson, 1974; Ladd & Mize, 1983), as they can provide a venue for social observation, rehearsal, and feedback. For instance, successful navigation through MMORPG environments necessitates the effective utilization of a variety of social skills (Ducheneaut & Moore, 2005), such as leadership and agreeableness. Thus, through progression within the gaming space, individuals are given the opportunity to further develop, hone, and master these abilities. Indirect social learning can also arise through the observation of other players. Similar to observing real-world models, players can observe the social behaviors modeled by others in a wide variety of situations. Through observation, one can acquire social knowledge relating to socially appropriate (and inappropriate) behaviors, which can be drawn upon in future social experiences (Bandura, 1962, 1977, 1986).

Steinkuehler and Williams (2006) have postulated that the beneficial social effects could be much broader and that OVGs have the potential to increase one's general sociability. As these game-based environments provide the almost unique opportunity to actively interact among a diverse group of individuals, players young and old, from near and far, are able to engage with individuals to whom they may not have otherwise been exposed. They hypothesize that this broad social immersion could expand and diversify one's worldviews and increase general sociability. Similar arguments have been voiced by Young and Whitty (2012), who contend that virtual worlds hold great potential for the psychological growth of their users.

However, if online gaming environments have the potential to be social learning communities, and expand one's social network, while online game players are somehow inherently socially inept, as argued by social compensation theorists, then "learning through practice" in these "communities of learning" could propagate the development of ineffective social skills (Galarneau, 2005) across the online game playing population. Further research is needed to evaluate this possibility as well as the potential for social learning within online game environments.

3.2.5   Empirical Links: Summary

Regardless of whether the significant relationships between social competence and OVG play are primarily driven by displacement or compensation phenomena, increased OVG involvement has been found to be associated with poor social outcomes, including declines in relationship quality and quantity, higher rates of loneliness, depression, and social anxiety, as well as ineffective social skills. However, before definitive conclusions can be drawn, a variety of methodological limitations need to be considered.

3.3 METHODOLOGICAL LIMITATIONS

3.3.1 Sample Selection and Assessment Focus

The samples in which the participants were drawn from also varied greatly across studies. While some researchers primarily utilized online samples recruited from game-related forums and websites (Kim et al., 2008; Liu & Peng, 2009; Shen & Williams, 2010; Visser et al., 2013; D. Williams et al., 2008), others enlisted school-based samples (Griffiths, 2010; Lemmens et al., 2011; Lo et al., 2005). Samples acquired through game-related forums are likely to include more involved gamers and exhibit greater play frequency and variation, as well as stronger ties to the social group of gamers, than broader, school-based samples. Average reported play frequency among the participants supports this supposition, as Lemmens et al.'s (2011) school-based sample reported playing video games an average of 11.2 hours a week, whereas the Internet-based samples enlisted by Liu and Peng (2009) averaged between 20 and 30 hours a week. By recruiting a highly active sample of online players, the conclusions drawn from these investigations become limited to the context of more involved, online players, who engage at a high frequency. If one's hypotheses were centered within populations of more avid players, drawing a game-centric Internet sample would be advantageous. However, if one aims to evaluate game players more generally, samples should be drawn from avenues that will produce a sample of players across the involvement spectrum (i.e., from highly involved players to less involved casual players) and across game modality (i.e., offline and online).

3.3.2 Outcome Measures

The conclusions drawn from any assessment are restricted to the measures that are enlisted. For example, Kim et al. (2008) concluded that there are inverse relationships between OVG involvement and the quality of interpersonal relationships. However, these conclusions are based on the outcome from a very broad four-item scale, one item of which was assessing social anxiety rather than interpersonal relationship quality. Similarly, the conclusions drawn from Shen and Williams (2010) are limited to differences in family communication and cannot be generalized to represent relationship quality/quantity in general.

The research assessing the links between psychosocial dispositions and OVG involvement has been more consistent, particularly in regards to loneliness. However, evaluations of depression, social anxiety, and OVG involvement have varied greatly. For example, one of the two studies that have evaluated the associations between depression and OVG involvement simply asked participants for a history of a diagnosis (D. Williams et al., 2008). While straightforward, it is likely that participants would not report such information. Social anxiety assessments have been similarly limited.

For example, the conclusions drawn by Kim et al. (2008) were based off of a single item asking participants if they feel "discomfort" in social situations. Although this measure displays high face validity, it is unclear if it is assessing social anxiety or something else, such as shyness or introversion.

Social skill assessments have also been somewhat inadequate. For example, Liu and Peng (2009) only administered the social control subscale of the SSI. Therefore, any possible relationships between social skills and video game involvement that are drawn from their results cannot be broadly attributed to social skills but are limited to a discussion of differences in social self-presentation. The conclusions that can be drawn from the work of Lemmens et al. (2011) are also restricted, as the social skills that were assessed were not specifically indicated. While they appeared to be assessing dimensions of social and emotional expressivity, the measure was described as appraising "social skills and interpersonal competence" (p. 147), making the outcomes difficult to interpret. Drawing conclusions from outcomes on the SSQ utilized by Griffiths (2010) is also tenuous, as it is unclear whether it is assessing social skills, social anxiety, or a combination of the two.

To comprehensively evaluate the relationship between social competence and OVG involvement, validated and unambiguous measures should be enlisted to allow for a more accurate evaluation of the social profile of video game players and the relationship between social competence and OVG involvement.

3.3.3 Conceptualization of Video Game Involvement

Across the literature, there has been a lack of consistency in determining what qualities identify an individual as a more involved 'gamer.' While play frequency has been the most commonly employed characteristic to differentiate between varying levels of video game involvement (M. Barnett et al., 1997; Colwell & Kato, 2003; Griffiths, 2010; Kolo & Baur, 2004; Kowert, Domahidi, & Quandt, 2014; Kowert, Festl, & Quandt, 2013; Lo et al., 2005; Senlow, 1984; Shen & Williams, 2010; Smyth, 2007; Visser et al., 2013), frequency alone may not be the most appropriate categorical criterion as multiple variables seem to contribute to the relationship between involvement and social skill outcomes. The reliance on play frequency as the sole differentiating variable of video game involvement is likely too simplistic, as it cannot account for the wide variety of other factors that may contribute to one's level of involvement within this activity.

In consideration of these limitations, researchers have begun to shy away from the reliance on frequency measures, instead choosing to categorize game players in terms of video game dependency or addiction (Caplan et al., 2009; Chiu et al., 2004; Colwell & Payne, 2000; Griffiths, 2010; Kim et al., 2008; Lemmens et al., 2011; D. Williams, Caplan, & Xiong, 2007), the extent to which negative life consequences are experienced due to play (Liu & Peng, 2009), or one's reported social identity with the community of gamers

(Kowert & Oldmeadow, 2010). While these measures may be slightly preferable, as they incorporate a wider variety of behaviors than play frequency alone (e.g., problematic behavior measures may incorporate elements of psychological dependency, consequences to play, mood modification, etc.), these categorizations are still one-dimensional in their reliance upon a single facet of video game involvement to classify participants.

Within these categorizations there has also been a lack of standardization. For example, Barnett et al. (1997) identified frequent video game players as those who played at least 1 hour per week of video games, Kolo and Baur (2004) identified frequent video game players as those who played between 5 and 15 hours a week, and Griffiths's (2010) criteria for a frequent player was more than 7 hours a week of video game play. In lieu of play frequency categories, other researchers have conceptualized play frequency on a spectrum (Colwell & Kato, 2003; Kowert et al., 2014, 2013; Lo et al., 2005; Shen & Williams, 2010). The calculation of problematic play has varied widely as well, from continuum approaches (Lemmens et al., 2011) to dichotomous classifications (Griffiths, 2010). Problematic play has also been conceptualized in terms of negative life consequences due to play rather than the psychological symptoms of addiction (Liu & Peng, 2009).

This inconsistency highlights the need for a systemization of the criteria used to differentiate individuals across varying degrees of video game involvement. Future researchers could consider expanding the conceptualization of play frequency to include a wider spectrum of measures to provide a more systematic assessment of video game involvement. For example, in addition to play frequency, researchers could consider incorporating game variety and social identity in order to create a more composite appraisal of one's level of video game involvement.

The addition of game variety would account for variation across individuals who engage in a wider range of gaming behaviors. This would allow for the differentiation between individuals who engage within one particular gaming environment (e.g., puzzle games) and those who disperse the same amount of time across a variety of environments (e.g., puzzle games, simulation games, and role-playing games). Engaging in a wider variety of gaming behavior is indicative of greater general involvement within video game environments and communities, a difference that is not detectable through the measurement of play frequency alone.

Social identity could also be incorporated into the composite evaluation of one's video game involvement. The rapid growth, and rising popularity, of video gaming as a leisure activity has stimulated the development of the 'gamer' identity. Television shows, movies, Web series, and print media have all acknowledged the emergence of the gamer. The gamer culture has been given mainstream recognition by popular television programs such as *South Park*, *The Big Bang Theory*, and *Law and Order: SVU*. There are entire television channels, such as *G4*, an American cable network, that are dedicated to video games, broadcast the latest game-related news, and review the latest video game releases. Hollywood has also acknowledged the influence of gamer culture by producing many movies based on video games or video game characters (e.g., *Tomb Raider*, *Street Fighter*, *Hitman*, *Resident Evil*, etc.). Several video game award shows have also developed, including the Spike Video Game Awards (first held in December 2003), the BAFTA Video Game Awards (first held in 2007), and the Canadian Videogame Awards (first held in 2010). Fashion trends have begun catering to this community as well, with numerous Web-based stores selling apparel that celebrates all things video game related. For example, jinx.com, a clothing website, describes their online store as providing unique clothing for "gamers and geeks." Video gaming clubs are also growing in popularity, ranging from university-based societies, such as FragSoc at the University of York, to national groups such as Video Games Club UK. There are even large-scale game-based conventions, such as Blizzcon, Blizzard Entertainment's yearly gaming convention held in California, which attracted over 8,000 in its first year (Perry, 2006) and over 26,000 attendees six years later (Holisky, 2011). The Electronic Entertainment Expo, or E3, is even more popular and drew a crowd of more than 45,000 attendees in 2011 (Sinclair, 2011).

These examples illustrate the emergence and worldwide growth of the gamer culture, which, in the last two decades, has evolved from a small, niche community of video game players to a large collective of like-minded individuals with a shared interest in video game–related fashion, entertainment, hobbies, and more. The gamer identity has developed alongside this cultural emergence, developing its own traditions and behaviors. However, despite this, consideration for one's identification with the social community of gamers remains largely absent from the literature. It is unknown why this is the case as one's identification with the social group of gamers has shown to be a strong predictor of play frequency and is implicated as an underlying source of social changes due to gaming (Ghuman & Griffiths, 2012). Furthermore, one's subjective identification has been acknowledged as a better predictor of group behavior than more behavioral measures (e.g., play frequency) (Jetten, Branscombe, Schmitt, & Spears, 2001; Turner, 1984). As such, the incorporation of social identity into a measure of video game involvement seems essential for a thorough assessment of the extent to which an individual is involved in video game play as an activity.

Whether one is assessing the game playing population more generally or focusing on problematic users, systematic criteria are necessary in order to be able to draw conclusions across studies within gaming populations. Future research could consider integrating psychological (e.g., play frequency and variety) and behavioral (e.g., social identity) measures of involvement to create a more systematic assessment of video game involvement that encompasses a variety of pertinent factors and allows for the evaluation of players across a broader spectrum of video game involvement than has previously been utilized.

3.3.4 Conceptualization of Social Competence

There has also been substantial variation in the conceptualization of social competence. While this is not inherently problematic, as social competence is a broad concept that can, and does, incorporate a wide variety of variables (Rose-Kransor, 1997, see chapter 2, this monograph), the inconsistency in quantifying this variable has made it difficult to establish the exact nature of the relationship between social outcomes and OVG involvement and brings into question whether such a broad concept is empirically or theoretically tenable. For example, despite the fact that inverse relationships between friendship quality and OVG involvement have been uncovered (Lo et al., 2005; Shen & Williams, 2010), the role OVG involvement plays in this relationship remains unclear. While researchers contend that the displacement of offline for online contacts underlies these inverse relationships, it is also possible that these findings are reflective of an underlying social anxiety, loneliness, or depression. Over time, these dispositions could have negatively influenced interpersonal relationships and motivated increased involvement, superseding any displacement effects. While compensation theorists have examined these possibilities, the work in this area has also largely failed to establish directional links, the magnitude of these relationships, and whether negative social outcomes are a cause or a consequence of play.

3.4 CONCLUSION

The online gaming industry continues to flourish, as people choose to spend substantial amounts of time playing games together (Wu, 2010). However, as online gaming grows so does the concern about the possible effects of prolonged interaction within these gaming environments, particularly in relation to social competence. While online communities may be thriving, it appears to be at the expense of offline relationships and activities, as online gamers themselves link being social online to being anti-social offline and report that participation within these environments has contributed to the breakdown of offline relationships (Cole & Griffiths, 2007; Hussain & Griffiths, 2009). Online games seem to have created a "communication paradox," as increased participation within these environments, which promote interaction and sociability, has been found to be associated with a range of negative social outcomes (Shen & Williams, 2010).

However, the consistency and magnitude of these relationships between social outcomes and OVG involvement remain somewhat unclear. While the empirical evidence suggests that online game players lack certain social skills and display greater rates of certain psychosocial predispositions as compared to their less active, or non-playing, counterparts, variability in the conceptualization of OVG involvement and social competence has made it difficult to generalize these findings and determine the precise nature of these relationships. It also remains unknown to what extent the inverse relationships between OVG involvement and social outcomes are attributable to social displacement and compensation phenomena or a combination of the two. While researchers tend to support one theory or the other, it is likely that compensation and displacement phenomena are intertwined in a 'Cycle Model of Use.' Certain social predispositions (e.g., loneliness, depression, and/or social anxiety) seem to motivate the initial engagement within online video gaming environments and, over time, may become exacerbated through the displacement of offline for online contacts, leading to tangible social declines. However, it has also been suggested that online game involvement may help develop certain forms of sociality, such as leadership skills, indicating the possibility that online game involvement may not inevitably lead to negative social outcomes.

Enlisting a social skills approach to social competence may be the first step to unraveling this debate, not only for the impact of involvement on social skills specifically but also for the broader relationship between OVG involvement and social competence and its underlying mechanisms. Social skills are a fundamental component of social competence, providing the foundation upon which other facets of sociability develop (Cavell, 1990; DuBois & Felner, 1996; Rose-Kransor, 1997). Maladaptive social skills can prevent effective communication and lead to an array of social difficulties, including poor communication quality and an inhibited ability to create and sustain friendships (Gottman, Gonso, & Rasmussen, 1975; Ladd, 1999). Furthermore, validity evidence has sufficiently demonstrated significant relationships between self-report measures of social skill and performance-based assessments (Baron & Markman, 2003; Ladd & Mize, 1983; Ladd, 1981), indicating that this approach is a valid measurement of both social skills and performance. Thus, any significant associations between social competence and OVG involvement should be quantifiable on this foundational level. Furthermore, a social skills approach can pinpoint the precise social abilities that may hold a relationship with OVG play. Identifying the specific social abilities that hold a relationship with OVG involvement will allow for a greater understanding of the extent to which online games provide individuals opportunities to learn (and perfect) social skills (Ducheneaut & Moore, 2005; Jakobsson & Taylor, 2003) or relate to negative social outcomes for their players directly (in the case of displacement effects) and/or indirectly (through an exacerbation of pre-existing dispositions).

REFERENCES

Back, M. D., Schmukle, S. C., & Egloff, B. (2008). How extraverted is honey. bunny77@hotmail.de? Inferring personality from e-mail addresses. *Journal of Research in Personality, 42*, 1116–1122. doi:10.1016/j.jrp.2008.02.001
Bandura, A. (1962). Social learning through imitation. In M. R. Jones (Ed.), *Nebraska Symposium on Motivation.* Lincoln: University of Nebraska Press.
Bandura, A. (1977). *Social learning theory.* Englewood Cliffs, NJ: Prentice-Hall.

Bandura, A. (1986). *Social foundations of thought and action: A social cognitive theory.* Englewood Cliffs, NJ: Prentice-Hall.

Bargh, J., & McKenna, K. (2004). The Internet and social life. *Annual Review of Psychology, 55*(1), 573–590.

Barnett, J., Coulson, M., & Foreman, N. (2009). *The WoW! factor: Reduced levels of anger after violent on-line play.* London: Middlesex University.

Barnett, M., Vitaglione, G., Harper, K., Quackenbush, S., Steadman, L., & Valdez, B. (1997). Late adolescents' experiences with and attitudes towards videogames. *Journal of Applied Social Psychology, 27*(15), 1316–1334.

Baron, R., & Markman, G. (2003). Beyond social capital: The role of entrepreneurs' social competence in their financial success. *Journal of Business Venturing, 18*(1), 41–60.

Bartholomew, K., & Horowitz, L. M. (1991). Attachment styles among young adults. *Journal of Personality and Social Psychology, 61*(2), 226–244.

Basak, C., Boot, W., Voss, M., & Kramer, A. (2008). Can training in a real-time strategy video game attenuate cognitive decline in older adults? *Psychology and Aging, 23*(4), 765–777.

Bessière, K., Kiesler, S., Kraut, R., & Boneva, B. (2004). Longitudinal effects of Internet uses on depressive affect: A social resources approach. Unpublished manuscript, Carnegie Mellon University, Philadelphia, PA.

Bjornskov, C. (2003). The happy few: Cross-country evidence on social capital and life satisfaction. *Kyklos, 56*, 3–16.

Blais, J., Craig, W. M., Pepler, D., & Connolly, J. (2008). Adolescents online: The importance of Internet activity choices on salient relationships. *Journal of Youth and Adolescence, 37*, 522–536. doi:10.1007/s10964–007–9262–7

Bourdieu, P., & Wacquant, L. (1992). *An invitation to reflexive sociology.* Chicago: University of Chicago Press.

Brightman, J. (2006). Study: Video games can promote sociability. *Game Daily.* Retrieved from http://www.gamedaily.com/articles/features/study-video-games-can-promote-sociability/69323/?biz=1

Bryant, B., & Trower, P. E. (1974). Social difficulty in a student sample. *British Journal of Educational Psychology, 44*, 13–21.

Caplan, S. (2003). Preference for online social interaction: A theory of problematic Internet use and psychosocial well-being. *Communication Research, 30*, 625–648.

Caplan, S., Williams, D., & Yee, N. (2009). Problematic Internet use and psychosocial well-being among MMO players. *Computers in Human Behavior, 25*(6), 1312–1319. doi:10.1016/j.chb.2009.06.006

Cassidy, J., Kirsh, S., Scolton, K., & Parke, R. (1996). Attachment and representations of peer relationships. *Developmental Psychology, 32*(5), 892–904.

Cavell, T. A. (1990). Social adjustment, social performance, and social skills: A tricomponent model of social competence. *Journal of Clinical Child Psychology, 19*, 111–122.

Chak, K., & Leung, L. (2004). Shyness and locus of control as predictors of Internet addiction and Internet use. *Cyberpsychology and Behavior, 7*(5), 559–570. doi:10.1089/cpb.2004.7.559.

Chan, D., & Cheng, G. (2004). A comparison of offline and online friendship qualities at different stages of relationship development. *Journal of Social and Personal Relationships, 21*(3), 305–320.

Chan, E., & Vorderer, P. (2006). Massively multiplayer online games. In P. Vorderer & J. Bryant (Eds.), *Playing video games: Motives, responses, and consequences* (pp. 77–88). Hillsdale, NJ: Erlbaum.

Chen, M. (2009). Communication, coordination, and camaraderie in *World of Warcraft. Games and Culture, 4*(1), 47–73.

Cherny, I. (2008). Mom, let me play more computer games: They improve my mental rotation skills. *Sex Roles, 59*, 776–786.

Chiu, S., Lee, J., & Huang, D. (2004). Video game addiction in children and teenagers in Taiwan. *Cyberpsychology and Behavior, 7*(5), 571–581.

Cole, H., & Griffiths, M. D. (2007). Social interactions in massively multiplayer online role-playing games. *Cyberpsychology and Behavior, 10*(4), 575–583. doi:10.1089/cpb.2007.9988

Coleman, J. S. (1988). Social capital in the creation of human capital. *American Journal of Sociology,* (94), 95–120.

Colwell, J., & Kato, M. (2003). Investigation of the relationship between social isolation, self-esteem, aggression and computer game play in Japanese adolescents. *Asian Journal of Social Psychology, 6*, 149–158.

Colwell, J., & Payne, J. (2000). Negative correlates of computer game play in adolescents. *British Journal of Psychology, 91*, 295–310.

Cornwell, B., & Lundgren, D. (2001). Love on the Internet: Involvement and misrepresentation in romantic relationships in cyberspace vs. realspace. *Computers in Human Behavior, 17*, 197–211.

Cummings, J., Butler, B., & Kraut, R. (2002). The quality of online social relationships. *Communications of the ACM, 45*, 103–108.

Davis, R. A. (2001). A cognitive behavioral model of pathologial Internet use. *Computers in Human Behavior, 17*(2), 187–195.

Davis, R. A., Flett, G., & Besser, A. (2002). Validation of a new scale for measuring problematic Internet use: Implications for pre-employment screening. *Cyberpsychology and Behavior, 5*(4), 331–345.

DiTommaso, E., Brannen-McNulty, C., Ross, L., & Burgess, M. (2003). Attachment styles, social skills and loneliness in young adults. *Personality and Indivdiual Differences, 35*(2), 303–312.

Dominick, J. R. (1984). Video games, television violence, and aggressoin in teenagers. *Journal of Communication, 34*(2), 136–147. doi:10.1111/j.1460-2466.1984.tb02165.x

DuBois, D. L., & Felner, R. D. (1996). The quadripartite model of social competence: Theory and applications to clinical intervention. In M. A. Reinecke (Ed.), *Cognitive therapy with children and adolescents: A casebook for clinical practice.* New York: Guilford Press.

Ducheneaut, N., & Moore, R. (2005). More than just "XP": Learning social skills in massively multiplayer online games. *Interactive Technology and Smart Education, 2*(2), 89–100.

Dye, M., Green, C., & Bavelier, D. (2009a). Increasing speed of processing with action video games. *Current Directions in Psychologial Science, 18*(6), 321–326.

Dye, M., Green, C., & Bavelier, D. (2009b). The development of attention skills in action video game players. *Neuropsychologia, 47*(8), 1780–1789.

Ellison, N., Steinfield, C., & Lampe, C. (2007). The benefits of Facebook "friends": Social capital and college students' use of online social network sites. *Journal of Computer-Mediated Communication,* (12), 1143–1168.

Engles, R., Finkenauer, C., Meeus, W., & Dekovic, M. (2001). Parental attachment and adolescents' emotional adjustment: The associations with social skills and relational competence. *Journal of Counseling Psychology, 48*(4), 428–439.

Evers-Pasquale, W., & Sherman, M. (1975). The reward value of peers. *Journal of Abnormal Child Psychology, 3*(3), 179–189.

Feng, J., Spence, I., & Pratt, J. (2007). Playing an action video game reduces gender differences in spatial cognition. *Psychologial Science, 18*(10), 850–855.

Gabbay, S. M., & Zuckerman, E. W. (1998). Social capital and opportunity in coporate R&D: The contingent effect of contact density on mobility expectations. *Social Science Research, 27*, 189–217.

Galarneau, L. (2005). Spontaneous communities of learning: Learning ecosystems in massively multiplayer online game environments. In *DiGRA 2005:.Changing Views—Worlds in Play*. Vancouver: DiGRA.

Galston, W. A. (2000). Does the Internet strengthen community? *National Civic Review, 89*(3), 193–202.

Garcia, A. C., & Jacobs, J. B. (1999). Eyes of the beholder: Understanding the turn-taking system in quasi-synchronous computer-mediated communication. *Research on Language and Social Interaction, 32*(4), 337–369.

Garthoeffner, J. L., Henry, C. S., & Robinson, L. (1993). The modified interpersonal relationship scale: Reliability and validity. *Psychologial Reports, 73*(3), 995–1004.

Gergen, K. J., Gergen, M. M., & Barton, W. H. (1973). Deviance in the dark. *Psychology Today, 7*, 129–130.

Ghuman, D., & Griffiths, M. D. (2012). A cross-genre study of online gaming: Player demographics, motivation for play, and social interactions among players. *International Journal of Cyber Behavior, Psychology, and Learning, 2*(1), 13–29.

Goffman, E. (1959). *The presentation of self in everyday life*. New York: Overlook Press.

Gottman, J., Gonso, J., & Rasmussen, B. (1975). Social interaction, social competence, and friendship in children. *Child Development, 46*(3), 709–718.

Granovetter, M. S. (1982). The strength of weak ties: A network theory revisted. In P. V. Mardsen & N. Lin (Eds.), *Social structure and network analysis* (pp. 105–130). Thousand Oaks, CA: Sage Publications.

Green, C., & Bavelier, D. (2010). Effect of action video games on the spatial distribution of visuospatial attention. *Journal of Experimental Psychologial Human Perception and Performance, 32*(6), 1465–1478.

Gresham, F., & Nagel, R. J. (1980). Social skills traning with children: Responsiveness to modeling and coaching as a function of peer orientation. *Journal of Consulting and Clinical Psychology, 48*, 718–729.

Griffiths, M. D. (2010). Computer game playing and social skills: A pilot study. *Aloma, 27*, 301–310.

Gunawardena, C., & Zittle, F. (1997). Social presence as a predictor of satisfaction within a computer-mediated conferencing envionrment. *American Journal of Distance Education, 11*(3), 8–26.

Halloran, J. (2011). Game changer? How VoIP is impacting the way we play. *International Journal of Interactive Worlds, 2*, 1–27.

Helliwell, J. F. (2006). Well-being, social capital and public policy: What's new? *Economic Journal, 16*(510), 34–45.

Helliwell, J. F., & Putnam, R. (2004). The social context of well-being. *Philosophical Transactions of the Royal Society, 359*(1149), 1435–1446.

Herring, S. (2001). Computer-mediated discourse. In F. Schriffen & D. Tannen (Eds.), *The handbook of discourse analysis* (pp. 612–634). Oxford, UK: Blackwell Publishing.

Holisky, A. (2011). *World of Warcraft: Mists of Pandaria* announced. *WoW Insider*. Retrieved from http://wow.joystiq.com/2011/10/21/world-of-warcraft-mists-of-pandaria/

Hsu, S., Wen, M., & Wu, M. (2009). Exploring user experiences as predictors of MMORPG addiction. *Computers and Education, 53*(3), 990–999.

Hussain, Z., & Griffiths, M. (2008). Gender swapping and socializing in cyberspace: An exploratory study. *Cyberpsychology and Behavior, 11*(1), 47–53.

Hussain, Z., & Griffiths, M. (2009). The attitudes, feelings, and experiences of online gamers: A qualitative analysis. *Cyberpsychology and Behavior, 12*(6), 747–753.

Iacono, C. S., & Weisband, S. (1997). Developing trust in virtual teams. In *Hawaii International Conference on System Sciences*. Hawaii.

Jakobsson, M., & Taylor, T. L. (2003). *The Sopranos* meets *EverQuest*: Social networking in massively multiplayer online games. In *Proceedings of the 2003 Digital Arts and Culture (DAC) conference, Melbourne, Australia* (pp. 81–90).

Jetten, J., Branscombe, N., Schmitt, M., & Spears, R. (2001). Rebels with a cause: Group identification as a response to perceived discrimination from the mainstream. *Personality and Social Psychology Bulletin, 27*(9), 1204–1213.

Joinson, A. (2001). Self-disclosure in computer-mediated communication: The role of self-awareness and visual anonymity. *European Journal of Social Psychology, 31*, 177–192.

Keller, M., & Carlson, P. (1974). The use of symbolic modeling to promote social skills in preschool children with low levels of social responsiveness. *Child Development, 45*, 912–919.

Kendall, L. (1998). Meaning and identity in "cyberspace": The performance of gender, class, and race online. *Symbolic Interaction, 21*, 129–153. doi:10.1525/si.1998.21.2.129

Kiesler, S., & Sproull, L. (1992). Group decision making and communicaiton technology. *Organizational Behavior and Human Decision Processes, 52*(1), 96–123.

Kim, E., Namkoong, K., Ku, T., & Kim, S. (2008). The relationship between online game addiction and aggression, self-control, and narcissistic personality traits. *European Psychiatry, 23*(3), 212–218. doi:10.1016/j.eurpsy.2007.10.010

Kolo, C., & Baur, T. (2004). Living a virtual life: Social dynamics of online gaming. *Game Studies, 4*(1), 1–31.

Kowert, R., Domahidi, E., & Quandt, T. (2014). The relationship between online video game involvement and gaming-related friendships among emotionally sensitive individuals. *Cyberpsychology, Behavior, and Social Networking, 17*(7), 447–453. doi:10.1089/cyber.2013.0656

Kowert, R., Festl, R., & Quandt, T. (2013). Unpopular, overweight, and socially inept: Reconsidering the stereotype of online gamers. *Cyberpsychology, Behavior, and Social Networking, 17*(3), 141–146. doi:10.1089/cyber.2013.0118

Kowert, R., Griffiths, M. D., & Oldmeadow, J. A. (2012). Geek or chic? Emerging stereotypes of online gamers. *Bulletin of Science, Technology & Society, 32*(6), 471–479. doi:10.1177/0270467612469078

Kowert, R., & Oldmeadow, J. A. (2010). Geek or chic: Perceptions of gamers. Paper presented at *Under the Mask*. Bedfordshire, UK: University of Bedfordshire.

Kowert, R., & Oldmeadow, J. A. (2012). The stereotype of online gamers: New characterization or recycled prototype. In *Nordic DiGRA: Games in Culture and Society conference proceedings*. Tampere, Finland: DiGRA.

Kraut, R., Patterson, M., Lundmark, V., Kiesler, S., Mukopadhyay, T., & Scherlis, W. (1998). Internet paradox: A social technology that reduces social involvement and psychological well-being? *American Psychologist, 53*(9), 1017–1031.

Ladd, G. W. (1981). Effectiveness of a social learning method for enhancing children's social interaction and peer acceptance. *Child Development, 52*(1), 171–178.

Ladd, G. W. (1999). Peer relationships and social competence during early and middle childhood. *Annual Review of Psychology, 50*, 333–359.

Ladd, G. W., & Mize, J. (1983). A cognitive-social learning model of social-skill tranining. *Psychologial Review, 90*(2), 127–157.

Lam, I., Chen, K., & Chen, L. (2008). Involuntary information leakage in social network services. *Lecture Notes in Computer Science: Advances in Information and Computer Security, 5312*, 167–183. doi:10.1007/978-3-540-89598-5_11

Lea, M., & Spears, R. (1995). Love at first byte? Building personal relationships over computer network. In J. T. Wood & S. W. Duck (Eds.), *Understudied relationships: Off the beaten track* (pp. 197–233). Newbury Park, CA: Sage.

Lea, M., Spears, R., & de Groot, D. (2001). Knowing me, knowing you: Anonymity effects on social identity processes within groups. *Personality and Social Psychology Bulletin.* doi:10.1177/0146167201275002

Leary, M., & Kowalski, R. (1995). *Social anxiety*. New York: Guilford Press.

Lemmens, J. S., Valkenburg, P. M., & Peter, J. (2009). Development and validation of a game addiction scale for adolescents. *Media Psychology*, 12(1), 77–95.

Lemmens, J., Valkenburg, P., & Peter, J. (2011). Psychological causes and consequences of pathological gaming. *Computers in Human Behavior*, 27(1), 144–152. doi:10.1016/j.chb.2010.07.015

Lewinsohn, P.M., Chaplin, M. W., & Barton, R. (1980). Social competence and depression: The role of illusory self-perceptions. *Journal of Abnormal Psychology*, (2), 203–212.

Liu, M., & Peng, W. (2009). Cognitive and psychological predictors of the negative outcomes associated with playing MMOGs (massively multiplayer online games). *Computers in Human Behavior*, 25(6), 1306–1311. doi:10.1016/j.chb.2009.06.002

Lo, S., Wang, C., & Fang, W. (2005). Physical interpersonal relationships and social anxiety among online game players. *Cyberpsychology and Behavior*, 8(1), 15–20. doi:10.1089/cpb.2005.8.15

Martey, R. M., Stromer-Galleyb, J., Banks, J., Wu, J., & Consalvo, M. (2014). The strategic female: Gender-switching and player behavior in online games. *Information, Communication & Society*, 17(3), 286–300.

Matson, J. L., Rotatori, A. F., & Helsel, W. J. (1983). Development of a rating scale to measure social skills in children: The Matson Evaluation of Social Skills with Youngsters (MESSY). *Behaviour Research and Therapy*, 21(4), 335–340.

McKenna, K., & Bargh, J. (2000). Plan 9 from cyberspace: The implications of the Internet for personality and social psychology. *Personality and Social Psychology Review*, 4(1), 57–75. doi:10.1207/S15327957PSPR0401_6

Mehrabian, A. (1969a). Significance of posture and position in the communication of attitude and status relationships. *Psychologial Bulletin*, 71, 359–372.

Mehrabian, A. (1969b). Some referents and measures of non-verbal behavior. *Behavior Resaerch Methods and Instrumentation*, 1, 203–207.

Milgram, S. (1965). Some conditions of obedience and disobedience to authority. *Human Relations*, 18(57), 57–76.

Moore, R., Ducheneaut, N., & Nickell, E. (2007). Doing virtually nothing: Awareness and accountability in massively multiplayer online worlds. *Computer Supported Cooperative Work*, 16(3), 265–305.

Morahan-Martin, J., & Schumacher, P. (2003). Loneliness and social uses of the Internet. *Computers in Human Behavior*, 19, 659–671.

Morio, H., & Buchholz, C. (2009). How anonymous are you online? Examining online social behaviours from a cross-cultural perspective. *AI & Society*, 23(2), 297–307.

Naumann, L., Vazire, S., Rentfrow, P., & Gosling, S. (2009). Personality judgments based on physical appearance. *Personality and Social Psychology Bulletin*, (35), 1661–1671.

Ng, B., & Wiemer-Hastings, P. (2005). Addiction to the Internet and online gaming. *Cyberpsychology and Behavior*, 8(2), 110–113.

Nie, N., & Erbring, L. (2002). Internet and mass media: A preliminary report. *IT & Society*, 1(2), 134–141.

Nie, N., & Hillygus, S. (2001). Eduation and democratic citizenship. In D. Ravitch & J. Viteritti (Eds.), *Making good citizens: Eduation and civial society*. New Haven, CT: Yale University Press.

Novaco, R. W. (1994). *Novaco Anger Scale and Provocation Inventory (NAS-PI)*. Los Angeles, CA: Western Psychological Services.

Parks, M. R., & Floyd, K. (1996). Making friends in cyberspace. *Journal of Communication*, 46, 80–97.

Parks, M. R., & Roberts, L. D. (1998). 'Making MOOsic': The development of personal relationships on line and a comparison to their off-line counterparts. *Journal of Social and Personal Relationships*, 15(4), 517–537.

Pena, J., & Hancock, J. T. (2006). An analysis of socioemotional and task communication in online multi-player video games. *Communication Research*, *33*(1), 92–109.

Perry, K. (2006). BlizzCon 2005—Part 1. *techFEAR*. Retrieved from http://www.techfear.com/articles/2005/11/blizzcon.shtml

Peters, C., & Malesky, A. (2008). Problematic usage among highly-engaged players of massively multiplayer online role playing games. *Cyberpsychology and Behavior*, *11*(4), 481–484.

Prensky, M. (2001). *Digital game-based learning*. New York: McGraw-Hill.

Putnam, R. (2000). *Bowling alone: The collapse and revival of American community*. New York: Simon & Schuster.

Rice, R. E. (1993). Media appropriateness: Using social presence theory to compare traditional and new organization media. *Human Communication Research*, *19*(4), 451–484.

Rice, R. E., & Love, G. (1987). Electronic emotion. *Communication Research*, *14*(1), 85–108.

Riggio, R. (1989). *Manual for the Social Skills Inventory*. Palo Alto, CA: Consulting Psychologists Press.

Riggio, R., & Carney, D.C. (2003). *Manual for the Social Skills Inventory* (2nd ed). Mountain View, CA: Mind Garden.

Riggio, R., Throckmorton, B., & DePaola, S. (1990). Social skills and self-esteem. *Personality and Indivdiual Differences*, *11*(8), 799–804.

Rose-Kransor, L. (1997). Nature of social competence: A theoretical review. *Social Developmental Psychology*, *6*(1), 111–135.

Rosser, J. C., Lynch, P. J., Haskamp, L. A., Yalif, A., Gentile, D. A., & Giammaria, L. (2004). Are video game players better at laparoscopic surgical tasks? Paper presented at the Medicine Meets Virtual Reality conference, Newport Beach, CA.

Sacks, H., Schegloff, E., & Jefferson, G. (1974). A simplest systematics for the organisation of turn-taking for conversation. *Language*, *50*, 696–735.

Schwartz, H. A., Eichstaedt, J. C., Kern, M. L., Dziurzynski, L., Ramones, S. M., Agrawal, M., . . . Ungar, L. H. (2013). Personality, gender, and age in the language of social media: The open-vocabulary approach. *PLoS ONE*, *8*. doi:10.1371/journal.pone.0073791

Segrin, C. (1990). A meta-analytic review of social skill deficits in depression. *Communication Monographs*, *57*(4), 292–308.

Segrin, C. (1993). Social skills deficits and psychosocial problems: Antecedent, concomitant, or consequent? *Journal of Social and Clinical Psychology*, *12*, 336–353.

Segrin, C. (1996). The relationship between social skills deficits and psychosocial problems. A test of a vulnerability model. *Communication Research*, *23*, 425–450.

Segrin, C. (1998). Interpersonal communication problems associated with depression and loneliness. In P. Andersen & L. Guerrero (Eds.), *Handbook of communication and emotion: Research, theory, applications, and contexts* (pp. 215–242). San Diego, CA: Academic Press.

Segrin, C. (2000). Social skills deficits assoicated with depression. *Clinical Psychology Review*, *20*(3), 379–403.

Segrin, C., & Flora, J. (2000). Poor social skills are a vulnerability factor in the development of psychosocial problems. *Human Commuication Research*, *26*(3), 489–514.

Senlow, G. (1984). Playing videogames: The electronic friend. *Journal of Communication*, *34*(2), 148–156.

Shen, C., & Williams, D. (2010). Unpacking time online: Connecting Internet and massively multiplayer online game use with psychological well-being. *Communication Research*, *20*(10), 1–27. doi:10.1177/0093650210377196

Short, J., Williams, E., & Christie, B. (1976). *The social psychology of telecommunicaitons*. London: Wiley.

Sinclair, B. (2011). E3 2011 attendance grows to 46,800. *UK GameSpot*. Retrieved from http://uk.gamespot.com/news/e3-2011-attendance-grows-to-46800-6318663

Slouka, M. (1995). *War of the worlds: Cyberspace and the high-tech assault on reality*. New York: Basic Books.

Smyth, J. (2007). Beyond self-selection in video game play. *Cyberpsychology and Behavior*, 10(5), 717–721.

Sproull, L., & Kiesler, S. (1986). Reducing social context cues: Electronic mail in organizational communication. *Management Science*, 32(11), 1492–1512.

Steinfield, C., Ellison, N., & Lampe, C. (2008). Social capital, self-esteem, and use of online social network sites: A longitudinal analysis. *Journal of Applied Developmental Psychology*, 29, 434–445.

Steinkuehler, C., & Williams, D. (2006). Where everybody knows your (screen) name: Online games as "third places." *Journal of Computer-Mediated Communication*, 11(4), 885–909.

Suler, J. (2004). The online disinhibition effect. *Cyberpsychology and Behavior*, 7(3), 321–326.

Tse, W., & Bond, A. (2004). The impact of depression on social skills: A review. *Journal of Nervous and Mental Disease*, 192(4), 260–268.

Turner, J. C. (1984). Social identification and psychologial group formation. In H. Tajfel (Ed.), *The social dimension* (Vol. 2, pp. 518–538). Cambridge: Cambridge University Press.

Visser, M., Antheunis, M. L., & Schouten, A. P. (2013). Online communication and social well-being: How playing *World of Warcraft* affects players' social competence and loneliness. *Journal of Applied Social Psychology*, 43, 1508–1517. doi:10.1111/jasp.12144

Walther, J. (1996). Computer-mediated communication: Impersonal, interpersonal, and hyperpersonal interaction. *Communication Research*, 23(1), 3–43.

Whitty, M. (2003). Cyber-flirting: Playing at love on the Internet. *Theory and Psychology*, 13, 339–357.

Whitty, M., & Carr, A. (2003). Cyberspace as potential space: Considering the Web as a playground to cyber-flirt. *Human Relations*, 56, 861–891.

Whitty, M., & Carr, A. (2006). *Cyberspace romance: The psychology of online relationships*. Basingstoke, UK: Palgrave Macmillan.

Whitty, M., & Gavin, J. (2001). Age/Sex/Location: Uncovering the social cues in the development of online relationships. *Cyberpsychology and Behavior*, 4(5), 623–630.

Wilkins, H. (1991). Computer talk: Long-distance conversations by computer. *Written Communication*, 8, 56–78.

Williams, D. (2006). Groups and goblins: The social and civic impact of online games. *Journal of Broadcasting and Electronic Media*, 50, 651–681. doi:10.1207/s15506878jobem5004_5

Williams, D. (2007). The impact of time online: Social capital and cyberbalkanization. *Cyberpsychology and Behavior*, 10(3), 398–406.

Williams, D., Caplan, S., & Xiong, L. (2007). Can you hear me now? The impact of voice in an online gaming community. *Human Communication Research*, 33(4), 427–449.

Williams, D., Yee, N., & Caplan, S. (2008). Who plays, how much, and why? Debunking the stereotypical gamer profile. *Journal of Computer-Mediated Communication Monographs*, 13(4), 993–1018. doi:10.1111/j.1083–6101.2008.00428.x

Williams, E. (1977). Experimental comparisons of face-to-face and mediated communicaiton: A review. *Psychologial Bulletin*, 84(5), 963–976.

Winkelmann, R. (2009). Unemployment, social capital, and subjective well-being. *Journal of Happiness Studies*, *101*(1), 1–24.

Wittenberg, M., & Reis, H. (1986). Lonliness, social skills, and social perception. *Personality and Social Psychology Bulletin*, *12*(1), 121–130.

Wolak, J., Mitchell, K., & Finkelhor, D. (2003). Escaping or connecting? Characteristics of youth who form close online relationships. *Journal of Adolescence*, *26*, 105–119.

Wu, J. (2010). Global video game market forecast. *Strategy Analytics*. Retrieved from   http://www.strategyanalytics.com/default.aspx?mod=ReportAbstract Viewer&a0=5282

Yee, N. (2002). Befriending ogres and wood-elves -Understanding relationship formation in MMORPGs. *Nickyee*. Retrieved from http://www.nickyee.com/hub/relationships/home.html

Yee, N. (2006). The demographics, motivations, and derived experiences of users of massively-multi-user online graphical environments. *Teleoperators and Virtual Environments*, *15*(3), 309–329.

Yee, N. (2007). Motivations of play in online games. *Journal of CyberPsychology and Behavior*, *9*(6), 772–775.

Yee, N., & Bailenson, J. (2007). The Proteus Effect: The effect of transformed self-representation on behavior. *Human Communication Research*, *33*(3), 271–290.

Yee, N., & Bailenson, J. (2008). A method for longitudinal behavorial data collection in second life. *Presence: Teleoperators and Virtual Environments*, *17*(6), 594–596.

Young, G., & Whitty, M. (2012). *Transcending taboos*. New York: Routledge.

4 Social Goals, Social Skills, and Online Video Game Involvement

Unlike traditional video games, OVGs have integrated play within an Internet-based, social context, creating a distinctive environment, reminiscent of both traditional video games and other mediated social spaces, such as chat rooms, but unique in their compilation of these features and enabling of *social play*. Researchers have found the social elements contained within these playful spaces to be one of the immersive factors of these spaces (Guitton, 2011) and a primary reason for continued play frequency (Ducheneaut, Yee, Nickell, & Moore, 2006; Griffiths, Davies, & Chappell, 2003; Kolo & Baur, 2004) and extended duration (Caplan, Williams, & Yee, 2009; Ducheneaut et al., 2006; Hsu, Wen, & Wu, 2009; Williams, Ducheneaut, Xiong, Yee, & Nickell, 2006). At a minimum, socializing with other players helps accomplish the game's objectives (e.g., asking questions about the location of a particular object). However, many players seek more. For instance, content analyses of the social interactions that take place within online gaming spaces have revealed that emotional communication vastly predominates task-oriented conversations (Pena & Hancock, 2006), indicating that in-game social connections are not strictly goal oriented. Co-players assist not only with instrumental goals but also relational ones. They are seen as valued sources of offline advice (Williams, 2006), and up to 75% of game players report having "good friends" within their gaming communities (Cole & Griffiths, 2007). Players have even been found to adjust their in-game spatial location in relation to other players in an effort to sustain close proximity when engaged in social activities, presumably to promote more intimate social interactions (Lomanowska & Guitton, 2012).

However, freed from the rules and pressures of traditional socialization, engagement within these spaces can be "a socially liberating experience" (Davis, Flett, & Besser, 2002, p. 332), and users may begin to perceive themselves as "safer, more efficacious, more confident, and more comfortable with online interpersonal interactions and relationships than traditional face-to-face social activities" (Caplan, 2003, p. 629). For example, a lack of non-verbal cues allows individuals to socially engage free from any judgments based upon physical attributes, while the use of a text-based environment grants the ability to carefully craft any outgoing communication.

Consequently, and largely because of the *"inelasticity of time"* (Nie, 2001, p. 420, italics added), one's online social community may begin to thrive at the expense of face-to-face interactions (Caplan et al., 2009; Chiu, Lee, & Huang, 2004; Kraut et al., 1998; Morahan-Martin & Schumacher, 2003; Nie & Erbring, 2002; Williams, 2006). This can be problematic, as friends supported by physical proximity are able to provide more social and emotional resources (e.g., social and emotional support) and/or physical resources (e.g., tangible favors) as compared to their online counterparts and, as such, are seen as more socially satisfying (Dunbar, 2012; Kraut et al., 1998; Lo, Wang, & Fang, 2005; Shen & Williams, 2010).

This potential displacement of offline for online contacts has been identified within a variety of Internet-based, mediated social spaces; however, OVGs have garnered particular concern as they not only provide a social space populated by relative strangers, but they are also characterized by shared, playful, and often novel activities. This difference is important, as these shared activities can contribute to the formation of long-lasting, highly intimate friendship bonds, with sustainable levels of self-disclosure and intimacy not traditionally found in other mediated spaces (Cole & Griffiths, 2007; Hsu et al., 2009; Iacono & Weisband, 1997; Williams, 2006; Yee, 2002). Over time, the formation of intimate, sustainable bonds between co-players could generate substantial displacement effects, leading to declines in the quantity and quality of offline communication and the size of one's social circle (Blais, Craig, Pepler, & Connolly, 2008; Cole & Griffiths, 2007; Hussain & Griffiths, 2009; Kim, Namkoong, Ku, & Kim, 2008; Lo et al., 2005; Shen & Williams, 2010; Williams, 2006). This, in turn, may hinder one's ability to form and maintain reciprocal offline relationships (Cole & Griffiths, 2007; Shen & Williams, 2010) and attenuate the development or maintenance of effective social and emotional skills (Chiu et al., 2004; Kim et al., 2008; Peters & Malesky, 2008; Shen & Williams, 2010) as having and maintaining face-to-face relationships are integral to developing effective social skills and learning socially appropriate behavior (Engles, Finkenauer, Meeus, & Dekovic, 2001).

However, others have suggested that video game players are not socially inept in the traditional sense, but instead place different values on offline and online socialization (Ng & Wiemer-Hastings, 2005). It is a difference in social goals (Ng & Wiemer-Hastings, 2005), rather than social skills, that has contributed to the perception of social ineptitude among video game players (Kowert, Griffiths, & Oldmeadow, 2012), particularly online players (Kowert & Oldmeadow, 2012). While researchers have considered this possibility, no known study has examined differences in social goals among game players.

4.1   PRESENT STUDY

The current study aims to clarify the veracity of previously drawn conclusions and determine the extent to which video game involvement may support, or undermine, the development and maintenance of traditional social skills, through an examination of the relationships between social goals, social skills, and video game involvement.

To account for the possibility that game players may demonstrate equal social abilities (i.e., social skills) as non-players, but be less interested in socializing with others, or perceive themselves to be socially ineffective (in the absence of actual social differences), an evaluation of the importance placed upon, and perceived likelihood to achieve, offline and online social goals will first be undertaken. An examination of this nature will provide insight into game players' desire to socially engage with others as well as their perceived ability to do so. Evaluating the interest in and perceived likelihood to achieve in both offline and online contexts will also allow for an assessment of the interactions between offline and online socialization among video game playing communities and uncover if one's interest in or perceived ability to achieve social goals differs across contexts (i.e., offline or online), across game playing categories (i.e., online game players and non-online game players), and with varying degrees of involvement. Additionally, this assessment will account for the possibility that game players may perceive themselves to be socially inefficient in the absence of objective social differences, as such differences have been noted in other samples (Glasgow & Arkowitz, 1975; Rapee & Lim, 1992).

Based on the research of Ng and Wiemer-Hastings (2005), the following prediction has been made:

H_1: More involved video game players will rate offline social goals as less important to them, and less likely to be achieved, than less involved video game players.

As researchers have also postulated that OVGs appeal to those who are socially unskilled (Chak & Leung, 2004; McKenna & Bargh, 2000; Peters & Malesky, 2008), and inverse relationships between social skills and OVG involvement were uncovered in the review of the literature (see section 3.2), differences in social goals are expected to be magnified within this subgroup of players. As such, the following prediction was made:

H_2: Online video game players will rate offline social goals as less important to them, and less likely to be achieved, than the broader video game playing population.

However, uncovering differences in social goals would not dismiss the potential for more objective differences in social ability among the video game playing community. Therefore, the relationships between social skills and video game involvement will also be assessed. To determine the extent to which OVG involvement may support (i.e., compensate), or undermine (i.e., displace), the development and maintenance of traditional social skills, clear, consistent relationships between social skills and video game involvement need to be established. A review of the literature (see section 3.2) revealed inverse relationships between emotional and social expressivity, social sensitivity and social control, and video game involvement, suggesting that more involved players perceive themselves as lacking self-presentation skills, as being less comfortable in social situations, and as being less verbally and emotionally expressive. However, variability in sample selection and inconsistencies in the conceptualization of OVG involvement and social competence has made it difficult to generalize these findings and determine the precise nature of the relationships between social outcomes and video game involvement. For example, the specific social skills assessed by Lemmens et al. (2011) were not specified, making it difficult to infer links between specific social skills and OVG involvement. The measure enlisted by Griffiths (2010) was similarly ambiguous, as it assessed elements of social skills and social anxiety. As such, it is not possible to attribute the differences uncovered between high and low frequency players to specific social abilities.

To clarify the relationships between social skills and OVG involvement, and determine the consistency of the relationships between these two variables, a comprehensive evaluation of the relationships between social skills and OVG involvement will be undertaken. In consideration of the findings and limitations of previous work (see section 3.3 for an overview of the methodological limitations), and the established theoretical links between social skills and OVG involvement, several predictions have been made. As it is unclear whether social displacement or compensation phenomena are underlying the relationships between social skills and video game involvement, sub-hypotheses were made for each prediction. Sub-hypothesis (a) predicts compensation phenomena, while (b) hypothesizes the presence of displacement effects.

H_3: **An inverse relationship between Social Control (SC) and video game Involvement will emerge.**

   H_{3a}: **An inverse relationship between Social Control (SC) and video game Involvement will emerge between subjects, with active game players exhibiting lower levels of SC than the broader sample.**

   H_{3b}: **An inverse relationship between SC and video game Involvement will emerge within subjects, with SC demonstrating an inverse linear relationship with video game involvement.**

The predictions outlined by H_3 refer to differences in social control. According to Riggio (1989), Social Control (SC) refers to one's competence at social self-presentation, role taking, and impression management in face-to-face interpersonal interactions. Previous research has found lower SC to be a strong predictor of increased social Internet use (Caplan, 2005; Korgaonkar & Wolin, 1999; Utz, 2000; Walther, 1996) and increased OVG involvement (Liu & Peng, 2009). Due to the visual anonymity, asynchronicity of communication, and lack of non-verbal cues, computer-mediated environments are able to provide substantially greater control over one's social self-presentation and impression formation than provided by face-to-face communication (Walther, 1996). Online video games may be particularly accommodating as they also provide the ability to actively manipulate one's physical presentation through the customization of avatars. This sense of control can mediate the typical social anxiety associated with a lack of Social Control (Leary & Kowalski, 1995; Segrin & Kinney, 1995) by allowing for the strategic, and potentially idealized, presentation of oneself. Consequently, these mediated spaces are perceived as less threatening than traditional socialization and may become highly desirable for those who lack effective self-presentational skills. As significant inverse relationships between SC and OVG involvement would reflect this desirability, they are predicted to emerge.

H_4: An inverse relationship between Social Expressivity (SE) and video game Involvement will emerge.

   H_{4a}: An inverse relationship between SE and video game Involvement will emerge between subjects, with active game players exhibiting lower levels of SE than the broader sample.

   H_{4b}: An inverse relationship between SE and video game Involvement will emerge within subjects, with SE demonstrating an inverse linear relationship with video game involvement.

H_4 predicts that the inverse associations between Social Expressivity (SE) and OVG play found in previous research (e.g., Lemmens et al., 2011) will replicate. Traditionally, individuals low in SE have difficulties in engaging others in social conversation and exhibit a lower verbal fluency (Riggio, 1989, 2005). For individuals low in SE, OVG play could be a particularly desirable activity, as active engagement within these spaces promotes socialization while reducing the pressure to engage and guide social interactions. Not only does social communication become intertwined with the activity itself, but the provision of asynchronous communication further accommodates for any hindrances in verbal fluency (de Kort & Ijsselsteijn, 2008; Gajadhar, de Kort, & IJsselsteijn, 2008; Sjöblom, 2008). Reflecting the social utility of OVGs to accommodate individuals with lower SE, inverse associations between SE and OVG play are predicted to emerge.

H_5: A positive relationship between Emotional Sensitivity (ES) and video game Involvement will emerge.

   H_{5a}: A positive relationship between ES and video game Involvement will emerge between subjects, with active game players exhibiting lower levels of ES than the broader sample.

H_{5b}: **A positive relationship between ES and video game Involvement will emerge within subjects, with ES demonstrating a positive linear relationship with video game involvement.**

H_5 predicts the emergence of positive relationships between Emotional Sensitivity (ES) and OVG involvement. While ES has not been widely evaluated in relation to OVG play (e.g., Kowert, Domahidi, & Quandt, 2014), high levels of ES are indicative of shyness (Riggio, 1987), which has been shown to hold significant relationships with social uses of the Internet (Caplan, 2002; Chak & Leung, 2004; Roberts, Smith, & Pollock, 2000; Yuen & Lavin, 2004) as well as problematic and addicted use of online video games (Liu & Peng, 2009; Peng & Liu, 2010). As Internet-based, social spaces are able to reduce inhibitions (Caplan, 2002; Chak & Leung, 2004; Liu & Peng, 2009; Peng & Liu, 2010; Roberts et al., 2000; Yuen & Lavin, 2004), shyness, or high ES, is not an obstacle to effective communication within these spaces (Scealy, Phillips, & Stevenson, 2002), which makes them highly desirable for timid individuals (Roberts et al., 2000). In this sense, OVGs may be exceptionally accommodating. Unlike chat rooms, where the primary purpose, and sole function, of the space is to directly socialize with others, OVGs provide a strong, social community even in the absence of direct socialization (Ducheneaut et al., 2006; Steinkuehler & Williams, 2006). As shy individuals can be socially self-conscious, hesitant, and potentially avoidant (Zimbardo, 1997), involvement within a shared, playful environment could be preferable to a mediated space that requires direct interaction with others. Demonstrating the established links between the behavioral manifestations of shyness and OVG involvement, significant, positive relationships between ES and Involvement are predicted to emerge.

Uncovering significant relationships between social skills, social goals, and video game involvement would illustrate the presence of significant relationships between these variables; however, it would not reveal the extent to which these relationships are underpinned by social displacement and/or compensation phenomena. To clarify the potential mechanisms underlying the relationships between social competence and video game involvement, targeted statistical analyses will be conducted. To examine broad differences in social outcomes between gaming groups, numerous between-group analyses will be enlisted. The presence of broad differences between groups would provide support for the assertions put forth by compensation theorists (i.e., the "a" hypotheses), as it would indicate that there are substantial social differences between those who choose to engage in video game play, either to a greater extent than other players (i.e., high-/low-involved players) or in online-specific play (i.e., online/non-online players). A group categorization scheme based on levels of involvement (high/low) and video game modality (online/non-online) will be enlisted in lieu of a genre-specific approach as the current research aims to assess the broad relationships between video game involvement and social outcomes. As such, there are no genre-specific predictions that would necessitate a genre-specific categorization. Thus, differentiating players by levels of involvement and the modality in which they engage is a more appropriate categorization criterion for examining differences in social outcomes based on users' level of participation within video gaming environments.

To examine the presence of displacement phenomena (i.e., the "b" hypotheses), within-group analyses will be conducted, whereby the linear relationships between social outcomes and video game involvement will be assessed and compared across gaming groups. Uncovering a linear correspondence between increased involvement and social outcomes would indicate the presence of displacement phenomena as it would indicate that social skill outcomes linearly correspond with increases in video game involvement, suggesting that players experience social change as their video game involvement increases.

In addition to examining the relationship between social goals, social skills, and video game involvement, a broad demographic profile of video game players will be cataloged. Previous demographic inquiries into the gaming community have been limited to more specialist gaming groups, such as MMORPG players (Cole & Griffiths, 2007; Griffiths, Davies, & Chappell, 2004a; Kolo & Baur, 2004; Shen & Williams, 2010; Williams et al., 2006; Williams, Yee, & Caplan, 2008; Yee, 2006, 2007) or addicted populations (Kim et al., 2008; Wan & Chiou, 2007), largely neglecting the game playing community as a whole. As relatively little information is available about video game players in general, the questionnaire utilized within this study will examine a wide variety of demographic variables. In addition to basic information (e.g., gender, age, ethnicity), gaming history and genre and modality preferences will also be documented.

4.1.1   Offline Versus Online Games as Social Environments

It is possible that the predicted relationships between social goals, social skills, and Involvement will be evident among the broader participant pool (i.e., all game players) as the academic community's original apprehensions about the social consequences of video game play grew from research that examined the potential negative social influence of offline gaming (i.e., arcade machine play) on its players (Dominick, 1984; Senlow, 1984). These findings are largely unacknowledged in recent research, as the concern about the social effects of video game involvement has shifted away from video games themselves and toward the potential consequences of socially mediated video game play.

However, as video game play itself can be socially accommodating, through its provision of a shared activity, it must be accounted for prior to evaluating relationships between social skills and Involvement among OVG players. A failure to do would greatly increase the likelihood of drawing unreliable and invalid conclusions. For example, video games can be a desired leisure activity for individuals who have difficulties initiating and guiding conversation (i.e., low SE). When actively engaged within a gaming space, social communication becomes intertwined with the activity itself, thereby reducing the pressure to maintain and direct socialization (Sjöblom, 2008). This can grant considerable communicative flexibility, as the shared activity takes the forefront of attention and thus largely guides the content of the conversation and mediates the pace. Without accounting for the potential relationships between SE and Involvement within offline video game playing populations, one cannot accurately evaluate the existence of unique relationships between these variables among online players. Significant associations between social skills and offline video game play would signify the extent to which video game play itself is socially accommodating, whereas only relationships of a greater magnitude, or unique to online-exclusive players, would demonstrate the influence of OVG play specifically.

To account for this, the relationships between video game involvement, social goals, and social skills will be examined across different game playing groups, including offline and online players. While it is possible that these relationships will be evident among the broader participant pool (i.e., all game players), these relationships are expected to be magnified, or show unique associations, within online game playing samples, due to the wider variety of social affordances provided by online, rather than offline, gaming environments. This prediction is reflected in the following hypothesis:

> **H6: All of the predicted relationships will be magnified among online video game players.**

4.2   MATERIAL AND METHODS

4.2.1   Variables of Interest

4.2.1.1   *Social Goals*

A modified version of Ford's (1982) social goals measure was enlisted to assess participants' interest in and likelihood of achieving offline and online social, and non-social, goals. This measure was originally developed to investigate the relationship between social competence and social cognition among adolescent participants. Ford (1982) found that individuals who assigned a high priority to interpersonal goals, and described themselves as more likely to achieve these goals, were also judged more socially competent by a third-party observer. As this measure was developed for adolescents, the wording was adjusted slightly to reflect an adult population (see appendix A).

Participants will first be presented with an adapted version of Ford's (1982) 'offline' goals, five social and five non-social, and asked to rate them based on their level of importance (1 = "*not important to me at all*," 7 = "*very important to me*"). As the definition of a goal was not explicitly stated in the original Ford (1982) study, a goal will be defined as "something you are actively working to attain."

Participants will then be presented with the same 10 goals and asked to rate how likely it is that they will achieve these goals. This was done on a 1–5 Likert scale, with 1 denoting *"not likely"* and 5 denoting *"extremely likely."* This deviated from Ford's (1982) study, which utilized a 1–3 Likert scale (1 = *"superior goal capabilities,"* 2 = *"average goal capability,"* 3 = *"deficient goal capability"*). The adjusted 1–5 scale measures the same underlying construct of self-efficacy but provides participants with a wider spectrum of response choices. Additionally, participants may be more likely to report that attaining a goal is *"not likely"* rather than reporting they are *"deficient"* in the ability to attain a particular goal.

Adapted from Ford's (1982) offline goals, a list of 10 online, social and non-social, goals was constructed. The online goals were loosely based on Yee's (2007) research into motivations for MMORPG play. As such, a separate set of instructions was provided to participants who had reported that they had never played MMORPG games before. These instructions outlined MMORPG environments and prompted participants to imagine the importance they would place on these virtual world goals if they were engaged in this type of gaming environment (the online social goals measure and instructions can be found in appendix B).

Offline and online social goals were summed and divided by the number of presented items in order to calculate the average rating given to each item within the scales. This created four separate outcome scores, reflecting the average importance and likelihood for offline and online social goals. The importance of and likelihood of achieving offline and online social goals was found to be highly correlated (offline, $r = .61$, $p < .001$; online $r = .95$, $p < .001$). The reliability of the offline and online social goal scales was computed prior to analysis, revealing acceptable levels of internal consistency for the importance of both offline (Cronbach's α ranged from .61 to .69) and online (Cronbach's α ranged from .77 to .78) social goals.

Differences in the importance of and perceived likelihood to achieve social goals will undergo between- and within-subject analyses. First, between-subject analyses will be conducted to identify any mean differences between groups (i.e., high- and low-involved video game players and online and non-online game players). Uncovering broad differences in social goals would indicate that individuals with different social profiles (e.g., less interest in achieving offline social goals, greater interest in achieving online social goals, etc.) are more highly involved in video game play, or online-specific play, and would suggest the presence of social compensation phenomena. Within-subject analyses will then be enlisted to assess the linear relationships between social goals and video game involvement within different gaming groups (i.e., all participants, online players only). These analyses will uncover if the interest in, or perceived ability to achieve, offline and online social goals corresponds with varying video game involvement (and to what extent it varies among online game players in particular), with significant linear relationships suggesting the presence of displacement phenomena. For example, a significant, inverse linear relationship between the interest in achieving offline social goals and video game involvement among online players would indicate that greater involvement in online gaming spaces corresponds with decreases in one's interest in offline socialization.

4.2.1.2   *Social Skills*

While social competence can, and has been, conceptualized in a multitude of ways, a social skills approach to measuring social competence will be enlisted. This approach operationalizes social competence as having, or not having, certain social skills (Rose-Kransor, 1997). The social skills approach was chosen because it forms the base of social competence models (Cavell, 1990; DuBois & Felner, 1996; Rose-Kransor, 1997), supplying the foundation for the other facets of social competence to build upon. This approach is also the most frequently employed within the social competence literature (Rose-Kransor, 1997) and has shown significant relationships with performance-based assessments (Baron & Markman, 2003; Riggio, Watring, & Throckmorton, 1993), suggesting that it is a valid methodology to assess social skills and social performance. Furthermore, according to the social skills deficit vulnerability hypothesis, an individual's psychosocial well-being can be threatened by a lack of social competence (Lewinsohn, Chaplin, & Barton, 1980; Segrin, 1990, 1993, 1998, 2000). Thus, variability in social skill outcomes among more active video game players may also be reflective of the behavioral symptoms associated with loneliness, depression, and/or social anxiety. Thus, any significant associations between social competence and OVG involvement should be quantifiable on this foundational level. Additionally, the social skills approach is the most adept for pinpointing the precise social abilities that may hold a relationship with video game play.

4.2.1.2.1   SOCIAL SKILLS INVENTORY (SSI)

To assess social skills, participants were asked to complete the Social Skills Inventory (SSI) in its entirety (Riggio, 1989). The SSI is a 90-item questionnaire that provides an overall score, as well as scores for each of its six separate subscales, allowing for a multidimensional assessment of social skills. The subscales fall along two dimensions, emotional and social, that assess non-verbal and verbal aspects of social ability, respectively. Each of these broad dimensions is further subdivided into expressivity, sensitivity, and control subscales (full descriptions of the subscales can be found in appendix C).

The expressivity subscales focus on one's ability to communicate, both verbally (Social Expressivity) and non-verbally (Emotional Expressivity). Social Expressivity (SE) assesses skill in verbal expression and the ability to engage others in social discourse (e.g., "*I always mingle at parties*"), whereas Emotional Expressivity (EE) measures the skills with which individuals communicate non-verbally, particularly the ability to accurately express felt emotional states (e.g., "*I am able to liven up a dull party*").

The sensitivity subscales assess one's ability to interpret verbal (Social Sensitivity) and non-verbal (Emotional Sensitivity) communication. Social Sensitivity (SS) specifically assesses one's ability to interpret the verbal communication of others and one's sensitivity to and understanding of the norms governing appropriate social behavior. Socially sensitive people are attentive to social behavior and are conscious and aware of the appropriateness of their own actions (e.g., "*Sometimes I think that I take things other people say to me too personally*"). Conversely, Emotional Sensitivity (ES) measures one's skill in receiving and interpreting the non-verbal communications of others. Individuals who are emotionally sensitive attend to, and accurately interpret, the subtle emotional cues of others (e.g., "*I sometimes cry at sad movies*"). In excess, high levels of ES can be indicative of shyness, or a hypersensitivity to the non-verbal signals of others (Riggio, 1987).

The control subscales of the SSI measure the ability to control and regulate non-verbal (Emotional Control) and verbal (Social Control) displays. While the Emotional Control (EC) subscale measures ability to control and regulate emotional and nonverbal displays (e.g., "*I am easily able to make myself look happy one minute and sad the next*"), the Social Control (SC) subscale assesses verbal control centering on social self-presentation. Individuals whose social control skills are well developed are generally adept, tactful, and self-confident in social situations and can fit in comfortably in just about any kind of social situation. Social Control is also important in guiding the direction and content of communication in social interaction (e.g., "*I am usually very good at leading group discussions*").

The SSI has shown to have high convergent validity with other self-report measures of non-verbal and social skill constructs (Riggio, 2005) and high test retest reliabilities (ranging from .81 to .96) (Riggio, 1989). While this inventory relies on self-report data, there has been little concern about socially desirable responding for the SSI (Riggio & Carney, 2003; Riggio, 1986).

Traditional scoring of the SSI includes summing all 90-items within the questionnaire (after adjusting for the reverse scored items) to produce an overall composite score, which represents the global level of social skill or social competence (Riggio, 1989). Although a global outcome can be calculated, the outcomes generated from each of the six subscales are often more informative as they provide quantitative scores for specific dimensions of social skill. The amount or degree to which an individual displays each skill is also important, as the balance among the various social abilities can also signify social effectiveness (Riggio, 1986). For example, a person who scores high on the Sensitivity subscales (ES and SS), but scores low to moderate on the Expressivity (EE and SE) and Social Control subscales, will understand others' social behavior, but will not be likely to actively socially engage. While one's global SSI score may be moderately high, a person displaying a skill imbalance may not be able to engage in effective socialization with others (Riggio, 1989). It is also important to note that Riggio (1989) intended the SSI to conceptualize social skills as existing on a continuum, rather than in terms of a deficit or surplus. This is key, as social skills are highly adaptive and can vary in importance across contexts, individuals, and relationships (Gresham & Elliot, 1987; Gresham, 1986; Walther, 1996).

Due to the limited amount of research investigating the links between social skills and video game use, the entire SSI will be administered. While only three specific predictions between OVG involvement and SSI outcomes were made, it is possible that additional relationships between the SSI and OVG involvement will emerge. There is simply not sufficient evidence to support further predictions. The administration of the SSI in its entirety will allow for a comprehensive and systematic evaluation of the relationship between social skills and video game involvement.

4.2.1.2.1.1   *PRINCIPAL COMPONENTS ANALYSIS*

To confirm that the SSI aligned upon the appropriate six-factor structure, a principal components analysis was conducted using Riggio's (1989) item sets and a six-factor solution (varimax rotation), utilizing the current sample ($N = 291$). The Kaiser-Meyer-Olkin (KMO) measure verified the sampling adequacy for the analysis (.87), and all KMO values for individual items were > .75, which is well above the acceptable limit of .50 (Field, 2009). Bartlett's test of sphericity (X^2 (153) = 3732.87, $p < .001$) indicated that the correlation between items was sufficient. The six factors explained 68.32% of the variance (see appendix D for factor loadings). The results indicated that a six-factor solution was the best fit for this model, with the intended factors emerging.

4.2.1.2.1.2   *RELIABILITY AND INTERCORRELATIONS*

Consistent with previous findings (Hamann, Lineburg, & Paul, 1998; Riggio, 1989), the SSI subscales were found to be highly intercorrelated (see Table 4.1). As the possession of one social skill will likely predispose an individual to develop other skills, the SSI subscales are generally positively intercorrelated (Hamann et al., 1998; Riggio, 1989). There are exceptions, however, where the attainment of one skill may impede the effective implementation of another. For example, Emotional Expressivity and Emotional Control are negatively correlated, as extremely emotionally expressive individuals may be unable to monitor and control their expression of emotion. Similarly, highly controlled individuals may be stifled in their expression of felt emotions (Riggio, 1989).

Reliability analyses confirmed an acceptable internal consistency for all six subscales, with alpha levels ranging from .70 to .89.

Table 4.1 Intercorrelations between SSI subscales in Study 1 (*N* = 291)

SSI Subscale	ES	EC	SE	SS	SC
Emotional Expressivity (EE)	.47**	−.35**	.57**	.18**	.41**
Emotional Sensitivity (ES)		−.07	.52**	.33**	.39**
Emotional Control (EC)			.06	−.41**	.26**
Social Expressivity (SE)				.09	.69**
Social Sensitivity (SS)					−.29
Social Control (SC)					

**p* < .01

4.2.1.2.1.3 GENDER, AGE, AND SOCIAL SKILLS

Prior to analysis, variation in the SSI across gender and age categories was examined as previous research has found SSI to vary significantly across gender (Riggio, 1989; Riggio and Carney, 2003). This effect was replicated here. SSI outcome scores across gender and age were assessed using a 5 (age group) by 2 (gender) by 6 (subscale) MANOVA. A significant main effect of gender was found on four of the six subscales. As seen in Figure 4.1, females scored higher than males on three of the six subscales (EE, ES and SS), whereas males scored higher than females on the EC subscale (*F*'s > 11, *p*'s < .01).

A significant main effect of age was also found for ES, SE, and SC subscales (*F*'s > 3.5, *p*'s < .01). This effect was marginally significant for the EE subscale, $F(4, 262) = 2.14$, $p = .08$. In general, younger participants obtained higher outcomes than older participants; however, the precise patterns were inconsistent across subscales.

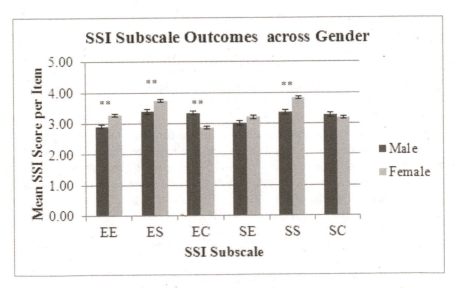

Figure 4.1 Mean SSI outcome scores across gender

A significant interaction between gender and age was found for the EE and ES subscales (F's > 3, p's < .02). These interactions are likely unique to this sample as they were centralized within the older age groups (e.g., after age 30), which were groups with very small sample sizes (males, n = 13; females, n = 12). Furthermore, previous research has not noted significant age effects for the SSI among an adult sample.

4.2.1.3 *Involvement*

In an effort to address the inconsistency in the conceptualization of video game involvement within the literature (see section 3.3.3), and move beyond assessments that rely on single facets of video game involvement, a single variable called 'Involvement' was developed to represent the degree to which participants are involved in video gaming as a form of activity. Involvement scores were generated as a composite of participants' reported weekly play frequency, game play variety, and social identity. The integration of behavioral (i.e., play frequency and variety) and psychological (i.e., social identity) measures of involvement will provide a more systematic assessment of video game involvement than has been employed previously. It also allows for the evaluation of players across a broad spectrum of video game involvement. The rationale for the selection of these three components of video game involvement is discussed in more detail in the following sections.

4.2.1.3.1 PLAY FREQUENCY

Play frequency has been commonly utilized to distinguish between varying degrees of video game involvement (Barnett et al., 1997; Colwell & Kato, 2003; Griffiths, 2010; Kolo & Baur, 2004; Lo et al., 2005; Senlow, 1984; Shen & Williams, 2010; Smyth, 2007). Play frequency has likely become the measurement of choice due to its ease of assessment and intrinsic relationship with video game involvement. A higher frequency of play indicates greater exposure to video game environments and, in the case of online-specific play, more time spent in mediated, social spaces. This increased time commitment also represents the degree of potential displacement from other activities due to play.

To assess play frequency, participants were asked to report their average weekly play time. This was chosen in lieu of a frequency multiplied by duration-per-session statistic, as recalling the average amount of sessions, and the length of those sessions, would likely generate a less accurate report of play time than a general estimation of the total amount of time dedicated to game play per week.

4.2.1.3.2 GAME VARIETY

To assess game variety, participants were asked to indicate which types of game genres (e.g., role-playing games, puzzle games, etc.), across modalities (i.e., single- or multiplayer), they were currently playing by choosing any that applied from a set list. Engaging in a wider variety of gaming behavior is indicative of greater general involvement within video game environments and communities, a difference that is not detectable through the measurement of play frequency alone. The incorporation of game variety into the Involvement factor will account for this variation, allowing for the differentiation between individuals who engage within one particular gaming environment (e.g., single-player puzzle games) and those who disperse the same amount of time across a variety of environments (e.g., single-player puzzle games, single-player simulation games, and multiplayer role-playing games).

The list of game types that participants could choose from included eight combinations of game genre and modality (see appendix E). The total number of game types selected by the participants was summed to create a game-variety outcome score. This broad, rather than genre-specific, approach to conceptualizing game variety was adopted as the research questions being evaluated here are not genre specific but rather related to the broader associations between video game play and social outcomes.

4.2.1.3.3 SOCIAL IDENTITY

How one identifies with a social group provides a vastly different determination of his or her categorization within it than a more objective measure. As Hall (1966) argues, identification is the self-definition of the individual, rather than categorizations based on static definitions of identity applied from the outside. As defined by Tajfel (1979), social identity is "that part of the individual's self-concept which derives from their knowledge of their membership of a social group (or groups) together with the value and emotional significance of that membership" (p. 255). This concept originates from Social Identity Theory, which is a theoretical framework that was developed to explain the tendency for individuals to categorize the social world into groups and, consequently, generate in-group and out-group biases in their thoughts and behavior (Tajfel & Turner, 1979; Tajfel, 1970, 1974, 1982; Turner, 1984). Individuals are continuously cataloging themselves and others into various social groups, such as ones based on organizational membership, religious affiliation, gender, and age (Tajfel & Turner, 1985). These categorizations bring order to the social environment and enable individuals to identify themselves within the social landscape. An individual can belong to multiple categories simultaneously (e.g., 'female' and 'gamer'); however, the extent to which an individual identifies with and values each category exists along a continuum. One's social identities are also comparative and relational in nature. Individuals who seek, and find, positive differences between themselves and other social groups achieve and retain a positive social identity (Tajfel, 1978). This is important, as a positive social identity fosters feelings of belongingness and self-worth (Branscombe & Wann, 1991) and can enhance self-esteem (Barreto & Ellemers, 2000; Branscombe, 1998).

Consideration for one's social identity within the social group of gamers is largely absent from the literature (one notable exception comes from Kowert & Oldmeadow, 2010), even though researchers have found social identity to be a strong predictor of play frequency and hypothesized it to be a potential underlying source of social changes due to gaming (Ghuman & Griffiths, 2012). Therefore, social identity was incorporated into the composite assessment of video game involvement. The incorporation of social identity will generate a more comprehensive evaluation of an individual's involvement within the online video gaming community than has previously been utilized by accounting for the various psychological factors that may be associated with involvement that are not measured by play frequency and variety alone. For example, when involvement categorizations are based on the objective assessment of play frequency, an individual who engages in OVG play five hours a week could be rated as a 'low-frequency' player. However, this same individual may socialize with their in-game contacts on a daily basis, be a member of game-related clubs, contribute to video game–related blogs, and/or work within the video game industry. All these factors suggest that this individual may be more reliant upon the community as a source of positive identity, entertainment, and socialization than was indicated by his or her reported play frequency. An assessment of the individual's social identity with the community of gamers would likely quantify these additional facets of OVG involvement, as greater levels of identity signify the internalization of the 'gamer identity' as a source of belongingness and self-esteem and indicate higher levels of social and psychological investment within the gaming community.

Participants' social identity with the community of gamers was assessed with a four-item scale based upon a measure developed by Doosje, Ellmers, and Spears (1995). Participants rated each statement ("*I see myself as a gamer*," "*I am pleased to be a gamer*," "*I identify with other gamers*," and "*I feel strong ties with other gamers*") on a 1–7 Likert scale, ranging from "*strongly disagree*" to "*strongly agree*." As different individuals may utilize different categorization schemas for any particular identity, gamer identity was assessed on a spectrum, rather than a dichotomous characterization. Reliability analyses confirmed that this measure was highly reliable (Cronbach's α = .96).

4.2.1.3.4 RELIABILITY AND INTERCORRELATIONS

The three components of Involvement (i.e., play frequency, game variety, and social identity) were found to be moderately intercorrelated (see Table 4.2) and, when combined, demonstrated a high internal consistency, producing an alpha coefficient of .81. These three variables were combined into a single component by summing the scores on each factor. Each indicator of Involvement was standardized prior to being summed in order to account for the variation in response options across constructs. Within the sample, Involvement scores ranged from −3.97 to 5.96 (SD = 2.54).

Table 4.2 Intercorrelations among Involvement variables in Study 1 (*n* = 250)

	Total play time	Number of games played
Social identity	.830***	.433***
Total play time		.400***

***p < .01

4.2.1.3.5 PRINCIPAL COMPONENTS ANALYSIS

A principal components analysis was conducted with the standardized Involvement outcomes from participants who completed all of the questions relating to Involvement (*n* = 250). The Kaiser-Meyer-Olkin measure verified the sampling adequacy for this analysis (KMO = .63), and all KMO values for individual items were above the acceptable limit of .50 (Field, 2009). Bartlett's test of sphericity (X^2 (3) = 369.42, *p* < .001) indicated that the correlation between items was sufficient. Supporting the established theoretical links between the components of Involvement, the results indicated that a one-factor solution was the best fit for this model (as only one component was extracted a rotation was not warranted). The three factors of Involvement explained 71.29% of the variance (see Table 4.3 for factor loadings).

While game variety was found to contribute less to the composite score of Involvement than play frequency or social identity, each component contributed a significant amount of variance to the model.

4.2.1.3.6 GENDER, AGE, AND INVOLVEMENT

Prior to analysis, Involvement was assessed across gender and age categories using a 5 (age group) by 2 (gender) MANOVA. Analyses revealed significant variation in Involvement across gender and age, with males (*M* = 1.85, *SD* = 2.07) reporting higher levels of video game involvement than females (*M* = −1.17, *SD* = 2.07), *F*(1, 240) = 32.71, *p* < .001, partial η^2 = .120. This effect varied slightly across all age groups; however, no consistent pattern was evident; *F*(4, 240) = 2.88, *p* < .05, partial η^2 = .046. While more females participate in this activity now than ever before, these results confirm that their level of video game involvement is still not equivalent to their male counterparts (Entertainment Software Association, 2012; Ghuman &

Table 4.3 Principal axis analysis of Involvement factor loadings for Study 1 participants

Component of Involvement	Factor Loading
Play frequency	.923
Game variety	.673
Social identity	.911

Griffiths, 2012; Williams et al., 2008). In consideration of the variation of Involvement across gender and age, these two variables will be held as covariates in subsequent analyses.

4.2.2 Procedure

To explore the association between social goals, social skills, and video game involvement, an online survey was conducted. In addition to reporting general demographic information (age, gender, etc.), participants were asked to complete a measure of offline and online social goals (adapted from Ford, 1982), the SSI in its entirety (Riggio, 1989), and a series of questions relating to their level of video game involvement.

4.3 PARTICIPANTS

4.3.1 Participant Recruitment

The concerns about OVG players are not limited to only the problematic and addicted subsample but to the population as a whole. As such, the current research aims to move away from the focus on problematic game playing populations and to evaluate the relationships between social skills and OVG involvement among a broad, adult sample. An adult game playing population was targeted in lieu of an adolescent sample to ensure evaluations between social skills and video game involvement were independent of any developmental influences on social competence.

   Participants were primarily recruited through the University of York's online experimental booking system. This system is primarily utilized by psychology undergraduate studies at the University of York in York, England. Students were given one hour of course credit for completion. Advertisements for participants were also placed on the popular social networking site Facebook. This allowed for the recruitment of a more diverse Western sample, including participants from the United States and United Kingdom. Once the survey had been completed, participants were encouraged to 'repost' the link across their social network to obtain 'snowball' sampling. To ensure the recruitment of more active game players, recruitment advertisements were also placed on online forums and websites oriented toward the gaming community. This included online realm forums, individual guild and clan forums, and gaming clubs and game-related websites. The advertisement stated that participants were being sought to complete a survey assessing individual differences in video game players.

4.3.1.1 Participant Selection

Substantial differences in video game culture and the quantification of social competence have been identified between Eastern and Western nations. For example, the integration of the 'video gamer' into popular culture in the East and West has taken vastly different paths. While in the East video game players are often held in very high esteem, much like sports figures (Ashcraft, 2010; Rossingnol, 2009; Veale, 2007), in the West they remain characterized as lazy, reclusive, and immature (Kowert et al., 2012; Kowert & Oldmeadow, 2012). MarineKing, one of the world's most famous 'cyberathletes,' would be considered a gaming addict by most Western standards, as he plays video games up to 20 hours a day (CNN, 2012). However, in South Korea his dedication to video game play has earned him fame and fortune. He is not characterized as a problematic or addicted player, but rather is lauded for his dedication to his craft (CNN, 2012).

As no known research has examined the stereotypes of video game players in Eastern cultures or noted concern over the potential social consequences of prolonged video game play within Eastern societies as is found in the West, it is unclear if prolonged interaction within these spaces is perceived with the same degree of negativity, socially or otherwise, that would warrant an investigation. However, even if there was evidence of a concern about the social consequences of video game play within Eastern societies, it would not be possible to assess the links between social competence and video game involvement without a culturally sensitive measure of social skills, as what is deemed 'socially competent' can vary greatly across cultures (Tannen, 1984; Ting-Toomey, 1999). As outlined by Ochs (1984), individuals socialize to achieve culturally organized goals. The differences in goals across cultures give rise to variation in the social skills of individuals within different social groups (Leontyev, 1981). For example, being direct or expressing one's emotions may be valued in some cultures but disapproved of in others. These cultural differences can then manifest into the development of culturally bound social skills. This has been evidenced in cross-cultural studies of children. For example, Jay (2010) found substantial differences in social skill development across children within Eastern and Western cultures. Western children were found to exhibit more "positive" social skills (i.e., friendship formation, empathy, sharing, and cooperation), while Eastern children exhibited more "negative" skills (i.e., fighting, anger, arguing). Jay (2010) suggests that this variation in skill use across cultures indicates that different societies may cultivate particular social skills, which, over time, may lead to differences in social skill development and variation in what is deemed socially competent behavior.

Due to these differences in the perception of video game players and the quantification of social competence across cultures, the enlisted sample will be limited to Western participants. Unfortunately, differentiation by region of residency was not possible. Therefore, ethnicity categorizations will be used to represent a participant's country of residence. As it is important to retain a Western sample, only those participants who identified as Caucasian will be retained. While not ideal, this kind of categorization is sufficient to differentiate participants from Eastern and Western cultures.

4.3.2   Age and Ethnicity

In total, 343 participants completed the online survey. As social competence is believed to rapidly develop before reaching adulthood (Bartholomew, 1993; Carstensen, 1995; Cassidy, Kirsh, Scolton, & Parke, 1996; Engles et al., 2001; Gross et al., 1997; Lawton, Kleban, Rajagopal, & Dean, 1992), the analysis was limited to adult participants only. Thus, participants under the age of 18 were removed from the analysis ($n = 1$). In order to reduce cross-cultural variance, the current analyses were restricted to participants who indicated their ethnicity as Caucasian ($N = 291$). Comparisons across ethnicities were not undertaken, as the sample of non-Caucasian participants was too small for reliable analyses ($n = 52$).[1] Within the Caucasian sample, 104 (35.7%) participants were male, and 187 (64.3%) were female. Age ranged from 17 to 56, with an average age of 23.77 ($SD = 7.75$).

4.3.3   Game Play Statistics

Of the 291 remaining participants, 264 (90.7%) reported having played video games at some point. Of these, 180 (68.2%) reported having played OVGs at some point. Only 9.3% of participants reported never having played video games. In terms of play frequency, the sample ranged from "never" through "20+ hours a week." The percentage of players who fell within each play frequency category, for total and online-exclusive play, is presented in Table 4.4.

Just over half of the sample reported playing video games at least once a week (50.6%), while the remaining participants reported playing less frequently. Online players engage at similar rates, as 54.5% of online players reported play frequencies of at least once a week. Almost 20% of the sample (18.9%) played video games more than 10 hours a week. This proportion was slightly higher among the online subsample, with almost one-quarter

Table 4.4 Percentage of players within play frequency categories for total ($N = 291$) and online play ($n = 180$) in Study 1

Amount of Time	Total Playing Time	Online Playing Time
Never	9.3	10.6
Less than once a month	28.5	23.9
About once a month	11.7	11.1
About once a week	9.3	10.6
1–5 hours a week	10.7	9.4
6–10 hours a week	11.7	11.1
10–20 hours a week	9.6	12.8
20+ hours a week	9.3	10.6

(23.4%) revealing similar play frequencies. Of the general sample, 9.3% reported spending more than 20 hours a week engaged in video game play. This proportion was comparable among the online subsample (10.6%).

In line with previous demographic assessments (e.g., Caplan et al., 2009; Griffiths et al., 2004a; Williams, Martins, Consalvo, & Ivory, 2009; Yee, 2006), a range of demographic variables were assessed across age categories (e.g., under 19 years, 20–24 years, 25–29 years, 30–34 years, 35–39 years, 40–44 years, 45–49 years, and over 50). However, this categorization revealed a disproportionate distribution of the sample across ages, with substantially fewer participants within the older age brackets (e.g., 40–44, 45–49, and over 50). As any age effects found within these age categories would likely be unreliable, participants over the age of 40 were excluded from further analysis (n = 19), leaving 272 participants. Evaluations of play frequency and preferences were further limited to those who reported a history of game play (n = 250).

Prior to analysis, the data was assessed for normality. As graphical inspections of normality are often more informative than statistical analyses in large data sets (Field, 2009), normality was evaluated with QQ plots. The plots showed evidence of a normal distribution for play frequency and preferences across gender and age categories.

4.3.3.1 *Play Frequency across Gender and Age*
To evaluate differences in play frequency across age, a univariate ANOVA analysis of gender, age, and play frequency was conducted. A significant effect of gender, $F(1, 240) = 34.04$, $p < .001$, partial $\eta^2 = .124$, and age, $F(1, 240) = 5.51$, $p < .001$, partial $\eta^2 = .084$, was found for overall play

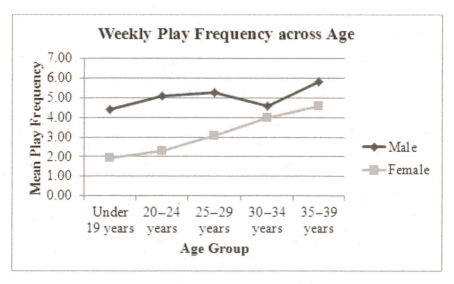

Figure 4.2 Frequency of overall game play across gender and age

frequency. An interaction between gender and age for overall play was not found ($p = .19$, *ns*). Males ($M = 4.98$, $SD = 1.67$) reported engaging in more overall game play than females ($M = 2.30$, $SD = 1.66$). In terms of the scale, males reported playing between 1 and 10 hours a week whereas females averaged between once a month and once a week. Over time, males' play frequency seems to remain relatively stable, while females' frequency steadily rises with age (see Figure 4.2).

4.3.3.1.1 ONLINE PLAY FREQUENCY

To evaluate differences in online play frequency across age and gender, a univariate ANOVA analysis of gender, age, and online play frequency was conducted among online game players ($n = 172$). A significant main effect of age, $F(1, 162) = 9.54$, $p < .001$, partial $\eta^2 = .191$, but not gender ($p = .13$, *ns*), was found. A marginally significant interaction between gender and age also emerged, $F(4, 162) = 2.31$, $p = .06$, partial $\eta^2 = .054$.

As with overall play frequency, male and female players under the age of 19 reported playing significantly less often than any other age group (p's < .01), with an average play frequency ranging from less than once a month to once a month ($M = 1.98$, $SD = 1.57$). Online play frequency showed a steady increase over time, with players over the age of 30 reporting an average of 6 to 20 hours a week ($M = 5.37$, $SD = 1.93$), as compared to between once a month and once a week ($M = 2.63$, $SD = 1.99$) for those under the age of 24. Additionally, by age 30, the play frequency of females reaches comparable levels to their male counterparts and continues to increase over time (see Figure 4.3).

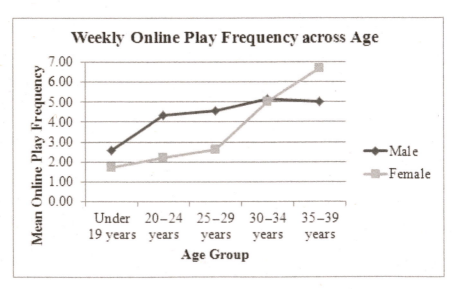

Figure 4.3 Frequency of online game play across gender and age

4.3.3.2   *Modality and Genre Preferences*

Participants were asked to indicate which genre of games, and in which modalities, they are currently playing by ticking any that applied from a list of eight (see Appendix E). The total number of selected game types was summed to create game variety totals for each participant. As seen in Figure 4.4, most participants (67.7%) played between one and three types of games, 16.9% of the sample played between four and five types of games, and 5.5% played more than five types of games. Game playing participants appear to enjoy a variety of games and do not typically limit themselves to one genre or modality. Of those participants who reported playing only one type of game, the largest percentage reported playing multiplayer party games (28.8%).

Roughly one-tenth (9.9%) of the sample indicated playing none of the possible game types. However, this statistic includes the 9.3% of players who reported no history of video game play. Thus, of the participants with a history of video game play, 0.6% appear to be non-active players. No participants reported playing all eight different types of games.

To assess genre preferences, participants were asked to indicate which types of game genres (i.e., first-person shooter, role-playing, simulation, sports, party, and other), across modalities (i.e., single- or multiplayer), they were currently playing by choosing any that applied from a set list of 14 combinations. Simulation (sim), sports, party, and other games could not be differentiated by modality and therefore are presented within the modality in which they are most likely to be experienced (e.g., multiplayer modality for party games). Games reported in the "other" category varied widely, but the

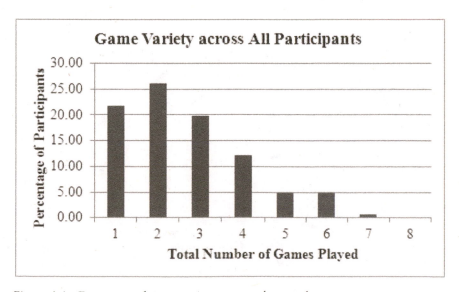

Figure 4.4   Frequency of game variety among the sample

most commonly reported genre was real-time strategy (RTS). Genre preferences, across modality (i.e., single- or multiplayer), are shown in Figure 4.5.

The most popular game genres were party and simulation, followed by first-person shooters (FPS) and role-playing games (RPG). Participants showed a slight preference for single-player games when able to choose across modalities (i.e., FPS and RPG). However, those who play with others are likely also to play at least occasionally in single-player mode, whereas those who play in single-player mode may not necessarily also play with others (through either an Internet connection or co-located gaming). Therefore, the percentage of individuals reporting to play in single-player modalities may be slightly overestimated and not representative of individuals who solely play without the presence of others.

4.3.3.2.1   GENRE PREFERENCES ACROSS AGE AND GENDER

To examine genre preferences across age and gender, single- and multiplayer FPS and RPG preferences were combined and averaged, in order to produce a score that would represent a participant's preference of genre regardless of modality. The results of an independent samples Kruskal-Wallis test indicated significant differences in preference for FPS ($p = .01$) and RPG ($p < .001$) genres across age. As seen in Figure 4.6, RPGs remain one of the most played genres across all the age groups, whereas sports steadily decline in popularity over time. FPSs show the opposite effect, as their popularity steadily increases over time.

Within-gender analyses revealed differences in the frequency of play for FPS ($p < .05$) and RPG ($p < .01$) genres among males (see Figure 4.7). An overall preference for FPSs is evident until age 29, where it sharply declines

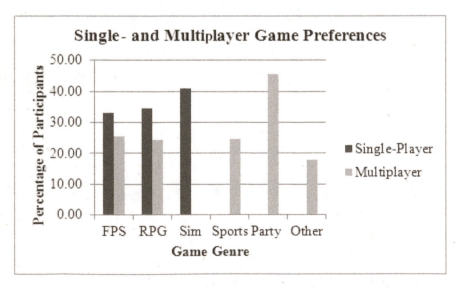

Figure 4.5   Single- and multiplayer game genre preferences among the sample

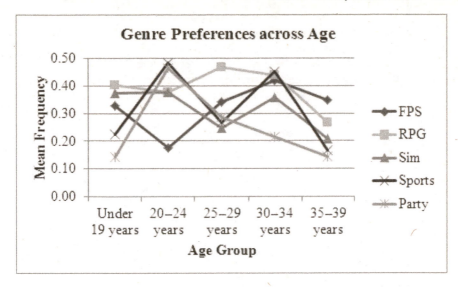

Figure 4.6 Game genre preferences across age

to equivalent levels of sim, sports, and party games preferences. Simultaneously, RPGs increase in popularity, overtaking FPSs as the most frequently played genre among males by age 30.

For females, no significant effects of age were found. However, as can be seen in Figure 4.8, female players seem to exhibit a greater frequency of play for sim and party games than the other genres.

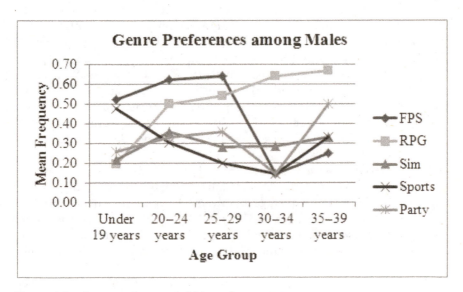

Figure 4.7 Genre preferences within males across age

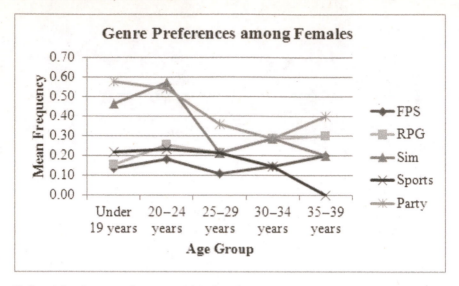

Figure 4.8   Genre preferences within females across age

4.3.3.2.2   MODALITY PREFERENCES ACROSS GENDER

To evaluate modality preferences, genres that were differentiated between single-player (FPS, RPG, and sim) and multiplayer (FPS, RPG, and party) modes were summed to create single- and multiplayer preference scores, which could range from 0 to 3. Those games that could not be distinguished by modality (i.e., sports games and other) were excluded from this analysis.

Independent samples Mann-Whitney U tests revealed a significant effect of gender for both single-player ($p < .001$) and multiplayer ($p < .001$) modalities. Male players reported playing more types of single-player ($M_{male} = 1.39$, $SD = .95$, $M_{female} = .91$, $SD = .87$) and multiplayer ($M_{male} = 1.23$, $SD = .89$, $M_{female} = .79$, $SD = .69$) games than female players (see Figure 4.9).

In general, participants under the age of 19 were found to exhibit less of a preference for either modality as compared to older participants. However, this pattern was not uniform, and it is likely that these age effects are reflective of the lower play frequency among younger players (see Figure 4.2).

4.3.3.3   Involvement across Genre and Modality

Variation in Involvement across game modality was also assessed. Figure 4.10 displays the average Involvement score for participants who engage in single- and multiplayer FPS and RPG games (analysis was limited to these genres as they were the only ones that could be differentiated across single- and multiplayer modalities). Independent t-tests revealed a significant difference in Involvement levels between players of single-player and multiplayer RPGs, $t(151) = -2.14$, $p < .05$, with multiplayer RPG players

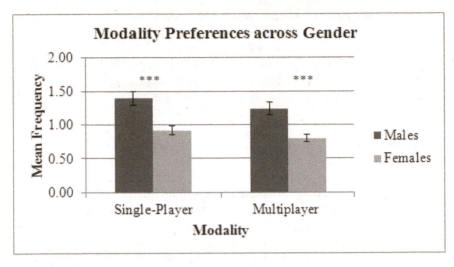

Figure 4.9   Modality preferences across gender collapsed across game types

exhibiting a significantly higher level of video game involvement than those who played in single-player mode. However, single- and multiplayer modalities are not necessarily mutually exclusive, as individuals who reported playing in multiplayer mode might also play in single-player mode, but not vice versa. This could have inflated the Involvement scores for players of multiplayer modalities.

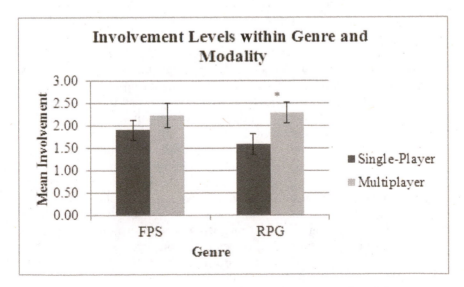

Figure 4.10   Mean Involvement scores within gender, genre, and modality

4.3.4 *Summary of Sample and Game Play Behavior*

Play frequency largely aligned with previous findings, as males were found to engage in more video game play and across a greater variety of genre categories than females (Ghuman & Griffiths, 2012; Griffiths et al., 2004a; Griffiths & Hunt, 1998; Williams et al., 2008; Yee, 2006). However, similar gender differences were not found within online play frequency. While previous demographic inquires have found that males also engage in online play to a greater extent than females (Griffiths et al., 2004a; Williams et al., 2008; Yee, 2006), this data has been largely based on MMORPG play. Moving past this niche community, the current results suggest that even though males may play more video games overall, females seem to devote a larger percentage of their total game time to online play, leading to equivalent levels of engagement within online gaming environments across gender.

The high levels of online play frequency among female players may be partially related to the recent rise of casual online games (i.e., games that do not require a substantial time investment or a set of special skills to progress through their content). These kinds of games are commonly played through social networking platforms (such as Facebook) and have been found to appeal to players who have no prior video game experience. A reported 20% of the U.S. population has played a casual social game through a social networking site, 35% of which had never played any other kind of video game (Patel, 2011). Additionally, 50% of Facebook users report signing into their account only to play these kinds of online games (Patel, 2011). Casual games are particularly popular among women; females comprise a reported 75% of the individuals who pay for these kinds of games (Caulfield, 2008). This shift in the consumption and accessibility of online gaming could be transforming the community into one that is more gender balanced than previously alleged.

The current sample also displayed significant age differences in play frequency, with the young females (under 19) engaging in significantly less overall and online specific play than any other age group. This finding was somewhat unexpected, as previous research has revealed that younger participants engage more frequently and are more likely than adults to sacrifice responsibilities to have more time for playing games (Griffiths, Davies, & Chappell, 2004b). However, as this difference was not found among male participants, it is possible that this finding is more reflective of gender differences in interest in the activity than an age-related phenomena. From an early age, video game environments are seen as an acceptable entertainment and socialization activity more so for males than females (Lucas & Sherry, 2004). Early and prolonged interaction within these environments is thought to promote, and help sustain, males' social relationships, as shared activities are an essential component for male bonding (Sherrod, 1987). Thus, males are socialized to engage in this activity more so than females, a difference that likely remains throughout the life span as males have consistently been found to engage in this activity to a greater extent than females (Ghuman & Griffiths, 2012; Griffiths et al., 2004a; Griffiths & Hunt, 1998; Williams et al., 2008; Yee, 2006).

Genre preferences also varied across gender and age, with males displaying a preference for FPSs and RPGs, and females preferring party and sim games. While previous demographic investigations have found that males prefer FPS and RPG genres more so than females (Ghuman & Griffiths, 2012), the current findings suggest that male players' preference for FPS and RPG games is age dependent: younger male players show a preference for FPSs and older male players a show preference RPGs. Female game players reported a general preference for sim and party games across all ages. The preference for sim games is not surprising, as it supports previous research that has found that women prefer less competitive games (Hartmann & Klimmt, 2006). There are typically no competitive elements within single-player simulation games, particularly with *The Sims*, a popular simulation game that has been pinpointed as being almost solely responsible for the popularity of the simulation genre among females (Steen, Greenfield, Davies, & Tynes, 2006). *The Sims* can be best described as a 'virtual dollhouse' in which players create virtual people, or 'sims,' and simulate their daily lives while ensuring their virtual needs are met. In 2008, *The Sims* sold its 100 millionth copy and was deemed the most popular computer game in the world, with versions in 22 languages across 60 countries (Huguenin, 2008). However, the preference for party games among female gamers contradicts the alleged partiality for non-competitive games among females, as party games are inherently competitive. Further research is needed to establish the reliability of these particular patterns.

Involvement levels were also found to vary across genre, suggesting that there are differences in the levels of time commitment and social identity between players of single- and multiplayer RPGs. This is not surprising, as individuals who play multiplayer RPGs have been shown to invest substantially more time online than other genres (Ghuman & Griffiths, 2012), with an average of up to 20 hours a week engaged in active game play (Ghuman & Griffiths, 2012; Griffiths et al., 2004a; Yee, 2006).

The sample for the current analysis captures a wide and representative cross-section of the (Caucasian) adult game playing population and displays a broad range of gaming behaviors, from the casual player to the dedicated gamer. The normativeness of gaming as an activity is reflected in that over 90% of the sample have played video games, and over 65% of participants have played online video games. The fact that almost 20% of all players play more than 10 hours a week reflects the frequency with which this activity plays a key role in people's lives as a form of entertainment, stimulation, and social interaction. Given these characteristics, the current sample would seem appropriate for exploring associations between video game involvement and social competence.

4.4 RESULTS

4.4.1 Social Goals and Video Game Involvement

To evaluate differences in offline and online social goals, between-group and within-group analyses were conducted. These analyses are discussed in the following sections. Prior to analysis, offline and online social goals were summed and divided by the number of presented items. Therefore, the scores indicate the average rating given to each item in the scale.

4.4.1.1 *Between-Group Analyses*

To assess the differences in the importance and likelihood of achieving online and offline social goals, two separate 2 (world: offline or online) by 2 (gaming status: high/low involved, online/offline) mixed ANOVAs with repeated measures on the first factor were conducted. As previous research has found general differences in sociability between males and females (Adler & Kless, 1992; Anastasi, 1984; Block, 1983; Crick & Dodge, 1994; DiPrete & Jennings, 2012; Eder & Hallinan, 1978; Eisenberg, Miller, Shell, McNalley, & Al, 1991; Friedman, Prince, Riggio, & DiMatteo, 1980; Nemeth, 1999; Riggio, 1986; Rosenthal, 1979), which may influence one's interest in and perceived likelihood of achieving social goals, gender was held as a covariate in these analyses.

It was predicted that more involved players would be less interested in, and perceive themselves as less likely to attain, offline social goals than less involved players (H_1). It was also predicted that these relationships would be magnified among the subgroup of online game players (H_2). Uncovering the predicted differences in social goals between gaming groups would support the contentions put forth by compensation theorists and suggest that more involved video game players, particularly online, are less interested in offline social goals, and perceive themselves as less able to attain offline social goals, than less involved players.

4.4.1.1.1 IMPORTANCE

To evaluate broad differences in offline and online social goals between players of varying degrees of Involvement, video game playing participants were differentiated into "high" and "low" Involvement categories based upon a median split. Of the 250 game playing participants, 124 were categorized as "low involvement," with Involvement scores less than –.2556, and 126 were categorized as "high involvement," with Involvement scores greater than –.2557.

A significant main effect of gender, $F(1, 247) = 6.92$, $p < .01$, partial $\eta^2 = .027$, but not Involvement ($F = 2.25$, $p = .135$, *ns*), was found. Within subjects, a significant main effect of world ($F = 86.92$, $p < .001$, partial $\eta^2 = .027$) also emerged. No significant interactions were found.

Controlling for Involvement, MANOVA analyses revealed that females ($M = 5.84$, $SD = .69$) placed slightly more importance on offline social goals than males ($M = 5.31$, $SD = .79$), $F(1, 247) = 10.09$, $p < .001$, partial $\eta^2 = .039$. There was no significant effect of gender for online goals ($p = .16$, *ns*).

Controlling for gender, MANOVA analyses revealed that less involved players ($M = 5.88$, $SD = .59$) placed more importance on offline social goals than more involved players ($M = 5.39$, $SD = .85$), $F(1, 247) = 6.94$, $p < .01$, partial $\eta^2 = .027$. No significant differences were found between high- and low-involved players for online social goals ($p = .80$, *ns*). However, both high-involved, $t(125) = -7.74$, $p < .001$, and low-involved, $t(123) = -4.78$, $p < .001$, players' mean importance of online goals fell significantly below the midpoint of the scale (i.e., 4 in the 1–7 scoring), in a negative direction, suggesting that the importance these goals hold for them is relatively minimal. These results can be seen in Figure 4.11.

Differences in the importance of offline and online social goals were also evaluated between online and non-online game players. This was done to determine the presence of broad differences in relation across these gaming groups, as would be contended by social compensation theorists and hypothesized by Ng and Wiemer-Hastings (2005). As was done previously, gender was held as a covariate in these analyses. A significant main effect of gender, $F(1, 247) = 11.57$, $p < .01$, partial $\eta^2 = .045$, but not a history of OVG play ($F = 1.97$, $p = .16$, *ns*), was found. Within subjects, a significant main effect of world ($F = 136.61$, $p < .001$, partial $\eta^2 = .356$) also emerged. No significant interactions were found.

Controlling for Involvement, MANOVA analyses revealed that females ($M = 5.84$, $SD = .69$) placed slightly more importance on offline social goals than males ($M = 5.31$, $SD = .78$), $F(1, 249) = 22.65$, $p < .001$, partial $\eta^2 = .084$. There was no significant effect of gender for online goals ($p = .18$, *ns*).

Again, both online, $t(171) = -8.80$, $p < .001$, and non-online, $t(77) = -2.99$, $p < .01$, players' mean importance of online goals fell significantly below the midpoint of the scale (i.e., 4 in the 1–7 scoring), in a negative direction, suggesting that the importance these goals hold for them is relatively minimal.

4.4.1.1.2 LIKELIHOOD

Between subjects, no significant main effect of gender ($F = 1.38$, $p = .24$, *ns*) or Involvement ($F = 2.39$, $p = .12$, *ns*) was found. A significant main effect of world ($F = 42.62$, $p < .001$, partial $\eta^2 = .15$) and an interaction between world and Involvement ($F = 10.33$, $p < .001$, partial $\eta^2 = .04$) also emerged.

Overall, offline social goals ($M = 3.94$, $SD = .57$) were rated as more likely to achieve than online goals ($M = 2.78$, $SD = .88$), with high- ($M = 3.85$, $SD = .64$) and low-involved ($M = 4.04$, $SD = .47$) players rating offline social goals as equally achievable, $F(1, 247) = 1.21$, $p = .27$, *ns*. Highly involved players ($M = 2.96$, $SD = .86$) did report a greater likelihood of obtaining online social goals non-gamers ($M = 2.61$, $SD = .87$), $F(1, 247) = 7.42$,

$p < .01$, partial $\eta^2 = .029$. However, low-involved players' mean likelihood of attaining online goals fell significantly below the midpoint of the scale (i.e., 3 on in the 1–5 scoring), in a negative direction), $t(98) = -4.94$, $p < .001$. This likely reflects a lack of interest in obtaining these goals rather than an inability. These results can be seen in Figure 4.11.

Differences in the likelihood of attaining offline and online social goals were also assessed between online and non-online game players. Between subjects, no significant main effect of gender ($F = .778$, $p = .38$, ns) or a history of online game play ($F = 2.21$, $p = .14$, ns) was found. However, a significant main effect of world ($F = 81.38$, $p < .001$, partial $\eta^2 = . 248$) and an interaction between world and gender ($F = 6.31$, $p < .05$, partial $\eta^2 = .025$) did emerge.

Overall, offline social goals ($M = 3.94$, $SD = .57$) were rated as more likely to achieve than online goals ($M = 2.78$, $SD = .88$), with online ($M = 3.91$, $SD = .60$) and non-online ($M = 4.01$, $SD = .49$) players rating offline social goals as equally achievable, $F(1, 249) = .003$, $p = .95$, *ns*. Online players ($M = 2.88$, $SD = .88$) did report a greater likelihood of obtaining online social goals than non-online players ($M = 2.59$, $SD = .85$), $F (1, 247) = 3.82$, $p = .052$, partial $\eta^2 = .015$.

However, non-online players' mean likelihood of attaining online goals fell significantly below the midpoint of the scale (i.e., 3 on in the 1–5 scoring), in a negative direction; $t(77) = -4.20$, $p < .01$. Thus, these differences are more likely reflective of a lack of interest in obtaining these goals rather than an inability.

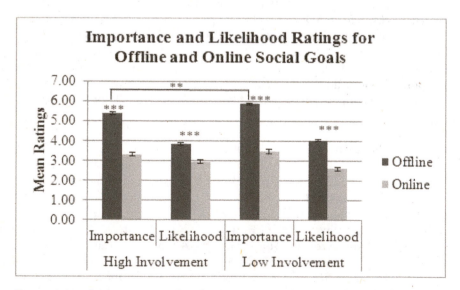

Figure 4.11 Average ratings for the importance of and likelihood of achieving social goals for high- and low-involved players

4.4.1.2 *Within-Group Analyses*

The linear relationships between social goals and video game involvement were also examined within game playing groups. Significant linear relationships would suggest that offline and online social goals change in conjunction with video game involvement. For example, uncovering a significant inverse relationship between Involvement and the importance of offline social goals in conjunction with a positive relationship between Involvement and the importance of online social goals among online players would suggest the exchange of online for offline social contacts as Involvement increases, providing support for social displacement theories. To determine the existence of displacement phenomena within the online game playing sample, the following analyses were first conducted within the general game playing sample and then the subgroup of OVG players. Following this, the two groups were comparatively evaluated.

A potential problem in this type of analysis is the correlational fallacy (Huff, 1954), in which two variables (e.g., Involvement and social skills) are correlated because they share variance with a third variable (e.g., gender). This can lead to an erroneous interpretation that the two variables are directly related when in fact they are not. The diversity of the current sample makes this problem particularly likely, as there are several variables that could potentially co-vary with both gaming involvement and social skills. Two such variables are gender and age. Therefore age and gender (dummy coded) were controlled for in the following analyses.

4.4.1.2.1 IMPORTANCE

Prior to analysis, standardized residuals were calculated in order to identify any outliers with residuals two or more standard deviations away from

Table 4.5 Total R^2 and unstandardized beta weights for individual predictors in the final model: Social goal importance

		All Participants ($N = 223$)	Online Players ($n = 151$)
Step 1			
	Age	.049*	.076**
	Gender	3.74***	3.16***
Step 2			
	Offline importance	−.354*	−.355*
	Online importance	.044	.266
R^2 Change		.011*	.014
Total R^2		.631	.581

* $p < .05$, ** $p < .01$, *** $p < .001$

Table 4.6   Total R^2 and unstandardized beta weights for individual predictors in the final model: Social goal likelihood

		All Participants (N = 235)	Online Players (n = 162)
Step 1			
	Age	.071***	.104***
	Gender	3.36***	2.67***
Step 2			
	Offline likelihood	−.582***	−.702**
	Online likelihood	.500***	.511**
R^2 Change		.037***	.050***
Total R^2		.555	.502

$**p < .01$, $***p < .001$

the mean. Of the 250 active game players, 27 outliers were identified and removed, leaving 223 participants (this includes participants who reported to be "inactive" players of video games but also a play frequency greater than "never"). Controlling for age and gender (dummy coded), Involvement was regressed by the importance of achieving offline and online social goals within the general game playing population as well as within the subgroup of OVG players. As seen in Table 4.5, a significant, inverse relationship between Involvement and the importance of offline socialization was found. This suggests that as players become more involved in video game play (both generally and with online specific play), the importance of offline socialization declines. No significant relationships emerged for online social goals.

4.4.1.2.2 LIKELIHOOD

The linear relationship between Involvement and the likelihood of achieving offline and online social goals was also examined. Prior to analysis, standardized residuals were calculated in order to identify any outliers with residuals two or more standard deviations away from the mean. Of the 250 active game players, 15 outliers were identified and removed, leaving 235 participants (this includes participants who reported to be "inactive" players of video games but also a play frequency greater than "never").

As can be seen in Table 4.6, a significant inverse relationship emerged between the likelihood of achieving offline goals and Involvement while a positive relationship emerged between the likelihood of achieving online social goals and Involvement. This effect was evident among gaming groups but increased in magnitude within the subgroup of OVG players. This suggests that as players become more Involved in video game play, and OVG play in particular, they experience a decline in the perceived ability to achieve offline social goals but an increase in the perceived ability to achieve online social goals.

4.4.1.3 Social Goals: Summary

The importance of and likelihood of achieving offline and online social goals were examined across and within different game playing groups. Broad differences in social goals were not found between high- and low-involved game players as both groups rated offline social goals as equally important, equally achievable, and significantly more important, and more achievable, than online social goals. A lack of broad differences between groups indicates the unlikelihood that highly involved video game players, and online players in particular, exhibit broad differences in relation to social goals prior to engagement.

However, significant linear relationships between the importance of, and likelihood of achieving, offline and online social goals and Involvement did emerge. Significant inverse links between involvement and offline social goals, and positive relationships between Involvement and online social goals, suggests that players may experience a decline in their perceived importance and likelihood of achieving offline social goals but an increase in the perceived ability to achieve online social goals as video game involvement increases. Among online players, these relationships were magnified. This particular pattern of findings is indicative of displacement phenomena and suggests an exchange of offline for online social contacts as Involvement increases. It is particularly concerning that inverse relationships were found for both offline importance and likelihood, as this suggests that diminished social self-confidence emerges alongside offline social disengagement.

4.4.2 Social Skills and Video Game Involvement

4.4.2.1 Between-Group Analyses

To examine broad differences in social skills between game playing categories, a MANOVA was conducted. To determine if individuals with poor social skills are attracted to OVGs in particular (as contended by social compensation theorists), participants were differentiated by their online game playing history.

When controlling for gender and age, no significant differences were found between those who reported a history of OVG play ($n = 172$) and video game players who did not report a history of OVG ($n = 78$) for any of the six SSI subscales (F's < 2.5, p's $< .12$), indicating a lack of broad social differences between online game players and non-online game players.

To examine differences between high- and low-involved online game players, participants who reported a history of OVG play were split differentiated into high- and low-involved players (median split; *Median* = 1.16). When controlling for gender and age no significant differences were found between high- ($n = 118$) and low-involved ($n = 54$) online game players for any of the six SSI subscales (F's < 1, p's $< .41$)

4.4.2.2 Within-Group Analyses

To uncover the statistical associations between social skills and Involvement, Involvement was regressed by all six of the SSI subscales across gaming

Table 4.7   Total R^2 and unstandardized beta weights for individual predictors in the final model: Social skills

		All Participants ($N = 237$)	Online Players ($n = 163$)
Step 2			
	EE	.009	−.003
	ES	.011	.039
	EC	−.002	−.120
	SE	**−.037***	−.029
	SS	−.015	−.016
	SC	.013	−.002
R^2 Change		.015	.020
Total R^2		.509	.460

*$p < .05$

groups (i.e., all players, online players). This type of analysis will allow for the identification of relationships between Involvement and social skills as well as the magnitude of these effects across different gaming groups. Significant relationships between social skills and Involvement would suggest the presence of social displacement effects as it would indicate that social skills fluctuate in correspondence with video game involvement. Due to theoretical and empirical links between social competence and video game involvement, it was predicted that inverse relationships between Social Control (SC) and Social Expressivity (SE), and a positive relationship between Emotional Sensitivity (ES) and video game involvement, would emerge (H_3—H_5). These relationships are predicted to either be unique to, or magnified within, the subgroup of OVG players (H_6).

As there were significant gender differences on four of the six SSI subscales, gender (dummy coded) was entered as a variable in the regression. Age was also imputed as a variable in the regression analyses, as Involvement and social skills showed some variation across groups, which could produce an illusory correlation between Involvement and social skills (Huff, 1954). Prior to analysis, standardized residuals were calculated in order to identify any outliers with residuals two or more standard deviations away from the mean. Of the 250 active game players, 13 outliers were identified and removed, leaving 237 participants (this includes participants who reported to be "inactive" players of video games but also a play frequency greater than "never"). In order to identify any potential differences between those who engage in general video game play and online play, analyses were conducted across the entire sample of game players and within the subgroup of participants who reported previous exposure to online gaming environments.

The total amount of variance explained in the final model and beta weights of each individual predictor are shown in Table 4.7. The addition of the SSI subscales in step 2 uncovered significant linear relationships between social skills and video game involvement.

Social Expressivity was the only subscale to emerge as a significant negative predictor of video game involvement, with lower outcomes on this subscale being predictive of higher levels of video game involvement. This pattern was retained within the subgroup of online players, although not to the same magnitude. A strong, positive association between Emotional Sensitivity and Involvement was also evident within online players, with higher outcomes on the ES subscale being predictive of higher levels of video game involvement. However, it did not reach significance ($p = .08$).

4.5 DISCUSSION

This primary aim of this study was to explore the relationship between social goals, social skills, and video game involvement. Prior to examining these relationships, an extensive evaluation of the demographic qualities of the current sample was performed. Play frequencies and preferences across gender and age were found to largely correspond with previously employed samples and encompassed a wide variety of game players, from the casual player to the dedicated gamer. Given these characteristics, this sample was considered appropriate for exploring associations between video game involvement and social competence.

The hypotheses put forth by Ng and Wiemer-Hastings (2005) were partially supported. While broad differences were not found between high- and low-involved video game players (H_1), or online and non-online players (H_2), linear relationships emerged between Involvement and the importance of and likelihood of achieving offline and online social goals. Increased video game involvement showed a positive linear relationship with the likelihood of achieving online social goals and a negative relationship with interest in, and likelihood of achieving, offline social goals. While these effects were found across all players, they were magnified among OVG players, suggesting that these effects are more pronounced when engaging in OVG play.

These results are suggestive of social displacement phenomena and indicate that video game players may experience a decline in interest for offline socialization as OVG involvement increases. Over time, this seems to negatively influence players' confidence in their ability to engage successfully in offline contexts (i.e., ability to achieve offline social goals), while boosting the perceived ability to socially engage with others online (i.e., ability to achieve social goals). In line with traditional descriptions of social displacement, these findings illustrate the potential for offline contacts to become replaced by online ones due to OVG involvement and, consequently, impede on one's ability to maintain real-world interpersonal relationships (Cole &

Griffiths, 2007; Hussain & Griffiths, 2009; Lo et al., 2005; Morahan-Martin & Schumacher, 2003; Shen & Williams, 2010).

To determine the extent to which there are tangible differences in social abilities between more involved and less involved video game players, an evaluation of social skills was conducted. As with the social goal outcomes, no broad differences were found between online players and non-online players, or within high- and low-involved OVG players, suggesting the unlikelihood that individuals with broad social skill deficits are attracted to, or highly engage in, online games in particular. However, significant linear relationships did emerge between video game involvement and social skills.

A significant inverse relationship between SE and Involvement was found (H_4), with lower outcomes on this subscale significantly predicting higher levels of Involvement. As the SE subscale assesses one's verbal speaking skill and the ability to engage others in social interaction (e.g., "*I always mingle at parties*") (Riggio, 1989, 2005), these results suggest that more involved game players perceive themselves as less verbally fluent, with difficulties in initiating and guiding conversation. While researchers have suggested that individuals who have difficulties engaging others may be drawn to OVG play as a leisure activity due to its opportunities for social interaction (de Kort & Ijsselsteijn, 2008; Ducheneaut & Moore, 2005; Gajadhar et al., 2008; Kolo & Baur, 2004) that is free from the rules and pressures of traditional social environments (Sjöblom, 2008), the current results indicate that that the relationships between SE and involvement are not driven by compensation phenomena and are not unique to online players. Instead, increased Involvement demonstrated an inverse relationship with the abilities associated with SE among the broader community of game players, both offline and online.

Characterized by visually anonymous, asynchronous, and hyperpersonal communication, online gaming spaces are considered to be ideal social outlets for individuals with social difficulties (Chak & Leung, 2004; Peters & Malesky, 2008). As online games provide a unique social arena in addition to a shared gaming space (Krotoski, 2004), it was expected that the relationships between social skills and Involvement would be magnified, or that unique relationships would emerge, within this subgroup (H_6). This prediction was partially supported. The relationship between SE and Involvement remained strong among online players, while a unique, linear relationship between ES and Involvement neared significance within this subgroup, with higher outcomes on this subscale predicting higher levels of Involvement.

Emotional Sensitivity refers to one's ability to receive and decode the non-verbal communication of others (e.g., "*I always seem to know what people's true feelings are no matter how hard they try to conceal them*") (Riggio, 1989). However, high levels of ES can be behaviorally exhibited in ways similar to shyness (Riggio, 1987), as an individual who is acutely mindful of the non-verbal signals of others (i.e., high Emotional Sensitivity) can become hypersensitive to the communicative messages of others. This can lead to a discomfort and/or inhibition in interpersonal situations, which behaviorally manifests itself as social self-consciousness or avoidance (Zimbardo, 1997). While there has not been extensive research evaluating the links between ES and OVG involvement (e.g., Kowert et al., 2014), research has found significant relationships between shyness and problematic Internet use (Caplan, 2002; Chak & Leung, 2004; Roberts et al., 2000; Yuen & Lavin, 2004) and problematic/addicted OVG play (Liu & Peng, 2009; Peng & Liu, 2010). Even though these are not identical behaviors, both are highly socially motivated (Caplan, 2003, 2005; Davis, 2001; Griffiths et al., 2011, 2004a; Morahan-Martin & Schumacher, 2003; Yee, 2007). Shy individuals are believed to be drawn to mediated social outlets due to the perceived sense of control over the communication process, such as visual anonymity and the lack of direct observation of others, which can accommodate for any difficulties that may have made traditional socialization ineffective (Carducci & Zimbardo, 1995; Young, Griffin-Shelley, Cooper, O'mara, & Buchanan, 2000). However, the current results found no broad differences in ES between online and non-online game playing samples (H_5), suggesting that there are not broad differences in ES levels between those who choose to play online games and those who do not. A significant, positive linear relationship between ES and Involvement within online players trended toward significance, suggesting a manifestation of the social skills associated with shyness among online game players as Involvement increases. However, future research is needed to explore this possibility, as the relationship between ES and Involvement within the subgroup of OVG players did not reach significance (this relationship is further explored in sections 5.4.1 and 6.6.2).

Contrary to predictions, there was no evidence of a significant relationship between SC and video game involvement (H_3). It is unclear why this is the case as research has suggested that individuals with low Social Control are motivated to engage within Internet-based social spaces for the variety of self-presentational strategies afforded by them (Caplan, 2005; McKenna & Bargh, 1999). However, it is possible that by only documenting participants' play history (i.e., if they had ever played video games and/or online video games), and not their current play patterns, the subgroup of 'online video game players' was not primarily comprised of active users. If true, this may have significantly influenced the findings, as the links between SC and video game play are believed to be specific to online interaction. Further research is needed to determine the consistency of the purported relationships between Social Control and OVG involvement (this relationship is further explored in sections 5.4.1 and 6.6.2).

4.5.1   Limitations

While this examination is the first known study to evaluate the relationship between video game involvement, social goals, and social skills among a general game playing population, there are limitations to this investigation that should be considered. As aforementioned, by only documenting participants' play history (i.e., if they had ever played video games and/or online video games), rather than their current play patterns, the applicability of the subgroup analyses are limited. Future research should document a player's current play patterns (i.e., active players of offline and online games, online-exclusive or offline-exclusive players only rather than a history of play) to more accurately evaluate the relationship between social skills and Involvement across different game playing communities and to reveal the nature of the relationships within and between them.

The current study was also limited by the opportunity sample that was employed. As participants were principally recruited via the University of York's online experimental booking system, they were predominantly young female psychology students. Due to this, sample sizes across gender and age categories were relatively small, limiting the generalizability of the findings. Increasing the pool of online players in particular would allow for more complete analyses into the relationship between social skills and Involvement within this subgroup of game players.

4.5.2   Conclusions

The current results provide preliminary evidence that there are significant relationships between social competence and video game involvement, the particular patterns of which suggest social displacement effects rather than compensation motivations. While broad differences were not found between high- and low-involved players for social goals or social skills, significant linear relationships between these variables were found. More involved players reported lower levels of importance for, and likelihood of achieving, offline social goals while online social goals were rated as more achievable (though not more important) as Involvement increased. This suggests that as players become more involved in video game play they may become less interested in offline socialization. Consequently, players may become socially disengaged from their offline contacts and, over time, experience a decrease in their social self-esteem.

Linear relationships between social expressivity, emotional sensitivity, and video game involvement also emerged, with more involved video game players reporting themselves to be less verbally fluent, with difficulties in initiating and guiding conversation. Online players also exhibited a positive, linear relationship between ES and Involvement that was not found within the broader game-playing sample, suggesting that a unique relationship between social skills and Involvement may exist within this subsample of players.

NOTE

1. While limiting the sample to Caucasian participants was determined a priori, substantial differences in video game play frequency ($F = 3.69$, $p = .056$), the perceived likelihood of achieving offline social goals ($F = 3.52$, $p = .06$), and outcomes on the EE and SE subscales of the SSI (F's > 5, p's $< .05$) were found between Caucasian and non-Caucasian participants (while controlling for age and gender). This variation in outcomes supports the theoretical differences in video game culture and social skills across Eastern and Western populations as outlined in section 4.3.1.1 and substantiates their exclusion from further analyses.

REFERENCES

Adler, P., & Kless, S. (1992). Socialziation to gender roles: Popularity among elementary school boys and girls. *Sociology of Education, 65*(3), 169–187.

Anastasi, A. (1984). Reciprocal relations between cognitive and affective development with implications for sex differences. In T. B. Sonderegger (Ed.), *Psychology and gender: Nebraska Symposium on Motivation* (pp. 1–35). Lincoln: University of Nebraska Press.

Ashcraft, B. (2010). Why is *StarCraft* so popular in Korea? *Kotaku*. Retrieved from http://kotaku.com/5595262/why-is-starcraft-so-popular-in-korea

Barnett, M., Vitaglione, G., Harper, K., Quackenbush, S., Steadman, L., & Valdez, B. (1997). Late adolescents' experiences with and attitudes towards videogames. *Journal of Applied Social Psychology, 27*(15), 1316–1334.

Baron, R., & Markman, G. (2003). Beyond social capital: The role of entrepreneurs' social competence in their financial success. *Journal of Business Venturing, 18*(1), 41–60.

Barreto, M., & Ellemers, N. (2000). You can't always do what you want: Social identity and self-presentational determinants of the choice to work for a low status group. *Personality and Social Psychology Bulletin,* (26), 891–906.

Bartholomew, K. (1993). From childhood to adult relationships: Attachment theory and research. In S. Duck (Ed.), *Understanding relationship processes: Learning about relationships* (Vol. 2). Beverly Hills, CA: Sage.

Blais, J., Craig, W. M., Pepler, D., & Connolly, J. (2008). Adolescents online: The importance of Internet activity choices on salient relationships. *Journal of Youth and Adolescence, 37,* 522–536.

Block, J. H. (1983). Differential premises arising from differential socialization of the sexes: Some conjectures. *Child Development, 54,* 1335–1354.

Branscombe, N. (1998). Thikning about one's gender group's privilieges or disadvantages: Consequneces for well-being in women and men. *British Journal of Social Psychology,* (37), 167–184.

Branscombe, N., & Wann, D. L. (1991). The positive social and self concept consequences of sports team identification. *Journal of Sport and Social Issues, 15*(2), 115–127.

Caplan, S. (2002). Problematic Internet use and psychosocial well being: Development of a theory-based cognitive-behavioral measurement instrument. *Computers in Human Behavior, 18,* 553–575.

Caplan, S. (2003). Preference for online social interaction: A theory of problematic Internet use and psychosocial well-being. *Communication Research, 30,* 625–648.

Caplan, S. (2005). A social skill account of problematic Internet use. *Journal of Communication, 55,* 721–736.

Caplan, S., Williams, D., & Yee, N. (2009). Problematic Internet use and psychosocial well-being among MMO players. *Computers in Human Behavior*, *25*(6), 1312–1319.

Carducci, B., & Zimbardo, P. (1995). Are you shy? *Psychology Today*, *28*(6), 34–82. Retrieved from http://www.psychologytoday.com/articles/200910/are-you-shy

Carstensen, L. L. (1995). Evidence for a life-span theory of socioemotional selectivity. *Current Directions in Psychologial Science*, *4*(5), 151–162.

Cassidy, J., Kirsh, S., Scolton, K., & Parke, R. (1996). Attachment and representations of peer relationships. *Developmental Psychology*, *32*(5), 892–904.

Caulfield, B. (2008). Games girls play. *Forbes*. Retrieved from http://www.forbes.com/2008/03/13/casual-gaming-women-tech-personal-cx_bc_0314casual.html

Cavell, T. A. (1990). Social adjustment, social performance, and social skills: A tricomponent model of social competence. *Journal of Clinical Child Psychology*, *19*, 111–122.

Chak, K., & Leung, L. (2004). Shyness and locus of control as predictors of Internet addiction and Internet use. *Cyberpsychology and Behavior*, *7*(5), 559–570.

Chiu, S., Lee, J., & Huang, D. (2004). Video game addiction in children and teenagers in Taiwan. *Cyberpsychology and Behavior*, *7*(5), 571–581.

CNN. (2012). Wired for success or destruction? *CNN News*. Retrieved from http://www.cnn.com/interactive/2012/08/tech/gaming.series/korea.html

Cole, H., & Griffiths, M. D. (2007). Social interactions in massively multiplayer online role-playing games. *Cyberpsychology and Behavior*, *10*(4), 575–583.

Colwell, J., & Kato, M. (2003). Investigation of the relationship between social isolation, self-esteem, aggression and computer game play in Japanese adolescents. *Asian Journal of Social Psychology*, *6*, 149–158.

Crick, N., & Dodge, K. A. (1994). A review and reformulation of social information-processing mechanisms in children's social adjustment. *Psychologial Bulletin*, *115*(1), 74–101.

Davis, R. A. (2001). A cognitive behavioral model of pathologial Internet use. *Computers in Human Behavior*, *17*(2), 187–195.

Davis, R. A., Flett, G., & Besser, A. (2002). Validation of a new scale for measuring problematic Internet use: Implications for pre-employment screening. *Cyberpsychology and Behavior*, *5*(4), 331–345.

de Kort, Y.A.W., & Ijsselsteijn, W. A. (2008). People, places, and play: Player experience in a socio-spatial context. *Computers in Entertainment*, *6*(2), 18.

DiPrete, T. A., & Jennings, J. L. (2012). Social and behavioral skills and the gender gap in early educational achievement. *Social Science Research*, *41*(1), 1–15.

Dominick, J. R. (1984). Video games, television violence, and aggression in teenagers. *Journal of Communication*, *34*(2), 136–147.

Doosje, B., Ellmers, N., & Spears, R. (1995). Perceived intragroup variability as a function of group status and identification. *Journal of Experimental Social Psychology*, *31*, 410–436.

DuBois, D. L., & Felner, R. D. (1996). The quadripartite model of social competence: Theory and applications to clinical intervention. In M. A. Reinecke (Ed.), *Cognitive therapy with children and adolescents: A casebook for clinical practice*. New York: Guilford Press.

Ducheneaut, N., & Moore, R. (2005). More than just "XP": Learning social skills in massively multiplayer online games. *Interactive Technology and Smart Education*, *2*(2), 89–100.

Ducheneaut, N., Yee, N., Nickell, E., & Moore, R. (2006). "Alone together?": Exploring the social dynamics of massively multiplayer online games. In *SIGCHI Conference on Human Factors in Computing Systems*. New York: ACM.

Dunbar, R. (2012). Social cognition on the Internet: Testing constraints on social network size. *Philosophical Transactions of the Royal Society*, *367*, 2192–2201.

Eder, D., & Hallinan, M. (1978). Sex differences in children's friendships. *American Sociologial Review, 43*, 237–250.

Eisenberg, N., Miller, P. A., Shell, R., McNalley, S., & Al, E. (1991). Prosocial development in adolescence: A longitudinal study. *Developmental Psychology, 27*, 849–857.

Engles, R., Finkenauer, C., Meeus, W., & Dekovic, M. (2001). Parental attachment and adolescents' emotional adjustment: The associations with social skills and relational competence. *Journal of Counseling Psychology, 48*(4), 428–439.

Entertainment Software Association. (2012). *Game player data*. Retrieved from http://www.theesa.com/facts/gameplayer.asp

Field, A. (2009). *Discovering statistics using SPSS*. London: SAGE Publications.

Ford, M. (1982). Social cognition and social competence in adolescence. *Developmental Psychology, 18*(3), 323–340.

Friedman, H. S., Prince, L. M., Riggio, R. E., & DiMatteo, M. R. (1980). Understanding and assessing nonverbal expressiveness: The Affective Communication Test. *Journal of Personality and Social Psychology, 39*, 333–351.

Gajadhar, B., de Kort, Y., & IJsselsteijn, W. (2008). Influence of social setting on player experience of digital games. In *CHI'08 extended abstracts on human factors in computing systems* (pp. 3099–3104). New York: ACM.

Ghuman, D., & Griffiths, M. D. (2012). A cross-genre study of online gaming: Player demographics, motivation for play, and social interactions among players. *International Journal of Cyber Behavior, Psychology, and Learning, 2*(1), 13–29.

Glasgow, R., & Arkowitz, H. (1975). The behavioral assessment of male and female social competence in dyadic heterosexual interactions. *Behavior Therapy, 6*(4), 488–498.

Gresham, F. (1986). Conceptual issues in the assessment of social competence in children. In P. Strain, M. Guralnick, & H. Walker (Eds.), *Children's social behavior: Development, assessment, and modification* (pp. 143–179). New York: Academic.

Gresham, F., & Elliot, S. (1987). The relationship between adaptive behavior and social skills. Issues in definition and assessment. *Journal of Special Education, 21*(1), 167–181.

Griffiths, M. D. (2010). Computer game playing and social skills: A pilot study. *Aloma, 27*, 301–310.

Griffiths, M. D., Davies, M., & Chappell, D. (2003). Breaking the stereotype: The case of online gaming. *Cyberpsychology and Behavior, 6*(1), 81–91.

Griffiths, M. D., Davies, M., & Chappell, D. (2004a). Demographic factors and playing variables in online computer gaming. *Cyberpsychology and Behavior, 7*, 479–487.

Griffiths, M. D., Davies, M., & Chappell, D. (2004b). Online computer gaming: A comparison of adolescent and adult gamers. *Journal of Adolescence, 27*(1), 87–96.

Griffiths, M. D., & Hunt, N. (1998). Dependence on computer games by adolescents. *Psychologial Reports, 82*, 475–480.

Griffiths, M. D., Hussain, Z., Grusser, S., Thalemann, R., Cole, H., Davies, M., & Chappell, D. (2011). Social interactions in online gaming. *International Journal of Game-Based Learning, 1*(4), 20–35.

Gross, J., Carstensen, L., Pasupathi, M., Tsai, J., Skorpen, C., & Hsu, A.Y.C. (1997). Emotion and aging: Experience, expression, and control. *Psychology and Aging, 12*, 590–599.

Guitton, M. (2011). Immersive role of non-required social actions in virtual settings: The example of trade role-play in the Second Life Gorean community. *An International Journal, 5*, 209–220.

Hall, P.M. (1966). Identification with the deliquent subculture and level of self-evaluation. *Sociometry, 29*(2), 146–158.

Hamann, D., Lineburg, N., & Paul, S. (1998). Teaching effectiveness and social skill development. *Journal of Research in Music Education, 46,* 87–101.

Hartmann, T., & Klimmt, C. (2006). Gender and computer games: Exploring females' dislikes. *Journal of Computer-Mediated Communication, 11*(4), 910–931.

Hsu, S., Wen, M., & Wu, M. (2009). Exploring user experiences as predictors of MMORPG addiction. *Computers and Education, 53*(3), 990–999.

Huff, D. (1954). *How to Lie With Statistics.* New York: Norton.

Huguenin, P. (2008). Women really click with *The Sims. NY Daily News.* Retrieved from http://www.nydailynews.com/life-style/women-click-sims-article-1.283191

Hussain, Z., & Griffiths, M. (2009). The attitudes, feelings, and experiences of online gamers: A qualitative analysis. *Cyberpsychology and Behavior, 12*(6), 747–753.

Iacono, C. S., & Weisband, S. (1997). Developing trust in virtual teams. In *Hawaii International Conference on System Sciences.* Hawaii.

Jay, A. (2010). *Cultural differences: Their effect on social skill development.* Providence, RI: Providence College.

Kim, E., Namkoong, K., Ku, T., & Kim, S. (2008). The relationship between online game addiction and aggression, self-control, and narcissistic personality traits. *European Psychiatry, 23*(3), 212–218.

Kolo, C., & Baur, T. (2004). Living a virtual life: Social dynamics of online gaming. *International Journal of Computer Game Research, 4*(1).

Korgaonkar, P., & Wolin, L. (1999). A mulitvariate analysis of Web usage. *Journal of Advertising Research,* 56–68.

Kowert, R., Domahidi, E., & Quandt, T. (2014). The relationship between online video game involvement and gaming-related friendships among emotionally sensitive individuals. *Cyberpsychology and Behavior, 17*(7), 447–453. doi:10.1089/cyber.2013.0656

Kowert, R., Griffiths, M. D., & Oldmeadow, J. A. (2012). Geek or chic? Emerging stereotypes of online gamers. *Bulletin of Science, Technology & Society, 32*(6), 471–479. doi:10.1177/0270467612469078

Kowert, R., & Oldmeadow, J. A. (2010). Geek or chic: Perceptions of gamers. Paper presented at *Under the Mask.* Bedfordshire, UK: University of Bedfordshire.

Kowert, R., & Oldmeadow, J. A. (2012). The stereotype of online gamers: New characterization or recycled prototype. In *Nordic DiGRA: Games in Culture and Society conference proceedings.* Tampere, Finland: DiGRA.

Kraut, R., Patterson, M., Lundmark, V., Kiesler, S., Mukopadhyay, T., & Scherlis, W. (1998). Internet paradox: A social technology that reduces social involvement and psychological well-being? *American Psychologist, 53*(9), 1017–1031.

Krotoski, A. (2004). *Chicks and joysticks: An exploration of women and gaming.* London: Entertainment and Leisure Software Publishers Association.

Lawton, M. P., Kleban, M. H., Rajagopal, D., & Dean, J. (1992). Dimensions of affective experience in three age groups. *Psychology and Aging, 7*(2), 171–184.

Leary, M., & Kowalski, R. (1995). *Social anxiety.* New York: Guilford Press.

Lemmens, J., Valkenburg, P., & Peter, J. (2011). Psychological causes and consequences of pathological gaming. *Computers in Human Behavior, 27*(1), 144–152.

Leontyev, A. N. (1981). *Problems of the development of mind.* Moscow: Progress Publishers.

Lewinsohn, P.M., Chaplin, M. W., & Barton, R. (1980). Social competence and depression: The role of illusory self-perceptions. *Journal of Abnormal Psychology, 89*(2), 203–212.

Liu, M., & Peng, W. (2009). Cognitive and psychological predictors of the negative outcomes associated with playing MMOGs (massively multiplayer online games). *Computers in Human Behavior, 25*(6), 1306–1311.

Lo, S., Wang, C., & Fang, W. (2005). Physical interpersonal relationships and social anxiety among online game players. *Cyberpsychology and Behavior, 8*(1), 15–20.

Lomanowska, A.M., & Guitton, M. J. (2012). Spatial proximity to others determines how humans inhabit virtual worlds. *Computers in Human Behavior, 28,* 318–323. doi:10.1016/j.chb.2011.09.015

Lucas, K., & Sherry, J. (2004). Sex differences in video game play: A communication-based explanation. *Communication Research, 31*(5), 499–523.

McKenna, K., & Bargh, J. (1999). Causes and consequences of social interaction on the Internet: A conceptual framework. *Media Psychology, 1*(3), 249–269.

McKenna, K., & Bargh, J. (2000). Plan 9 from cyberspace: The implications of the Internet for personality and social psychology. *Personality and Social Psychology Review, 4*(1), 57–75.

Morahan-Martin, J., & Schumacher, P. (2003). Loneliness and social uses of the Internet. *Computers in Human Behavior, 19,* 659–671.

Nemeth, E. (1999). Gender differences in reaction to publich achievement feedback. *Educational Studies, 25,* 297–310.

Ng, B., & Wiemer-Hastings, P. (2005). Addiction to the Internet and online gaming. *Cyberpsychology and Behavior, 8*(2), 110–113.

Nie, N. (2001). Sociability, Interpersonal relations, and the Internet: Reconciling conflicting findings. *American Behavioral Scientist, 45,* 420–435.

Nie, N., & Erbring, L. (2002). Internet and mass media: A preliminary report. *IT & Society, 1*(2), 134–141.

Ochs, E. (1984). Clarification and culture. In D. Shiffrin (Ed.), *Georgetown University Round Table on Langugaes and Lingusitics.* Washington, DC: Georgetown Press.

Patel, S. (2011). Social gaming: The good, the bad, & the ugly. *SingleGrain.* Retrieved from http://www.singlegrain.com/blog/social-gaming-the-good-the-bad-the-ugly/

Pena, J., & Hancock, J. T. (2006). An analysis of socioemotional and task communication in online multi-player video games. *Communication Research, 33*(1), 92–109.

Peng, W., & Liu, M. (2010). Online gaming depdendency: A preliminary study in China. *Cyberpsychology and Behavior, 13*(3), 329–333.

Peters, C., & Malesky, A. (2008). Problematic usage among highly-engaged players of massively multiplayer online role playing games. *Cyberpsychology and Behavior, 11*(4), 481–484.

Rapee, R. M., & Lim, L. (1992). Discrepancy between self-and observer ratings of performance in social phobics. *Journal of Abnormal Psychology, 101,* 728–731. doi:10.1037/0021–843X.101.4.728

Riggio, R. (1986). Assessment of basic social skills. *Journal of Personality and Social Psychology, 51*(3), 649–660.

Riggio, R. (1987). *The charisma quotient: What it is, how to get it, how to use it.* New York: Dodd Mead.

Riggio, R. (1989). *Manual for the Social Skills Inventory.* Palo Alto, CA: Consulting Psychologists Press.

Riggio, R. (2005). The Social Skills Inventory (SSI): Measuring nonverbal and social skills. In V. Manusov (Ed.), *The sourcebook of nonverbal measures: Going beyond words* (pp. 25–33). Mahwah, NJ: Lawrence Erlbaum.

Riggio, R., & Carney, D.C. (2003). *Manual for the Social Skills Inventory* (2nd ed). Mountain View, CA: Mind Garden.

Riggio, R., Watring, K., & Throckmorton, B. (1993). Social skills, support, and psychosocial adjustment. *Personality and Individual Differences, 15*(3), 275–280.

Roberts, L. D., Smith, L., & Pollock, C. (2000). "U r a lot bolder on the net": Shyness and Internet use. In *Shyness, development, consolidation, and change* (pp. 121–135). New York: Routledge.

Rose-Kransor, L. (1997). Nature of social competence: A theoretical review. *Social Developmental Psychology, 6*(1), 111–135.

Rosenthal, R. (1979). *Skill in nonverbal communication.* Cambridge, MA: Oelgeschlager, Gunn, & Hain.

Rossingnol, J. (2009). *This gaming life.* Ann Arbor: University of Michigan Press.

Scealy, M., Phillips, J., & Stevenson, R. (2002). Shyness and anxiety as predictors of patterns of Internet usage. *Cyberpsychology and Behavior, 5*(6), 507–515.

Segrin, C. (1990). A meta-analytic review of social skill deficits in depression. *Communication Monographs, 57*(4), 292–308.

Segrin, C. (1993). Social skills deficits and psychosocial problems: Antecedent, concomitant, or consequent? *Journal of Social and Clinical Psychology, 12,* 336–353.

Segrin, C. (1998). Interpersonal communication problems associated with depression and loneliness. In P. Andersen & L. Guerrero (Eds.), *Handbook of communication and emotion: Research, theory, applications, and contexts* (pp. 215–242). San Diego, CA: Academic Press.

Segrin, C. (2000). Social skills deficits assoicated with depression. *Clinical Psychology Review, 20*(3), 379–403.

Segrin, C., & Kinney, T. (1995). Social skills deficits among the socially anxious: Loneliness and rejection from others. *Motivation and Emotion, 19*(1), 1–24.

Senlow, G. (1984). Playing videogames: The electronic friend. *Journal of Communication, 34*(2), 148–156.

Shen, C., & Williams, D. (2010). Unpacking time online: Connecting Internet and massively multiplayer online game use with psychological well-being. *Communication Research, 20*(10), 1–27.

Sherrod, D. (1987). The bonds of men: Problems and possibilities in close male relationships. In H. Brod (Ed.), *The making of masculinities: The new men's studies* (pp. 213–293). Boston: Allen & Unwin.

Sjöblom, B. (2008). Language and perception in co-located gaming. Paper presented at the Language, Culture, Mind III conference, Odense, Denmark.

Smyth, J. (2007). Beyond self-selection in video game play. *Cyberpsychology and Behavior, 10*(5), 717–721.

Steen, F., Greenfield, P., Davies, M., & Tynes, B. (2006). What went wrong with *The Sims Online*: Cultural learning and barriers to identification in a massively multiplayer online role-playing game. In P. Vorderer & J. Bryant (Eds.), *Playing video games: Motives, responses, and consequences* (pp. 307–324). Mahwah, NJ: Lawrence Erlbaum.

Steinkuehler, C., & Williams, D. (2006). Where everybody knows your (screen) name: Online games as "third places." *Journal of Computer-Mediated Communication, 11*(4), 885–909.

Tajfel, H. (1970). Experiments in intergroup discrimination. *Scientific American, 223*(2), 96–102.

Tajfel, H. (1974). Social identity and intergroup behaviour. *Social Science Information, 13,* 65–93.

Tajfel, H. (1978). The achievement of group differentiation. In *Differentiation between social groups. Studies in the social psychology of intergroup relations* (pp. 77–98). London: Academic Press.

Tajfel, H. (1982). Social psychology of intergroup relations. *Annual Review of Psychology, 33,* 1–39.

Tajfel, H., & Turner, J. C. (1979). An integrative theory of intergroup conflict. In W. G. Austin & S. Worchel (Eds.), *The social psychology of intergroup relations* (pp. 33–47). Monterey: Brooks-Cole.

Tajfel, H., & Turner, J. C. (1985). The social identity theory of intergroup behavior. In S. Worcehl & W. G. Austin (Eds.), *Psychology of intergroup relations.* Chicago: Nelson-Hall.

Tannen, D. (1984). Cross-cultural communication. In *California Association of Teachers of English Speakers of Other Languages State Conference*. Los Angeles, CA.

Ting-Toomey, S. (1999). *Communicating across cultures*. New York: Guilford Press.

Turner, J. C. (1984). Social identification and psychologial group formation. In H. Tajfel (Ed.), *The social dimension* (Vol. 2, pp. 518–538). Cambridge: Cambridge University Press.

Utz, S. (2000). Social information processing in MUDs: The development of friendships in virtual worlds. *Journal of Online Behavior*, 1(1).

Veale, J. (2007). Where playing video games is a life. *Time*. Retrieved from http://www.time.com/time/world/article/0,8599,1620799

Walther, J. (1996). Computer-mediated communication: Impersonal, interpersonal, and hyperpersonal interaction. *Communication Research*, 23(1), 3–43.

Wan, C., & Chiou, W. (2007). The motivations of adolescents who are addicted to online games: A cognitive perspective. *Adolescence*, 42(165), 179–197.

Williams, D. (2006). Groups and goblins: The social and civic impact of online games. *Journal of Broadcasting and Electronic Media*, 50, 651–681.

Williams, D., Ducheneaut, N., Xiong, L., Yee, N., & Nickell, E. (2006). From tree house to barracks. *Games and Culture*, 1(4), 338–361.

Williams, D., Martins, N., Consalvo, M., & Ivory, J. (2009). The virtual census: Representations of gender, race and age in video games. *New Media & Society*, 11(5), 815–834.

Williams, D., Yee, N., & Caplan, S. (2008). Who plays, how much, and why? Debunking the stereotypical gamer profile. *Journal of Computer-Mediated Communication Monographs*, 13(4), 993–1018.

Yee, N. (2002). Befriending ogres and wood-elves—Understanding relationship formation in MMORPGs. *Nickyee*. Retrieved from http://www.nickyee.com/hub/relationships/home.html

Yee, N. (2006). The demographics, motivations, and derived experiences of users of massively-multi-user online graphical environments. *Teleoperators and Virtual Environments*, 15(3), 309–329.

Yee, N. (2007). Motivations of play in online games. *Journal of CyberPsychology and Behavior*, 9(6), 772–775.

Young, K., Griffin-Shelley, E., Cooper, A., O'mara, J., & Buchanan, J. (2000). Online infidenlity: A new dimension in couple relationships with implications for evaluation and treatment. *Sexual Addiction and Compulsivity*, 7, 59–74.

Yuen, C. N., & Lavin, M. J. (2004). Internet dependence in the collegiate population: The role of shyness. *Cyberpsychology and Behavior*, 7(4), 379–383.

Zimbardo, P. (1997). *Shyness: What it is, what to do about it*. Reading, MA: Addison-Wesley.

5 Social Skills and Video Game Involvement

A Replication

5.1 PRESENT STUDY

The current study aims to explore, identify, and confirm the relationships between social skills and video game involvement uncovered in chapter 4 by evaluating the relationship between these variables within a broader, and more diverse, sample of adult video game players. To determine the extent to which OVG involvement may support, or undermine, the development and maintenance of traditional social skills, the relationships between social skills and OVG involvement will be evaluated. The social skills approach to evaluating social competence was chosen as social skills are a fundamental component of social competence, providing the foundation upon which other facets of sociability develop (Cavell, 1990; DuBois & Felner, 1996; Rose-Kransor, 1997). Maladaptive social skills can prevent effective communication and lead to an array of social difficulties, including poor communication quality and an inhibited ability to create and sustain friendships (Gottman, Gonso, & Rasmussen, 1975; Ladd, 1999). As validity evidence has sufficiently demonstrated significant relationships between self-report measures of social skill and performance-based assessments (Baron & Markman, 2003; Gifford & O'Connor, 1987; Moskowitz, 1990), this approach is also a valid measurement of social performance. Thus, any significant associations between social competence and OVG involvement should be quantifiable on this foundational level.

While there have only been a few empirical assessments directly evaluating the links between social skills and video game involvement (e.g., Barnett, Coulson, & Foreman, 2009; Chiu, Lee, & Huang, 2004; Griffiths, 2010; Kowert, Domahidi, & Quandt, 2014; Lemmens, Valkenburg, & Peter, 2011; Liu & Peng, 2009), significant relationships between these variables have been found to lie within the domains of emotional and social expressivity, emotional and social sensitivity, and social control. This research suggests that more involved players perceive themselves as lacking self-presentation skills, as being less comfortable in social situations, as being less verbally and emotionally expressive, and as being more emotionally sensitive. However, due to the ambiguity and questionable validity of some of the measures utilized within these assessments (see section 3.3), it is not clear whether these relationships are consistent or reliable. An assessment of the linear relationships between social skills and video game involvement was undertaken in Study 1 (see chapter 4); however, due to a lack of power and an inability to differentiate between active and inactive OVG players it was difficult to interpret the findings. In consideration of this, the hypotheses from Study 1 were retained.

> H_3: An inverse relationship between Social Control (SC) and video game involvement will emerge.
>> H_{3a}: An inverse relationship between SC and video game involvement will emerge between subjects, with active game players exhibiting lower levels of SC than the broader sample.
>> H_{3b}: An inverse relationship between SC and video game involvement will emerge within subjects, with SC demonstrating an inverse linear relationship with video game involvement.

According to Riggio (1989), Social Control refers to one's competence at social self-presentation, role taking, and impression management in face-to-face interpersonal interactions. Previous research has found lower SC to be a strong predictor of increased social Internet use (Caplan, 2005; Utz, 2000; Walther, 1996) and increased OVG involvement (Liu & Peng, 2009). Due to the visual anonymity, asynchronicity of communication, and lack of non-verbal cues, computer-mediated environments are able to provide substantially greater control over one's social self-presentation and impression formation than provided by face-to-face communication (Walther, 1996). Online video games may be particularly accommodating as they also provide the ability to actively manipulate one's physical presentation through the customization of avatars. This sense of control can mediate the typical social anxiety associated with a lack of Social Control (Leary & Kowalski, 1995; Segrin & Kinney, 1995) by allowing for the strategic, and potentially idealized, presentation of oneself. Consequently, these spaces are perceived as less threatening than traditional socialization and may become highly desirable for those who lack effective self-presentational skills. As significant inverse relationships between SC and OVG involvement would reflect this desirability, they are predicted to emerge.

No significant links between SC and OVG involvement were found in Study 1. However, it is possible that this was due to the differentiation of participants by their video game play history (i.e., if they had ever played video games and/or online video games) rather than their current play patterns, as this kind of categorization did not allow for the distinction between active and inactive online players. This is important, as the links between SC and video game play are believed to be specific to online engagement (Caplan, 2005; Korgaonkar & Wolin, 1999; Liu & Peng, 2009; Utz, 2000; Walther, 1996). Reporting a history of online play does not necessarily confirm active participation within this type of gaming space. In consideration of this, alterations were made to the demographic questionnaire, and participants were asked to report their current level of play in addition to play history. This will allow for more extensive evaluations across different game playing communities (i.e., players of offline and online games, offline-exclusive players, online-exclusive players) and more accurate subgroup analyses.

H_4: An inverse relationship between Social Expressivity (SE) and video game involvement will emerge.

H_{4a}: An inverse relationship between SE and video game involvement will emerge between subjects, with active game players exhibiting lower levels of SE than the broader sample.

H_{4b}: An inverse relationship between SE and video game involvement will emerge within subjects, with SE demonstrating an inverse linear relationship with video game involvement.

Traditionally, individuals low in SE have difficulties engaging others in social conversation and exhibit a lower verbal fluency (Riggio, 1989, 2005). For individuals low in SE, OVG play could be a particularly desirable activity, as active engagement within these spaces promotes socialization while reducing the pressure to engage and guide social interactions. Not only does social communication become intertwined with the activity itself (de Kort & Ijsselsteijn, 2008; Gajadhar, de Kort, & IJsselsteijn, 2008; Sjöblom, 2008), but the provision of asynchronous communication further accommodates for any hindrances in verbal fluency. Inverse associations between SE and OVG play have been found in previous research (e.g., Lemmens et al., 2011), reflecting the social utility of these spaces to accommodate individuals with lower SE, and are expected to replicate here.

A significant linear relationship between SE and Involvement emerged in Study 1 within the broader group of video game players but not within the subgroup OVG players. However, it is possible that this was due to a lack of power, rather than a lack of a relationship. Therefore, the original predictions will be retained for the current study.

H_5: A positive relationship between Emotional Sensitivity (ES) and video game involvement will emerge.

H_{5a}: A positive relationship between ES and video game involvement will emerge between subjects, with active game players exhibiting lower levels of ES than the broader sample.

H_{5b}: A positive relationship between ES and video game involvement will emerge within subjects, with ES demonstrating a positive linear relationship with video game involvement.

While ES has not been widely evaluated in relation to OVG play (e.g., Kowert et al., 2014), high levels of ES are indicative of shyness (Riggio, 1987), which has been found to hold significant relationships with social uses of the Internet (Caplan, 2002; Chak & Leung, 2004; Roberts, Smith, & Pollock, 2000; Yuen & Lavin, 2004), including problematic and addicted use of OVGs (Liu & Peng, 2009; Peng & Liu, 2010). As Internet-based social spaces are able to reduce inhibitions (Caplan, 2002; Chak & Leung, 2004; Liu & Peng, 2009; Peng & Liu, 2010; Roberts et al., 2000; Yuen & Lavin, 2004), shyness is not an obstacle to effective communication within these spaces (Scealy, Phillips, & Stevenson, 2002), which makes them highly desirable for timid individuals (Roberts et al., 2000). In this sense, OVGs may be exceptionally accommodating. Unlike chat rooms, where the primary purpose, and sole function, of the space is to directly socialize with others, OVGs provide a strong, social community even in the absence of direct socialization (Ducheneaut, Yee, Nickell, & Moore, 2006; Steinkuehler & Williams, 2006). As shy individuals can be socially self-conscious, hesitant, and potentially avoidant (Zimbardo, 1997), involvement within a shared, playful environment could be preferable to a mediated space that requires direct interaction with others. Demonstrating the established links between the behavioral manifestations of shyness and OVG involvement, significant, positive relationships between ES and Involvement are predicted to emerge.

In Study 1, the linear relationship between ES and Involvement found among the broader game playing sample was substantially magnified among online game players. While this relationship did not reach significance, the patterns indicated a correspondence between higher outcomes on this subscale and higher levels of Involvement for the subgroup of online players. As it is possible that the failure to reach significance was due to a lack of power, rather than a lack of effect, it is predicted that a significant linear relationship between these variables will emerge within the subgroup of online players.

As offline and online video gaming environments both provide a range of social affordances, it is possible that the predicted relationships will not be limited to online players only. However, as online gaming spaces are characterized by visually anonymous, asynchronous, and hyperpersonal communication, and are considered to be ideal social outlets for individuals with social difficulties (Chak & Leung, 2004; Peters & Malesky, 2008), it is expected that the predicted relationships between social skills and Involvement will be magnified, or unique, to online game players. This prediction is reflected in the following hypothesis:

H_6: **All of the predicted relationships will be magnified among online video game players.**

To determine the extent to which relationships between social skills and video game involvement are evident across different game playing categories, the relationships between social skills and video game involvement will be examined within different game playing groups (i.e., all players, offline-excusive players, online-exclusive players).

5.2   MATERIAL AND METHODS

5.2.1   Variables of Interest

5.2.1.1   *Social Skills*

To assess social skills, participants were asked to complete the Social Skills Inventory (SSI) in its entirety (Riggio, 1989) (see section 4.2.1.2 for an overview of the SSI). Consistent with previous findings (see Hamann, Lineburg, & Paul, 1998; Riggio, 1989), the SSI subscales were found to be highly intercorrelated (see Table 5.1). Reliability analyses confirmed an acceptable internal consistency for all six subscales, with alpha levels ranging from .74 to .88.

5.2.1.1.1   GENDER, AGE, AND SOCIAL SKILLS

SSI outcomes have been found to vary significantly across gender (Riggio & Carney, 2003; Riggio, 1989), an effect that was replicated here. SSI subscale scores were assessed across gender and age using a 5 (age group) by 2 (gender) by 6 (subscale) MANOVA. A significant effect of gender was found for four of the six subscales (F's > 19, p's < .001). As was found in Study 1, females scored higher than males on EE, ES, and SS whereas males outperformed females on EC (see Figure 5.1). No main effect of age was found; however, an interaction between gender and age was found for the SE subscale, $F(4, 527) = 2.39$, $p = .05$. Females retained a higher ability in the skills associated with this subscale from an early age, but showed a slight decline over time, whereas males displayed the opposite pattern. While it is not within the scope of this monograph to discuss the possible underlying mechanisms behind this interaction, it is interesting to note that the interaction emerged across both samples, even though previous research has made no mention of significant age and gender interactions for any of the SSI subscales among an adult sample.

Table 5.1   Intercorrelations between SSI subscales in Study 2 ($n = 615$)

SSI Subscale	ES	EC	SE	SS	SC
Emotional Expressivity (EE)	.470**	−.220**	.632**	.045	.505**
Emotional Sensitivity (ES)		−.063	.539**	.153**	.413**
Emotional Control (EC)			.100*	−.419**	.319**
Social Expressivity (SE)				−.055	.735**
Social Sensitivity (SS)					−.357**
Social Control (SC)					

*p < .05, **p < .01

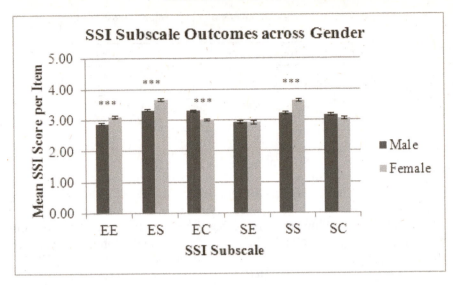

Figure 5.1 Mean SSI outcome scores across gender

5.2.1.2 Involvement

A single variable called Involvement was created to represent the degree to which participants are involved in gaming as a form of activity. Involvement levels were calculated as a composite of three variables: frequency of total video game play time, number of different types of games played, and social identification as a gamer (see section 4.2.1.3 for an overview of the components of Involvement). These three variables were combined into a single component by summing the scores on each factor. Each indicator of Involvement was standardized prior to being summed in order to account for the variation in response options across constructs.

5.2.1.2.1 RELIABILITY AND INTERCORRELATIONS

As was found in Study 1, the three variables of Involvement were also found to be highly intercorrelated (see Table 5.2). Once combined, this scale demonstrated a high internal consistency, producing an alpha coefficient of .77. Among the sample, Involvement scores ranged from –4.60 to 6.42 ($SD = 2.53$).

Table 5.2 Intercorrelations among Involvement variable in Study 2 ($N = 537$)

	Total play time	Number of games played
Social identity	.733**	.501**
Total play time		.474**

**$p < .01$

Table 5.3 Principal axis analysis of Involvement factor loadings for Study 2 participants

Component of Involvement	Factor Loading
Play frequency	.882
Game variety	.775
Social identity	.893

5.2.1.2.2 PRINCIPAL COMPONENTS ANALYSIS

Replicating the procedure of Study 1, a principal components analysis was conducted with the standardized Involvement outcomes from participants who completed all of the questions relating to Involvement (N = 537). The Kaiser-Meyer-Olkin measure verified the sampling adequacy for this analysis (KMO = .66), and all KMO values for individual items were above the acceptable limit of .50 (Field, 2009). Bartlett's test of sphericity (X^2 (3) = 583.08, $p < .001$) indicated that the correlation between items was sufficient. Supporting the established theoretical links between the components of Involvement, the results indicated that a one-factor solution was the best fit for this model (as only one component was extracted a rotation was not warranted). The three factors of Involvement explained 71.56% of the variance (see Table 5.3 for factor loadings).

5.2.1.2.3 GENDER, AGE, AND INVOLVEMENT

Variation in Involvement across gender and age was evaluated using a 5 (age group) by 2 (gender) MANOVA. Involvement was found to vary across gender categories, with males (M = .876, SD = 2.31) reporting higher levels of video game involvement than females (M = −1.03, SD = 2.39), $F(1, 527)$ = 58.17, $p < .001$, partial η^2 = .099. This effect remained stable across all age groups (p = .39, ns). This replicates the findings of Study 1, as males exhibited higher levels of video game involvement than females across all age groups, confirming that females' level of video game involvement is still not equivalent to their male counterparts (Entertainment Software Association, 2012; Ghuman & Griffiths, 2012; Williams, Yee, & Caplan, 2008).

5.2.2 Procedure

To explore the association between social skills and video game involvement, an online survey was constructed. In addition to reporting general demographic information (age, gender, etc.), participants were asked to complete the SSI in its entirety (Riggio, 1989) and a series of questions relating to their level of video game involvement.

In consideration of the limitations of Study 1, slight alterations were made to the demographic questionnaire. In addition to play history, participants were asked to report their current level of play. This was done to allow for more extensive evaluations across different game playing communities (i.e., players of offline and online games, offline-exclusive players, online-exclusive players). The video game play preferences section of the questionnaire was also expanded from 8 to 15 different game types, 6 of which spanned modality (increased from 2 in Study 1).

5.3   PARTICIPANTS

5.3.1   Participant Recruitment

To obtain a larger and more diverse participant pool, recruitment primarily took place through Amazon's Mechanical Turk (MTurk), which is an online open marketplace that allows individuals to advertise jobs that require human intelligence to complete (Buhrmester, Kwang, & Gosling, 2011; Paolacci, Chandler, & Ipeirotis, 2010). MTurk allows social scientists to recruit a large sample, quickly and inexpensively, while accommodating for the limitations that have previously troubled the social sciences, such as sample diversity. Participants, or "workers," as referred to by MTurk, represent a more demographically diverse sample than the typically recruited undergraduate university population (Buhrmester et al., 2011; Paolacci et al., 2010) and, therefore, should produce a sample of video game players across a broader spectrum and a greater range of backgrounds than would be found within a sample of undergraduate students only.

Research has found little evidence to suggest that the data collected online is of poorer quality than that collected from more traditional subject pools (Gosling, Vazire, Srivastava, & John, 2004; Paolacci et al., 2010). Test-retest reliabilities are similar to those found in traditional methods of testing, and the quality of data has been shown to meet or exceed the standards associated with published research (Buhrmester et al., 2011). Furthermore, MTurk workers have been found to be intrinsically motivated to complete the tasks they undertake (Buhrmester et al., 2011).

The online survey was posted on MTurk and offered 300 workers $0.50 USD for completion of the survey. Completion took less than 45 minutes. This quota was reached in less than 24 hours of posting the job, or HIT as it is referred to on the MTurk website. Upon reviewing the responses, it became evident that a majority of the workers who had completed the questionnaire were residents of India. This was unforeseen, as research had indicated that a majority of workers on MTurk were based in Western countries (Buhrmester et al., 2011; Paolacci et al., 2010). In order to balance the demographics of the sample, an additional 600 HITs were placed online at the payment rate of $0.25 USD (the rate was lowered in order to allow for a greater amount of HITs). The deduction in payment should not have influenced data quality, as MTurk payment levels have been found to only affect the speed of data collection (Buhrmester et al., 2011).

Advertisements for participants were placed on the popular social networking site Facebook. This allowed for the recruitment of a more diverse Western sample, including participants from the United States and United

Kingdom. Once a particular survey had been completed, participants were encouraged to 'repost' the link across their social network to obtain 'snowball' sampling. To ensure the recruitment of more active game players, advertisements were also placed on online forums and websites oriented toward the gaming community. This included online realm forums, individual guild and clan forums, and gaming clubs and game-related websites. The advertisement stated that participants were being sought to complete a survey assessing individual differences in video game players.

5.3.2 Age and Ethnicity

In total, 997 individuals completed the online survey. In order to reduce cross-cultural variance, the current analyses were restricted to participants who indicated their ethnicity as Caucasian (n = 629). Comparisons across ethnicities were not undertaken, as non-Caucasian subsamples varied greatly and contained too few participants across groups for reliable analyses.[1]

As social competence is believed to rapidly develop before reaching adulthood (Bartholomew & Horowitz, 1991; Carstensen, 1995; Cassidy, Kirsh, Scolton, & Parke, 1996; Engles, Finkenauer, Meeus, & Dekovic, 2001; Gross et al., 1997; Lawton, Kleban, Rajagopal, & Dean, 1992), the analysis was limited to adult participants only. Therefore, participants under the age of 18 were removed from the sample (n = 4). An additional 10 participants who did not indicate their age were removed, leaving 615 participants. Within the Caucasian sample, 316 (51.4%) were male, and 299 (48.6%) were female. Age ranged from 18 to 81, with an average age of 28.50 (SD = 10.32).

5.3.3 Game Play Statistics

Of the remaining 615 participants, 599 (97.4%) reported having played video games at some point, and 488 (79.3%) reported having played OVGs at some point. The majority of these individuals reported exposure to both offline video games and OVGs (80.6%). Only 15 participants reported having never played video games. Participants were also asked to indicate their current level of game play. Most were active players of both offline and online games (34.3%, or 211 individuals). However, some participants reported playing offline (19.5%, or 120 individuals) or online (6.7%, 41 individuals) games exclusively. In total, 60.5% of the sample actively played video games of some sort. In terms of play frequency, the sample ranged from "never" through "20+ hours a week." The percentage of players who fell within each play frequency category, for total and online-exclusive play, is presented in Table 5.4.

Over half of the sample (65%) played video games at least once a week, while the remaining participants played less frequently. Just under half of the sample played online games at least once a week (44.2%). About 20% of the sample reported playing video games more than 10 hours a week, while 9.1% of the sample reported spending more than 20 hours a week engaged in video game play.

Table 5.4 Percentage of players within play frequency categories for total (N = 599) and online play (n = 488) in Study 2

Amount of Time	Total Playing Time	Online Playing Time
Never	7.3	24.9
Less than once a month	15.1	19.2
About once a month	12.5	11.7
About once a week	10.1	9.6
1–5 hours a week	20.3	14.0
6–10 hours a week	13.5	10.1
10–20 hours a week	12.0	5.5
20+ hours a week	9.1	5.0

In line with previous demographic assessments (e.g., Caplan, Williams, & Yee, 2009; Griffiths, Davies, & Chappell, 2004; Williams, Martins, Consalvo, & Ivory, 2009; Yee, 2006), a range of demographic variables were assessed across age categories (e.g., under 19 years, 20–24 years, 25–29 years, 30–34 years, 35–39 years, 40–44 years, 45–49 years, and over 50). However, this categorization revealed a disproportionate distribution of the sample across ages, with substantially fewer participants within the older age brackets (e.g., 40–44, 45–49, and over 50). As any age effects found in these age categories would likely be unreliable, participants over the age of 40 were excluded from further analysis (n = 78), leaving 537 participants.

Prior to analysis, the data was assessed for normality. As graphical inspections of normality are often more informative than statistical analyses in large data sets (Field, 2009), normality was evaluated with QQ plots. The plots showed evidence of a normal distribution for play frequency and preferences across gender and age categories.

5.3.4 Summary of Sample and Game Play Behavior

The demographic data obtained within this sample was subjected to extensive analyses, as undertaken in Study 1 (see Appendix F for a full overview of the demographic findings). The play patterns and preferences exhibited by the current sample largely correspond with previous findings. In terms of play frequency, male game players were again found to engage in more frequent video game play, and across a greater variety of genre categories, than female players (Ghuman & Griffiths, 2012; Griffiths et al., 2004; Griffiths & Hunt, 1998; Williams et al., 2008; Yee, 2006). However, unlike in Study 1, gender differences were also detected for online-exclusive play, with male players engaging at a higher rate than female players. While females are participating in video game play (offline and online) more than ever, their levels of play frequency have not reached the same levels as their male counterparts.

Game genre preferences across gender also corroborated previous findings. Overall, FPS and puzzle games were the most actively played genres. Within gender, males displayed a preference for FPS games, whereas females preferred party and puzzle games. The expansion of the demographic questionnaire allowed for the uncovering of females' preference for puzzle and party games, as females had previously identified sim and party games as their preferred genres. However, as women have historically preferred less competitive games (Hartmann & Klimmt, 2006), it seems counterintuitive to have found party games to again emerge as a favorite among female players. However, the reported preferences for party, puzzle, and sim games for female players across Studies 1 and 2 could be less related to competitiveness and more related to a preference for casual games (i.e., games that do not require a special set of skills or a long-term time commitment to complete) (Kuittinen, Kultima, Niemelä, & Paavilainen, 2007). A recent surge in the development of casual online games is beginning to propel them into the mainstream. Individuals with no prior experience with video games are now playing casual social online games at a staggering rate. A reported 20% of the U.S. population has played a casual social game through a social networking site, 35% of which had never played any other kind of video game (Patel, 2011). This is particularly the case for females, as they comprise a reported 75% of the individuals who pay for these kinds of games (Caulfield, 2008). This preference for casual games among female players is important, as it likely explains some of the variability in play frequency across gender.

Corroborating previous findings, Involvement was found to vary across game modality. Across genre, participants who reported playing in multiplayer modalities trended toward slightly higher Involvement levels. Multiplayer FPS, sim, turn-based strategy (TBS), and puzzle game players were found to exhibit higher levels of Involvement than those who play the same genres in single-player modalities. Uncovering no significant differences in Involvement levels across modality for RPG players is particularly surprising, as players of multiplayer RPGs were found to engage at a significantly higher rate than players of single-player RPGs in Study 1. Additionally, previous research has found players of MMORPGs (one of the most popular multiplayer RPG game types) to invest substantially more time playing than players of other genres (Ghuman & Griffiths, 2012), with an average of up to 20 hours a week engaged in active game play (Ghuman & Griffiths, 2012; Griffiths et al., 2004; Yee, 2006).

The largest discrepancies in Involvement across modalities were found for puzzle games. However, the divergence in Involvement levels across modality within this genre may have less to do with puzzle games themselves and more to do with the intrinsic qualities of those who choose play these kinds of video games. Single-player puzzle games are highly popular and widely available, as they often come standard on home computers (Kuittinen et al., 2007). Due to their accessibility, even the most sporadic video game player is likely to engage in these kinds of games. Thus, the Involvement levels of individuals who play single-player puzzle games are likely reflective of intermittent, casual gamers, whereas players of the less popular, and less accessible, multiplayer puzzle games are likely to be more devoted video game players.

As the current sample is a large, diverse, adult population, with a considerable distribution of participants across age and gender categories, the play patterns uncovered here are likely representative of play behaviors across the (Caucasian) adult game playing community. While the current sample does contain slightly more active players than previously employed, with 65% of the participants reporting a play frequency of at least once a week as compared to 50% in Study 1, almost 20% of all players report more than 10 hours a week of video game play, indicating a consistency between the two samples. Similarly, over 95% of participants in both samples reported a history of video game play. This stability across samples reiterates the normativeness of this leisure activity and reflects the frequency with which video games play a role in people's lives as a form of entertainment, stimulation, and social interaction. Given these characteristics, the current sample would seem appropriate for exploring associations between levels of video game involvement and social competence.

5.4   RESULTS

5.4.1   Social Skills and Video Game Involvement

5.4.1.1   *Between-Group Analyses*

To examine broad differences in social skills between game playing categories, a MANOVA was conducted. Replicating the methods from Study 1, participants were first differentiated by their online game playing history in order to determine if individuals with poor social skills are attracted to OVGs in particular, as contended by social compensation theorists. When controlling for gender and age, no significant differences were found between those who reported a history of OVG play ($n = 442$) and those who did not ($n = 95$) for any of the six SSI subscales (F's < 3.97, p's < .05).

Participants were then categorized by their current play patterns, and players who reported only engaging in OVG play were compared to the general sample (i.e., all other participants). This kind of assessment allows for a more accurate appraisal of broad social differences between individuals who engage in OVG play exclusively and video game players who engage in more varied game playing behavior (i.e., online and offline). If social compensation phenomena underlie the motivation to engage in OVG play, online-exclusive game players should exhibit lower social skill outcomes as compared to those who do not exclusively engage in OVG play. When controlling for gender and age, no significant differences were found between online-exclusive players ($n = 37$) and non-online-exclusive players ($n = 500$) for any of the six SSI subscales (F's < 3.69, p's $< .05$), indicating an absence of broad social differences between online-exclusive players and non-online-exclusive players.

5.4.1.2   *Within-Group Analyses*

To uncover the statistical associations between social skills and Involvement, Involvement was regressed by all six of the SSI subscales across gaming groups (i.e., all participants, active offline and online players, offline-exclusive players, and online-exclusive players). This type of analysis allows for the identification of social differences across different gaming groups and the magnitude of these relationships, as well as the identification of any potential displacement effects of video game involvement on social skills, as significant, inverse, linear relationships between social skills and Involvement would suggest a correspondence between lower social skills and increased video game involvement.

As before, significant gender differences were found on four of the six SSI subscales. Therefore, gender (dummy coded) was entered as a variable in the regression. Age was also imputed as variable in the regression analyses, as Involvement and social skills showed some variation across groups, which could produce an illusory correlation between Involvement and social skills (Huff, 1954). Prior to analysis, standardized residuals were calculated in order to identify any outliers with residuals two or more standard deviations away from the mean. Of the 537 game players, 22 outliers were identified and removed, leaving 515 participants (this includes participants who reported to be "inactive" players of video games but also a play frequency greater than "never").

To evaluate the potential differences in the relationship between Involvement and social skills across different game playing communities, analyses were conducted within current play level categories (i.e., active players of online and offline games, active players of offline games only, active players of online games only). It is predicted that significant inverse relationships between SC and SE, and a positive relationship with ES, and Involvement would emerge (H_3—H_5) and be unique to, or magnified among, online-exclusive players (H_6).

The total amount of variance explained in the final model and beta weights of each individual predictor are shown in Table 5.5. The addition of the SSI subscales in Step 2 uncovered significant linear relationships between social skills and video game involvement.

Multiple SSI subscales emerged as significant predictors of video game involvement. Across all participants, increased levels of EE, ES, and EC, and lower SE outcomes, were found to be predictive of increased Involvement. These relationships remained equivalent in magnitude among active

Table 5.5   Total R^2 and unstandardized beta weights for individual predictors in the final model: Social skills

		All Participants ($n = 515$)	Active Online and Offline ($n = 182$)	Offline Only ($n = 107$)	Online Only ($n = 37$)
Step 2					
	EE	.524*	.488	.152	–.888
	ES	.476*	.606*	.296	.848
	EC	.921**	.824**	.660*	–.778
	SE	–.649**	–.655*	–.532	–.140
	SS	–.175	.165	–.235	–1.02
	SC	.252	.170	.317	.267
R^2 Change		.084**	.119**	.106*	.174
Total R^2		.280	.219	.200	.293

$**p < .001, *p < .05$

game players (i.e., active on and offline) and those who only reported a history of game play (i.e., all participants) despite the difference in sample size. Among offline-exclusive players, EC remained as a significant positive predictor, with higher levels of EC predicting higher levels of offline video game involvement. The predictive power of ES and SE remained trending the same direction within this subgroup though it did not reach significance. None of the SSI subscales significantly predicted increased Involvement among the subgroup of online-exclusive players. However, the positive relationships between EE, EC, and Involvement found among the broader sample reversed among online players, with lower outcomes corresponding with higher levels of online-exclusive play.

5.5   DISCUSSION

The current study sought to explore, identify, and confirm the relationships between social skills and video game involvement uncovered in Study 1. Prior to examining the relationships between Involvement and social competence, an extensive demographic evaluation of the current sample was undertaken. Play frequencies and preferences across gender and age categories were found to largely correspond with previously employed samples, encompassing a wide variety of game players, from the casual player to the dedicated gamer. Given these characteristics, this sample was considered appropriate for exploring associations between video game involvement and social competence.

Corroborating the results from Study 1, no mean differences in social skills were found between those who reported a history of OVG play and those who did not. Broad differences between online-exclusive players and non-online-exclusive players were also not found. The lack of mean differences between groups indicates the unlikelihood that individuals with vastly different social profiles are drawn to OVG play, at least in terms of social skills. While these results do not definitively demonstrate that social differences within the online gaming population do not exist prior to engagement, they do indicate that broad social differences between online and non-online gaming groups are not evident at the social skills level.

While Study 1 only uncovered a significant linear relationship between SE and Involvement, the current study found significant, linear relationships for four of the six SSI subscales. Significant positive, linear relationships with video game involvement were found for all three of the emotional subscales of the SSI, with higher outcomes predicting higher levels of Involvement. A negative relationship with SE also emerged, with lower outcomes predicting increased Involvement. These findings corroborate previous research and extend the links between social skills and Involvement uncovered in Study 1. Taken together, the results suggest that more involved video game players may have an enhanced ability to express (EE) and regulate their emotions (EC) but may exhibit higher levels of emotional sensitivity (ES) and be less able to engage others socially (SE).

Replicating the findings from Study 1, a significant negative relationship between SE and Involvement emerged among the broader game playing sample (H_4), but not the subgroup of online-exclusive players, confirming that more involved video game players perceive themselves as less verbally fluent, with difficulties in initiating and guiding conversation (Riggio, 1989, 2005). While previous research has uncovered significant inverse relationships between SE and OVG involvement among the problematic online game playing community (Lemmens et al., 2011), the current results indicate that this relationship is not limited to online play. Highly involved offline and OVG players are reporting difficulties with initiating and guiding conversation. As the relationship between SE and Involvement was strongest among active video game players, it can be postulated that active engagement in video game spaces may lead to the atrophy of the skills associated with SE.

The current analysis also uncovered a significant, positive relationship between ES and Involvement among the broader game playing sample (H_5). While ES did not emerge as a significant individual predictor of Involvement among the broad sample in Study 1, the predictive power of ES on Involvement was substantially stronger among participants who reported a history of OVG play. These findings were replicated here, as online-exclusive players exhibited a positive, linear relationship between ES and Involvement of a greater magnitude than any other game playing subgroup. However, the relationship between these variables only reached significance within the general game playing samples (i.e., all participants and active offline and online players).

Emotional Sensitivity refers to one's ability in receiving and decoding the non-verbal communication of others (e.g., "*I always seem to know what peoples' true feelings are no matter how hard they try to conceal them*") (Riggio, 1989). High levels of ES can behaviorally manifest in ways similar to shyness (Riggio, 1987). An individual who is acutely mindful of the non-verbal signals of others (i.e., high Emotional Sensitivity) can become hypersensitive to others' communicative messages, which can lead to discomfort and/or inhibition in interpersonal situations, which behaviorally manifests itself as social self-consciousness or avoidance (Zimbardo, 1997). While the results from Study 1 suggested that the relationship between ES and Involvement was limited to online players, the current results indicate the broader community of game players exhibit higher levels of ES in relation to their level of Involvement. The linear relationship between these variables was particularly strong among online-excusive players in the current sample, as well as in Study 1, suggesting a stronger correspondence between high ES and online play rather than video game play generally.

Contrary to predictions, a significant linear relationship with SC and Involvement did not emerge (H_3). While previous research has found lower SC to be a strong predictor of problematic Internet use (Caplan, 2005; Parks & Floyd, 1996; Roberts et al., 2000; Utz, 2000; Walther, 1996) and problematic/addicted OVG play (Liu & Peng, 2009), SC did not show a significant, linear relationship with Involvement among the current sample of online-exclusive players. The absence of significant links between SC and Involvement suggests that OVG players may not explicitly be drawn to online games for their ability to accommodate social self-presentation.

However, it is also possible that the previously uncovered links between lower SC and increased Involvement were driven by a third factor. For example, Liu and Peng (2009) found lower Social Control skills to be negatively related to increased OVG involvement and a preference for a virtual life. Thus, lower SC not only predicted increased play frequency, but also a psychological preference for online social environments. Similarly, Caplan (2005) found lower Social Control skills to predict a preference for online social interaction as well as the degree to which participants were unable to control their impulses to use Internet-based social spaces. Lower SC not only predicted a preference of online, versus offline, social interaction, but also an inability to control one's use of this medium. Thus, it is possible that the previously uncovered relationships between SC and Involvement were being driven by an extraneous factor associated with problematic or addicted use, such a self-regulatory deficiency. Future research is needed to explore this possibility.

5.5.1 Additional Findings

Additional relationships between social skills and Involvement were not predicted to emerge. However, due to the lack of comprehensive evaluations between social skills and video game involvement, uncovering additional relationships is not necessarily surprising. The regression analyses indicated significant relationships between EE, EC, and Involvement among the broader video game playing population. Broadly speaking, these subscales assess one's ability to effectively express (EE) and control (EC) emotional and non-verbal communication. Significant positive relationships between Involvement and these subscales suggest that individuals who are more involved in video game play are more emotionally expressive and controlled. Among online-exclusive players, the direction of the relationships between EE, EC, and Involvement reversed, suggesting that more involved online-exclusive players are less emotionally expressive and controlled than the broader video game playing sample. However, these relationships did not reach significance. As previous research has not identified consistent links between EE, EC, and Involvement, it is tenuous to draw broad conclusions from these findings. Additional research is needed to verify the consistency of these associations before interpretations of these findings can be postulated (these relationships are further assessed in section 6.6.2).

5.5.2   Limitations

Similar to Study 1, the relatively small sample size across age and gender categories limits the generalizability of the findings. Future research should aim to recruit a larger pool of online-exclusive players. In the current investigation, no significant effects were found within online-exclusive players, which, considering their magnitude, was likely due to a lack of power. Future research should aim to enlist a larger pool of online-exclusive players to better assess any differences within this particular subgroup in relation to others.

5.5.3   Conclusions

The current findings suggest that more involved game players display different social profiles than their less involved counterparts. Partially supporting previous research (e.g., Griffiths, 2010; Kowert et al., 2014; Lemmens et al., 2011; Liu & Peng, 2009), video game involvement showed significant relationships with SE and ES. However, significant relationships between Involvement and SC again failed to emerge. The broad video game playing population exhibited linear relationships between increased Involvement and greater emotional sensitivity (ES) and social hesitancy (SE) and an enhanced ability to express (EE) and regulate emotions (EC), while the only unique link found between Involvement and social skills among online-exclusive players was a magnified relationship between ES and Involvement. The particular patterns of relationships between social skills and video game involvement that emerged (i.e., linear rather than mean differences) suggest that social skill outcomes are influenced by social displacement effects, rather than being representative of social compensation motivations, and are not limited to the subgroup of online players.

Taken together, the current results demonstrate that there are consistent relationships between social skills and video game involvement and implicate displacement phenomenon as the underlying impetus. However, it would not be prudent to draw definitive conclusions as to the role of social displacement or compensation without further exploration of the potential mechanisms that may underlie the relationships between these variables. Further research is needed to explore the possible mechanisms that may underlie the significant and consistent relationships found between social skills and video game involvement. This is the primary aim of Study 3, as discussed in the following chapter (chapter 6).

NOTE

1. While limiting the sample to Caucasian participants was determined a priori, significant differences in video game play frequency ($F = 4.96$, $p < .05$) and outcomes on the SE ($F = 12.71$, $p < .001$) and SS ($F = 4.44$, $p < .05$) subscales of the SSI between Caucasian and non-Caucasian participants were found (while controlling for age and gender). This variation in outcomes supports the theoretical differences in video game culture and social skills across Eastern and Western populations as outlined in section 4.3.1.1 and substantiates their exclusion from further analyses.

REFERENCES

Barnett, J., Coulson, M., & Foreman, N. (2009). *The WoW! factor: Reduced levels of anger after violent on-line play*. London: Middlesex University.

Baron, R., & Markman, G. (2003). Beyond social capital: The role of entrepreneurs' social competence in their financial success. *Journal of Business Venturing, 18*(1), 41–60.

Bartholomew, K., & Horowitz, L. M. (1991). Attachment styles among young adults. *Journal of Personality and Social Psychology, 61*(2), 226–244.

Buhrmester, M., Kwang, T., & Gosling, S. (2011). Amazon's Mechanical Turk: A new source of inexpensive, yet high-quality, data? *Perspectives on Psychological Science, 6*(1), 3–5.

Caplan, S. (2002). Problematic Internet use and psychosocial well being: Development of a theory-based cognitive-behavioral measurement instrument. *Computers in Human Behavior, 18,* 553–575.

Caplan, S. (2005). A social skill account of problematic Internet use. *Journal of Communication, 55,* 721–736.

Caplan, S., Williams, D., & Yee, N. (2009). Problematic Internet use and psychosocial well-being among MMO players. *Computers in Human Behavior, 25*(6), 1312–1319.

Carstensen, L. L. (1995). Evidence for a life-span theory of socioemotional selectivity. *Current Directions in Psychologial Science, 4*(5), 151–162.

Cassidy, J., Kirsh, S., Scolton, K., & Parke, R. (1996). Attachment and representations of peer relationships. *Developmental Psychology, 32*(5), 892–904.

Caulfield, B. (2008). Games girls play. *Forbes*. Retrieved from http://www.forbes.com/2008/03/13/casual-gaming-women-tech-personal-cx_bc_0314casual.html

Cavell, T. A. (1990). Social adjustment, social performance, and social skills: A tri-component model of social competence. *Journal of Clinical Child Psychology*, *19*, 111–122.

Chak, K., & Leung, L. (2004). Shyness and locus of control as predictors of Internet addiction and Internet use. *Cyberpsychology and Behavior*, *7*(5), 559–570.

Chiu, S., Lee, J., & Huang, D. (2004). Video game addiction in children and teenagers in Taiwan. *Cyberpsychology and Behavior*, *7*(5), 571–581.

de Kort, Y.A.W., & Ijsselsteijn, W. A. (2008). People, places, and play: Player experience in a socio-spatial context. *Computers in Entertainment*, *6*(2), 18.

DuBois, D. L., & Felner, R. D. (1996). The quadripartite model of social competence: Theory and applications to clinical intervention. In M. A. Reinecke (Ed.), *Cognitive therapy with children and adolescents: A casebook for clinical practice*. New York: Guilford Press.

Ducheneaut, N., Yee, N., Nickell, E., & Moore, R. (2006). "Alone together?": Exploring the social dynamics of massively multiplayer online games. In *SIGCHI Conference on Human Factors in Computing Systems*. New York: ACM.

Engles, R., Finkenauer, C., Meeus, W., & Dekovic, M. (2001). Parental attachment and adolescents' emotional adjustment: The associations with social skills and relational competence. *Journal of Counseling Psychology*, *48*(4), 428–439.

Entertainment Software Association. (2012). *Game player data*. Retrieved from http://www.theesa.com/facts/gameplayer.asp

Field, A. (2009). *Discovering statistics using SPSS*. London: SAGE Publications.

Gajadhar, B., de Kort, Y., & IJsselsteijn, W. (2008). Influence of social setting on player experience of digital games. In *CHI'08 extended abstracts on human factors in computing systems* (pp. 3099–3104). New York: ACM.

Ghuman, D., & Griffiths, M. D. (2012). A cross-genre study of online gaming: Player demographics, motivation for play, and social interactions among players. *International Journal of Cyber Behavior, Psychology, and Learning*, *2*(1), 13–29.

Gifford, R., & O'Connor, B. (1987). The interpersonal circumplex as a behavior map. *Journal of Personality and Social Psychology*, *52*(5), 1019–1026.

Gosling, S., Vazire, S., Srivastava, S., & John, O. (2004). Should we trust Web-based studies? A comparative analysis of six preconceptions about Internet questionnaires. *American Psychologist*, *59*, 93–104.

Gottman, J., Gonso, J., & Rasmussen, B. (1975). Social interaction, social competence, and friendship in children. *Child Development*, *46*(3), 709–718.

Griffiths, M. D. (2010). Computer game playing and social skills: A pilot study. *Aloma*, *27*, 301–310.

Griffiths, M. D., Davies, M., & Chappell, D. (2004). Demographic factors and playing variables in online computer gaming. *Cyberpsychology and Behavior*, *7*, 479–487.

Griffiths, M. D., & Hunt, N. (1998). Dependence on computer games by adolescents. *Psychologial Reports*, *82*, 475–480.

Gross, J., Carstensen, L., Pasupathi, M., Tsai, J., Skorpen, C., & Hsu, A.Y.C. (1997). Emotion and aging: Experience, expression, and control. *Psychology and Aging*, *12*, 590–599.

Hamann, D., Lineburg, N., & Paul, S. (1998). Teaching effectiveness and social skill development. *Journal of Research in Music Education*, *46*, 87–101.

Hartmann, T., & Klimmt, C. (2006). Gender and computer games: Exploring females' dislikes. *Journal of Computer-Mediated Communication*, *11*(4), 910–931.

Huff, D. (1954). *How to Lie With Statistics*. New York: Norton.

Korgaonkar, P., & Wolin, L. (1999). A mulitvariate analysis of Web usage. *Journal of Advertising Research*, 56–68.

Kowert, R., Domahidi, E., & Quandt, T. (2014). The relationship between online video game involvement and gaming-related friendships among emotionally sensitive individuals. *Cyberpsychology, Behavior, and Social Networking, 17(7),* 447–453. doi:10.1089/cyber.2013.0656

Kuittinen, J., Kultima, A., Niemelä, J., & Paavilainen, J. (2007). Casual games discussion. In *Proceedings of the 2007 conference on Future Play* (pp. 105–112). New York: ACM.

Ladd, G. W. (1999). Peer relationships and social competence during early and middle childhood. *Annual Review of Psychology, 50,* 333–359.

Lawton, M. P., Kleban, M. H., Rajagopal, D., & Dean, J. (1992). Dimensions of affective experience in three age groups. *Psychology and Aging, 7(2),* 171–184.

Leary, M., & Kowalski, R. (1995). *Social anxiety.* New York: Guilford Press.

Lemmens, J., Valkenburg, P., & Peter, J. (2011). Psychological causes and consequences of pathological gaming. *Computers in Human Behavior, 27(1),* 144–152.

Liu, M., & Peng, W. (2009). Cognitive and psychological predictors of the negative outcomes associated with playing MMOGs (massively multiplayer online games). *Computers in Human Behavior, 25(6),* 1306–1311.

Moskowitz, D. S. (1990). Convergence of self-reports and independent observers: Dominance and friendliness. *Journal of Personality and Social Psychology, 58(6),* 1096–1106.

Paolacci, G., Chandler, J., & Ipeirotis, P. (2010). Running experiments on Amazon Mechanical Turk. *Judgment and Decision Making, 5(5),* 411–419.

Parks, M. R., & Floyd, K. (1996). Making friends in cyberspace. *Journal of Communication, 46,* 80–97.

Patel, S. (2011). Social gaming: The good, the bad, & the ugly. *SingleGrain.* Retrieved from http://www.singlegrain.com/blog/social-gaming-the-good-the-bad-the-ugly/

Peng, W., & Liu, M. (2010). Online gaming dependency: A preliminary study in China. *Cyberpsychology and Behavior, 13(3),* 329–333.

Peters, C., & Malesky, A. (2008). Problematic usage among highly-engaged players of massively multiplayer online role playing games. *Cyberpsychology and Behavior, 11(4),* 481–484.

Riggio, R. (1987). *The charisma quotient: What it is, how to get it, how to use it.* New York: Dodd Mead.

Riggio, R. (1989). *Manual for the Social Skills Inventory.* Palo Alto, CA: Consulting Psychologists Press.

Riggio, R. (2005). The Social Skills Inventory (SSI): Measuring nonverbal and social skills. In V. Manusov (Ed.), *The sourcebook of nonverbal measures: Going beyond words* (pp. 25–33). Mahwah, NJ: Lawrence Erlbaum.

Riggio, R., & Carney, D. C. (2003). *Manual for the Social Skills Inventory* (2nd ed). Mountain View, CA: Mind Garden.

Roberts, L. D., Smith, L., & Pollock, C. (2000). "U r a lot bolder on the net": Shyness and Internet use. In *Shyness, development, consolidation, and change* (pp. 121–135). New York: Routledge.

Rose-Kransor, L. (1997). Nature of social competence: A theoretical review. *Social Developmental Psychology, 6(1),* 111–135.

Scealy, M., Phillips, J., & Stevenson, R. (2002). Shyness and anxiety as predictors of patterns of Internet usage. *Cyberpsychology and Behavior, 5(6),* 507–515.

Segrin, C., & Kinney, T. (1995). Social skills deficits among the socially anxious: Loneliness and rejection from others. *Motivation and Emotion, 19(1),* 1–24.

Sjöblom, B. (2008). Language and perception in co-located gaming. Paper presented at the Language, Culture, Mind III conference, Odense, Denmark.

Steinkuehler, C., & Williams, D. (2006). Where everybody knows your (screen) name: Online games as "third places." *Journal of Computer-Mediated Communication, 11(4),* 885–909.

Utz, S. (2000). Social information processing in MUDs: The development of friendships in virtual worlds. *Journal of Online Behavior, 1*(1).

Walther, J. (1996). Computer-mediated communication: Impersonal, interpersonal, and hyperpersonal interaction. *Communication Research, 23*(1), 3–43.

Williams, D., Martins, N., Consalvo, M., & Ivory, J. (2009). The virtual census: Representations of gender, race and age in video games. *New Media & Society, 11*(5), 815–834.

Williams, D., Yee, N., & Caplan, S. (2008). Who plays, how much, and why? Debunking the stereotypical gamer profile. *Journal of Computer-Mediated Communication Monographs, 13*(4), 993–1018.

Yee, N. (2006). The demographics, motivations, and derived experiences of users of massively-multi-user online graphical environments. *Teleoperators and Virtual Environments, 15*(3), 309–329.

Yuen, C. N., & Lavin, M. J. (2004). Internet dependence in the collegiate population: The role of shyness. *Cyberpsychology and Behavior, 7*(4), 379–383.

Zimbardo, P. (1997). *Shyness: What it is, what to do about it*. Reading, MA: Addison-Wesley.

6 Social Skills, Insecure Attachment, and Video Game Involvement

Studies 1 and 2 uncovered reliable relationships between social skills and video game involvement and indicated that more involved video game players, both offline and online, report higher degrees of emotional sensitivity, less verbal fluency, and greater difficulties in initiating and guiding conversation, than their less involved counterparts. These particular patterns of findings (i.e., linear relationships within game playing categories but not broad differences between groups) suggest that relationships between video game involvement and social outcomes are attributable to displacement, rather than compensation effects. However, this is curious, as historically the main effect of media use has been behavior reinforcement (Perse, 2008), not change. As interaction within a particular medium is only one possible source of influence among other possible influences (Rosengren, 1974; Rubin, 2002), it would not be prudent to attribute the relationships between social skills and video game involvement to displacement mechanisms without consideration for the personal attributes of game players that may be underlying these relationships. As explained by Schramm, Lyle, and Parker (1961) in their research on the impact of television watching, "in order to understand television's impact and effect[s] . . . we first have to get away from the unrealistic concept of what television does to children and substitute the concept of what children do with television" (p. 169). Thus, to fully understand the relationships between media consumption and behavioral outcomes, consideration needs to be given to influences apart from the media use itself.

Some researchers have attempted to do so and have drawn links between video game involvement, social skills, and a variety of underlying psychosocial dispositions, such as loneliness (Kim, Namkoong, Ku, & Kim, 2008; Morahan-Martin & Schumacher, 2003), depression (Williams, Yee, & Caplan, 2008), and social anxiety (Kim et al., 2008; Lo, Wang, & Fang, 2005), as these dispositions have been independently acknowledged as potential precursors to OVG engagement and have shown significant, inverse relationships with social skills (DiTommaso, Brannen-McNulty, Ross, & Burgess, 2003; Riggio, Throckmorton, & DePaola, 1990; Segrin & Flora, 2000; Segrin, 1996, 1998). Others have linked the associations between social outcomes and video game involvement to an increased prevalence of Asperger syndrome (AS) within the video game playing population. Characteristically, individuals with AS struggle in social situations, as they are not able to effectively utilize social skills (Mullen, 2009). Along with a skill deficit, individuals with AS tend to have higher levels of social anxiety (Tatum, 2000) and depression (Barnhill, 2011; Myles & Adreon, 2001), as well as a heightened interest in video games (Fattig, 2008). As skill deficits, social anxiety, and depression have all been independently linked to OVG players (Kim et al., 2008; Lo et al., 2005; Williams et al., 2008), the link between OVG and AS has become widely discussed (Langlois, 2011). In line with the social compensation hypothesis, it is believed that the inability to effectively socialize draws individuals with AS into gaming environments (Mullen, 2009). However, as the estimated prevalence of AS in the world's population is believed to range between .003% and .5%, and approximately 22.4% of the world's population plays OVGs (Bureau, 2008; Fombonne & Tidmarsh, 2003; TMachine.org, 2008), it seems unlikely that a substantial portion of OVG players have AS. Additionally, individuals with AS often display a wide range of social skill deficits, including those associated with emotional expressivity (Barnhill, 2011; Moyes, 2001) and sensitivity (Attwood, 2000; Church, Alisanski, & Amanullah, 2000; Safran, Safran, & Ellis, 2003), which are patterns that have not been consistently found within OVG playing populations.

While AS is unlikely underpinning the relationship between social skills and video game involvement, it is possible that the particular mechanism underlying the relationship between these variables is attributable to a fundamental construct, such as attachment. While no known research has explored the relationships between insecure attachment and video game involvement directly, insecure attachment styles have independently displayed significant links with decreased social skills (Allen et al., 2002; Bartholomew & Horowitz, 1991; DiTommaso et al., 2003; Engles, Finkenauer, Meeus, & Dekovic, 2001; Gutstein & Whitney, 2002; Schneider & Younger, 1996), increased loneliness (Deniz, Hamarta, & Ari, 2005; Wiseman, Mayseless, & Sharabany, 2006), increased depression (Bifulco, Moran, Ball, & Bernazzani, 2002; Roberts, Gotlib, & Kassel, 1996), and higher degrees of social anxiety (Eng, Heimberg, Hart, Schneier, & Liebowitz, 2001; Irons & Gilbert, 2005; Lee & Hankin, 2009). Furthermore, researchers have found that individuals higher in attachment anxiety and avoidance utilize mediated social environments, such as chat rooms and social networking sites, in different ways than their securely attached peers (Buote, Wood, & Pratt, 2009; Oldmeadow, Quinn, & Kowert, 2013; Ponder, 2009). For example, a study by Buote, Wood, and Pratt (2009) found that, unlike securely attached individuals, participants high in attachment anxiety or avoidance approach online friendships differently than offline ones. Individuals with high attachment anxiety reported being equally satisfied with the level of intimacy, approval, and responsiveness of their friendships, irrespective of whether they were based offline or online. While online friendships are often assumed to be less fulfilling than offline friendships, as they are not supported by physical proximity (Wellman & Wortley, 1990) and therefore are less able to provide tangible resources, this research suggests that friendships made online may be well suited for highly anxious individuals, as Internet-based social spaces provide an additional outlet in which friendships can be created and sustained. Individuals high in attachment avoidance emerged as the most likely to disclose personal information online and were the only group to report being equally forthcoming to both offline and online friends. Thus, for avoidant individuals, Internet-based mediated spaces seem to provide a less risky social environment where they can overcome their traditional social difficulties and form intimate bonds online.

However, not all mediated social spaces are well suited to serve attachment functions. When evaluating the social utility of social networking sites for the insecurely attached, Oldmeadow et al. (2013) found individuals high in attachment anxiety to be more likely to utilize social networking services, such as Facebook, to generate closeness with others. However, no links were found between attachment avoidance and the use of Facebook. While the researchers speculate that avoidant individuals may not be drawn to social networking sites due to their desire to retain their sense of autonomy, such individuals may also neglect social networks due to their perceived lack of anonymity. This sense of anonymity provides individuals with a greater sense of social freedom, promoting open and intimate conversation while removing the fear of any social repercussions (Morahan-Martin & Schumacher, 2003; Walther, 1996). Research has found visually anonymous, mediated socialization to be particularly beneficial for avoidant individuals, as those high in attachment avoidance report a greater likelihood to disclose personal information to their online contacts (Buote et al., 2009) as well as a greater comfort with self-disclosure and intimacy in their semi-anonymous, online relationships as compared to their offline counterparts (Ponder, 2009). As self-disclosure is an integral component of developing intimacy (Miell & Duck, 1986; Reis & Shaver, 1988) and an inability to self-disclose has been a fundamental hindrance to the formation of intimate friendship bonds among avoidant individuals, contributing to their potential social isolation (Buote et al., 2009; E. Smith, Murphy, & Coats, 1999), the provision of a visually anonymous social space may be more suited to serve attachment needs for these individuals. As social networking sites provide mediated connections between real-world social contacts, there is little reason to suggest that the traditional social patterns of avoidant individuals would not remain. Therefore, while this research indicates the potential for Internet-based social services to serve beneficial attachment functions for the highly anxious or avoidant, it also highlights that different social services may serve different attachment functions. As a highly social, mediated, and visually anonymous space, online games may be well suited to provide the sense of closeness, belonging, and security needed to satisfy attachment needs (particularly for those high in attachment avoidance), while compensating for any associated social difficulties.

The current study will explore these possibilities and examine the relationship between social skills and OVG involvement through the perspective of attachment theory. Examining the relationships between social skills and Involvement through the theoretical perspective of attachment will help further unravel the directional connections between social skills and video game involvement. As attachment forms in childhood, which is likely prior to video game exposure, significant links between attachment, social skills, and Involvement would signify that social differences among game players are, at least partially, attributable to an underlying construct that existed prior to video game exposure and would support the claims put forth by social compensation theorists. Uncovering significant links between attachment, social skills, and Involvement would also further elucidate why individuals are becoming increasingly involved in this activity, how they are utilizing this medium, and what they are potentially gaining or losing as a result of continued participation. Prior to examining the relationships between attachment, social skills, and Involvement, an overview of attachment theory and its associations with social skills will be discussed.

6.1   ADULT ATTACHMENT THEORY

Attachment theory is a developmental framework that emphasizes the role of early experience in influencing the expectations, beliefs, and behaviors of an individual's responsiveness and trustworthiness of others (Ainsworth, Blehar, Wathers, & Wall, 1978; Bowlby, 1969, 1973, 1979; Fraley, 2002). Depending upon the nature of the relationship between an individual and his or her caregiver, a secure or insecure attachment bond can develop. Those who experience responsive and reliable care develop the expectation that others will be available and supportive when needed and become securely attached. However, individuals who were raised by inconsistent or neglectful caregivers may form an insecure attachment (Ainsworth et al., 1978; Bartholomew & Horowitz, 1991).

An insecure attachment can be characterized along two dimensions: anxious or avoidant (Brennan, Clark, & Shaver, 1998; Collins & Allard, 2004). If one's primary caregiver was inconsistent, an individual will likely develop a cognitive model in which he or she fears and expects rejection from others. This is attachment anxiety, which can be formally defined as an anxious or fearful preoccupation with relationships (E. Smith et al., 1999). As adults, individuals high in attachment anxiety are less trusting of others and hold higher levels of worry and impulsiveness in their relationships (Bartholomew & Horowitz, 1991; Hazan & Shaver, 1987, 1990, 1994) while desiring intimacy, approval, and responsiveness from others

(Buote et al., 2009). This combination of high anxiety and desire for intimacy can result in an overdependence on others through a pursuit for excessive closeness (Buote et al., 2009).

Conversely, if a child's primary caregiver was neglectful, the child will develop a working model of others as undependable. These individuals, who can be described as attachment avoidant, view themselves as self-sufficient, with no need for close relationships (Feeny & Noller, 1990), putting them at a higher risk for social isolation in adulthood (Buote et al., 2009). Avoidant individuals tend to dismiss or *avoid* intimate relationships due to the belief that they will eventually be disappointed (Buote et al., 2009; E. Smith et al., 1999).

One's initial attachment organization has been found to remain stable across the lifespan (Fraley, 2002; Hamilton, 2000; Urban, Carlson, Egeland, & Sroufe, 1991; Waters, Merrick, Treboux, Crowell, & Albersheim, 2000) and generations (Benoit & Parker, 1994). Thus, this ingrained system of thoughts, beliefs, expectations, and behaviors about the self in relation to others established in infancy contributes to the development and maintenance of all subsequent relationships (Fraley, 2002).

6.2 ATTACHMENT AND SOCIAL SKILLS

A secure attachment is a fundamental component for the development of skills associated with social competence (Gutstein & Whitney, 2002), as it provides individuals with a set of expectations about how to effectively interact with others (Sroufe & Fleeson, 1986) and the ability to develop the skills necessary for establishing and maintaining reciprocal interpersonal relationships (Allen et al., 2002; Bartholomew & Horowitz, 1991; Cassidy, Kirsh, Scolton, & Parke, 1996; Engles et al., 2001). Not only have researchers found that securely attached infants develop into more socially competent adults than their insecure counterparts (Schaffer, 2007), but they have also linked secure attachment to increases in social skill levels across adolescence (Allen et al., 2002) and significantly higher scores on skills measured at university age (Deniz et al., 2005). Secure attachment has been specifically linked with the development of a range of social skills such as negotiation, giving and receiving critiques, and the ability to provide positive feedback to others (Bell, Avery, Jenkins, Feld, & Schoenrock, 1985; Nada Raja, McGee, & Stanton, 1992; Rice, Cunningham, & Young, 1997; Rice, 1990; Schneider & Younger, 1996). More broadly, social and emotional expressivity have displayed positive associations with secure attachment (Deniz et al., 2005) and inverse relationships with insecure attachment (DiTommaso et al., 2003). Researchers have also found insecurely attached individuals to be more vulnerable to developing social problems (Berlin, Cassidy, & Appleyard, 2008), including ineffective social skills (Berlin et al., 2008; Schaffer, 2007), than their securely attached counterparts.

6.3 PRESENT STUDY

The current study aims to explore the relationships between social skills and video game involvement through the perspective of attachment theory. Examining the potential foundational role of attachment will help further unravel the connections between social skills and OVG involvement and help determine why individuals are becoming increasingly involved in this activity, how they are utilizing this medium, and what they are gaining or losing (socially) as a result. Significant relationships between attachment, social skills, and Involvement, among online-exclusive players, would suggest that online players engage within these spaces for their ability to compensate for social difficulties and to obtain a sense of closeness, belonging, and security that satisfies attachment needs. Furthermore, as attachment forms in childhood (Ainsworth et al., 1978; Bowlby, 1969, 1973, 1979), which is likely prior to video game exposure, these links would signify that social differences among game players are at least partially attributable to an underlying construct that existed *prior* to video game exposure.

As playful, social communities that provide a sense of anonymity and encourage the creation of intimate friendship bonds, OVGs are likely particularly suited to serve attachment needs for those high in attachment avoidance. Avoidant individuals desire autonomy above all else. While the relative anonymity and invisibility provided by online games substantially diminishes any fear and consequences of social rejection (Morahan-Martin & Schumacher, 2003; Suler, 2004; Walther, 1996), the shared activities experienced by co-players help create close bonds between them (Cole & Griffiths, 2007; Hsu, Wen, & Wu, 2009; Iacono & Weisband, 1997; Williams, 2006; Yee, 2002), which would allow avoidant individuals to develop and maintain intimate interpersonal relationships in the absence of physical proximity. Furthermore, OVG environments can provide a sense of social community even in the absence of direct socialization with others (Ducheneaut, Yee, Nickell, & Moore, 2006; Steinkuehler & Williams, 2006) as, at their core, video games are achievement-based activities (i.e., the primary goal is to complete in-game objectives). Thus, avoidant individuals may be particularly drawn to participate in a shared, achievement-based environment that provides a sense of social presence but does not require direct socialization. In consideration of this, the following predictions have been made:

H$_7$: A positive relationship between attachment avoidance and online video game involvement will emerge.

    H$_{7a}$: A positive relationship between attachment avoidance and online video game involvement will emerge between subjects, with online-exclusive players exhibiting higher levels of attachment avoidance than non-online-exclusive players.

H_{7b}: **A positive relationship between attachment avoidance and online video game involvement will emerge within subjects, with attachment avoidance demonstrating a positive, linear relationship with video game involvement within the subgroup of online-exclusive players.**[1]

As individuals high in attachment anxiety have been found to utilize a wide variety of media to supplement their need for excessive closeness (e.g., chat rooms, social networking sites), it is possible that significant relationships between attachment anxiety and OVG involvement will also be found. However, as OVGs are a less accessible and less mainstream form of mediated communication than online chat rooms or social networking websites,[2] it seems unlikely that individuals high in attachment anxiety will display a preference for online gaming spaces more so than those high in attachment avoidance. Furthermore, anxious individuals have been shown to utilize a wide range of mediated outlets to serve their attachment needs (Buote et al., 2009; Oldmeadow et al., 2013; Ponder, 2009), both visually anonymous and non-visually anonymous, while avoidant individuals seem to require a space where self-disclosure is promoted and intimate social contacts can be formed, but self-sufficiency can be retained. As such, OVGs are likely providing a social space that is particularly suited to serve the social needs of individuals high in attachment avoidance.

In addition to assessing the linear relationships between insecure attachment, social skills, and Involvement, emotional motivations for OVG play will be evaluated.[3] If OVG players are becoming increasingly involved for their social functionality and ability to serve attachment needs, then there should be a discernible motivation to engage for social comfort, rather than entertainment, which is often viewed as the primary function of video game play. Thus, the following predictions have been made:

H_8: **A significant positive correlation will be found between attachment avoidance and playing online video games for social comfort.**
H_9: **Playing online video games for the purpose of entertainment will be negatively correlated with attachment avoidance.**

It is also predicted that the relationships between social skills and Involvement uncovered in Studies 1 and 2 will be replicated within the current sample:

H_{10}: **An inverse relationship between Social Expressivity (SE) and video game involvement will emerge within subjects, with SE demonstrating an inverse linear relationship with video game involvement.**
H_{11}: **A positive relationship between Emotional Sensitivity (ES) and video game involvement will emerge within subjects, with ES demonstrating a positive linear relationship with video game involvement.**

6.4 MATERIAL AND METHODS

6.4.1 Variables of Interest

6.4.1.1 *Social Skills*

Due to the length of the Social Skills Inventory (SSI, consisting of 90 items), and the overall size of the current questionnaire, an abridged version of the SSI was devised by choosing four items to measure each of the six subscales (i.e., 24 items in total). A principal components analysis (varimax rotation) was run on the SSI outcomes from the Study 2 sample, which contained over 500 participants, in order to identify the items to be included within the abridged measure. The Kaiser-Meyer-Olkin measure verified the sampling adequacy for the analysis of the Study 2 participants, KMO = .913, and Bartlett's test of sphericity (X^2 (4005) = 23306.75, $p < .001$) indicated that the correlation between items was sufficiently large for PCA. Nineteen items emerged with eigenvalues over Kaiser's criterion of 1 and explained 62.27% of the variance.

The four items from each subscale with the highest factor loading (rotated component matrix, varimax rotation) were then selected (i.e., 24 items in total). Only items that loaded highly on their primary factor were chosen (see appendix G for factor loadings).

The general pattern of intercorrelations between subscales within the abridged SSI is similar to what previous research has found when examining the SSI subscales in their entirety (see Hamann, Lineburg, & Paul, 1998; Riggio, 1989). While the magnitude of the intercorrelations are somewhat lower, this is likely because it is an abridged measure with a smaller pool of items and, therefore, holds less statistical power (see Table 6.1).

Enlisting a smaller pool of items also influenced the internal consistency of the subscales. While reliability analyses confirmed a high internal consistency for five of the six subscales (Cronbach's α levels ranged from .78 to .91), the EE subscale emerged with a somewhat low internal consistency (Cronbach's α = .46). Considering the relatively small number of items (4),

Table 6.1 Intercorrelations between subscales for abridged SSI ($n = 386$)

SSI Subscale	ES	EC	SE	SS	SC
Emotional Expressivity (EE)	–.08	–.13*	.29*	–.09	.30*
Emotional Sensitivity (ES)		.05	.17*	.01	.23*
Emotional Control (EC)			–.07	–.33*	.02
Social Expressivity (SE)				.09	.59*
Social Sensitivity (SS)					–.06
Social Control (SC)					

* $p < .01$

this is not necessarily incongruous and therefore was deemed adequate (a copy of the abridged SSI can be found in appendix H). However, any interpretations made from significant associations with this abridged EE subscale will be approached cautiously.

6.4.1.2   *Attachment*

To measure adult attachment, the Experiences in Close Relationships (ECR) scale (Brennan et al., 1998) was administered (a copy of the ECR can be found in appendix I). This 36-item, self-report measure of adult attachment conceptualizes attachment on a continuum, rather than assigning individuals to a particular attachment style category (Ainsworth et al., 1978; Bartholomew & Horowitz, 1991), thus making it ideal for assessing linear relationships between social skills, video game involvement, and attachment.

The ECR assesses the two major dimensions of adult attachment, anxiety and avoidance, as they have been found to underlie all previously constructed self-report adult romantic attachment measures and are believed to be key to capturing individual differences in adult attachment (Brennan et al., 1998). The development of this measure incorporated years of attachment research, as it was created from the results of a principal components analysis of 60 constructs, representing 482 items, obtained from previous attachment measure research (Brennan et al., 1998).

The ECR is the scale of choice among attachment researchers as it has shown excellent reliability and validity across hundreds of studies (Mikulincer & Shaver, 2007). Reliability analyses confirm the scale's reliability, as a high internal consistency was found for both the avoidant ($\alpha = .91$) and anxious ($\alpha = .92$) attachment subscales. These two subscales were found to be positively correlated ($r = .216$, $p < .001$), suggesting that individuals who score higher on the avoidance dimension also report being more anxiously attached. This slight correlation was not considered to be problematic, as it was relatively weak and similar patterns have been noted in previous research enlisting the ECR (e.g., Butzer & Campbell, 2008; Sibley, Fischer, & Liu, 2005; Wei, Russell, Mallinckrodt, & Vogel, 2007).

6.4.1.2.1   GENDER, AGE, AND ATTACHMENT

Variation of the ECR across age and gender was assessed using a 5 (age group) by 2 (gender) by 2 (subscale) MANOVA. A marginally significant main effect of gender was found for avoidant, $F(1, 498) = 3.39$, $p = .07$, but not anxious ($p = .61$, *ns*) attachment (see Figure 6.1). Males ($M = 3.61$, $SD = .92$) obtained slightly higher outcome scores than females ($M = 3.39$, $SD = 1.09$) on this subscale. No significant main effects of age or interactions between gender and age were found.

6.4.1.2.2   ATTACHMENT AND SOCIAL SKILLS

Previous research has found securely attached individuals to display high levels of Social and Emotional Expressivity, Social Control, and lower levels

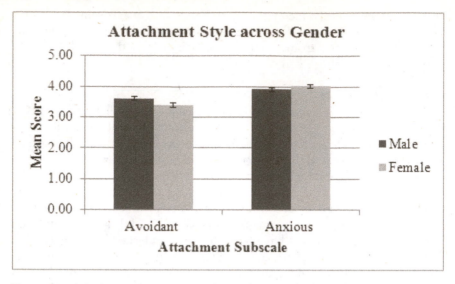

Figure 6.1   Attachment outcome scores by gender (error bars represent standard error).

Table 6.2   Partial correlations (controlling for age and gender) between insecure attachment and SSI

SSI Subscale	Anxious	Avoidant
EE	−.193**	−.533**
ES	−.028	−.082
EC	−.320**	.045
SE	−.127*	−.434**
SS	.469**	−.011
SC	−.177**	−.311**

**$p < .001$, *$p < .05$

of Social Sensitivity (Deniz et al., 2005; DiTommaso et al., 2003). Largely corroborating previous findings, insecure attachment styles exhibited negative relationships on the EE, SE, and SC subscales (see Table 6.2).

While both anxious and avoidant attachment showed a significant relationship with an inability to emotionally express oneself (EE), engage others (SE), and display confidence in social endeavors (SC), the magnitude of these relationships was intensified among avoidant individuals. Anxious attachment also emerged with a positive relationship with SS (e.g., "*I am very sensitive of criticism*") and a negative relationship with

EC (e.g., "*I am very good at maintaining a calm exterior even if I am upset*").

6.4.1.2.3 EXPERIENCES IN CLOSE RELATIONSHIPS: SUMMARY

Reliability analyses confirmed that the ECR is an internally consistent measure of adult attachment. Unexpectedly, a marginally significant main effect of gender was found for avoidant attachment. Gender differences in attachment are largely absent within current literature (Thompson, 2010); however, some research has suggested that attachment processes operate similarly, though not identically, across gender (Cooper, Shaver, & Collins, 1998). Age effects were not uncovered, confirming previous research that has found that attachment remains stable over time (Baldwin & Fehr, 1995; Bowlby, 1969; Fraley, 2002; Klohnen & Bera, 1998; Scharfe & Bartholomew, 1994; Waters et al., 2000). The relationships between attachment and social skills predominantly exhibited the predicted effects, as insecure attachment styles exhibited negative relationships with SE, EE, and SC. Attachment anxiety also displayed a positive relationship with SS, and a negative relationship with EC, indicating that individuals with high attachment anxiety also perceive themselves to have less control over their emotions and a higher sensitivity to social criticism.

6.4.1.3 *Emotional Motivations for Play*

To evaluate emotional motivations for play, participants responded to a series of six questions relating to game play motivations (i.e., *I play video games when I feel: stressed, anxious, sad, lonely, happy, excited*) on a 1–5 scale ranging from "*strongly disagree*" to "*strongly agree.*" These six items were subjected to a principal components analysis (varimax rotation) to determine if different constructs underlie emotional motivations for play. The Kaiser-Meyer-Olkin measure verified the sampling adequacy for the analysis of the sample, KMO = .744, and Bartlett's test of sphericity, X^2 (15) = 949.26, $p < .001$, indicated that the correlation between items was sufficiently large for PCA. Two distinct components emerged (see appendix J for factor loadings). Items loading highly on the first factor included those related to playing video games when feeling negative emotions (stressed, anxious, sad, and lonely) and were labeled "Playing for Social Comfort" (α = .81). The items loading on the second factor related to playing video games when feeling positive emotions (happy and excited) and were labeled "Playing for Entertainment" (α = .80). Playing for social comfort and entertainment were moderately correlated (r = .443, $p < .001$).

6.4.1.4 *Involvement*

A single variable called Involvement was created to represent the degree to which participants are involved in gaming as a form of activity. Involvement levels were calculated as a composite of three variables: frequency of total video game play time, number of different types of games played, and social identification as a gamer (see section 4.2.1.3 for an overview of the components of Involvement). These three variables were combined into a single component by summing the scores on each factor. Each indicator of Involvement was standardized prior to being summed in order to account for the variation in response options across constructs.

6.4.1.4.1   RELIABILITY AND INTERCORRELATIONS

The three variables that comprise Involvement were again found to be highly intercorrelated (see Table 6.3) and demonstrated a high internal consistency, producing an alpha coefficient of .77. Scores ranged from –3.71 to 5.97, with an average score of .77 (SD = 2.49).

6.4.1.4.2   PRINCIPAL COMPONENTS ANALYSIS

A principal components analysis was conducted with the standardized Involvement outcomes from participants who completed all of the questions relating to Involvement (n = 409). The Kaiser-Meyer-Olkin measure verified the sampling adequacy for this analysis (KMO = .71), and all KMO values for individual items were above the acceptable limit of .50 (Field, 2009). Bartlett's test of sphericity (X^2 (3) = 530.54, p < .001) indicated that the correlation between items was sufficient. Supporting the established theoretical links between the components of Involvement, the results indicated that a one-factor solution was the best fit for this model (as only one component was extracted a rotation was not warranted). The three factors of Involvement explained 76.47% of the variance (see Table 6.4 for factor loadings).

Table 6.3   Intercorrelations among Involvement variables in Study 3 (n = 409)

	Total play time	Number of games played
Social identity	.727**	.581**
Total play time		.734**

**p < .01

Table 6.4   Principal axis analysis of Involvement factor loadings for Study 3 participants

Component of Involvement	Factor Loading
Play frequency	.903
Game variety	.836
Social identity	.882

6.4.1.4.3   GENDER, AGE, AND INVOLVEMENT

As was found in Studies 1 and 2, Involvement varied across gender categories, with males reporting higher levels of video game involvement than females. Also confirming previous findings, engaging within a multiplayer modality did not guarantee higher levels of involvement, as the only consistent difference within genre, but across modality, has been for FPS and puzzle games, suggesting that there are not general differences in Involvement across genres and modalities.

6.4.2   Procedure

To explore the association between attachment, social skills, and video game involvement an online survey was constructed. In addition to reporting general demographic information (age, gender, etc.), participants were asked to complete the Social Skills Inventory (Riggio, 1989), the Experiences in Close Relationships (ECR) scale (Brennan et al., 1998), and a series of questions relating to video game involvement and play motivations.

6.5   PARTICIPANTS

6.5.1   Participant Recruitment

Participant recruitment was primarily conducted through Amazon's Mechanical Turk (MTurk) (see section 5.3.1 for an overview of MTurk). Advertisements for participants were placed on the popular social networking site Facebook. This allowed for the recruitment of a more diverse Western sample, including participants from the United States and United Kingdom. Once a particular survey had been completed, participants were encouraged to 'repost' the link across their social network to obtain 'snowball' sampling. To ensure the recruitment of more active game players, advertisements were also placed on online forums and websites oriented toward the gaming community. This included online realm forums, individual guild and clan forums, and gaming clubs and game-related websites. The advertisement stated that participants were being sought to complete a survey assessing individual differences in video game players.

6.5.2   Age and Ethnicity

In total, 797 individuals completed the online survey. In order to reduce cross-cultural variance, the current analyses were restricted to participants who indicated their ethnicity as Caucasian ($n = 568$). Comparisons across ethnicities were not undertaken, as non-Caucasian subsamples varied greatly and contained too few participants across groups for reliable analyses.[4] Within the Caucasian sample, 311 (54.8%) participants were male, and 257 (45.2%) were female. Age ranged from 18–67 ($M = 26.68$, $SD = 8.66$).

6.5.3   Game Play Statistics

Of the remaining 568 participants, 449 (79.0 %) reported having played video games at some point, and 372 (86.4%) reported having played OVGs at some point. Thus, the majority of participants reported an exposure to both offline and online games.

Participants were also asked to indicate their current level of game play. Just over one-quarter of all participants reported to be active players of offline and online games (26.9% or 153 individuals), with slightly fewer reporting being offline- (19.4%, or 110 individuals) or online-exclusive (12.7%, or 72 individuals) players. Just over 20% of the sample (21.0%, 119 participants) reported that they do not actively engage in video game play. In terms of play frequency, the sample ranged from "never" through "20+ hours a week." The percentage of players who fell within each play frequency category, for total and online-exclusive play, is presented in Table 6.5.

Over half of the sample (58.8%) played video games at least once a week, while the remaining participants played less frequently. Just under half of the sample reported playing online games at least once a week (44.2%). Just over 20% of the sample could be considered 'heavy' players, playing video games more than 10 hours a week, whereas 11.1% of the sample could be considered 'very heavy' gamers, spending more than 20 hours a week engaged in video game play. The proportion of participants engaging in very heavy online play was 6.7%.

In line with previous demographic assessments (e.g., Griffiths, Davies, & Chappell, 2004; Williams, Martins, Consalvo, & Ivory, 2009; Yee, 2006), a range of demographic variables were assessed across age categories (e.g., under 19 years, 20–24 years, 25–29 years, 30–34 years, 35–39 years, 40–44 years, 45–49 years, and over 50). However, this categorization revealed a disproportionate distribution of the sample across ages, with substantially fewer participants within the older age brackets (e.g., 40–44, 45–49, and

Table 6.5 Percentage of players within play frequency categories for total ($N = 568$) and online play ($n = 372$) in Study 3

Amount of Time	Total Playing Time	Online Playing Time
Never	21.0	34.6
Less than once a month	12.7	13.7
About once a month	7.6	7.6
About once a week	10.7	9.5
1–5 hours a week	13.7	11.8
6–10 hours a week	12.7	8.6
10–20 hours a week	10.6	7.6
20+ hours a week	11.1	6.7

over 50). As any age effects found in these age categories would likely be skewed, and therefore unreliable, participants over the age of 40 were excluded from further analysis ($n = 55$), leaving 514 participants.

Prior to analysis, the data was assessed for normality. As graphical inspections of normality are often more informative than statistical analyses in large data sets (Field, 2009), normality was evaluated with QQ plots. The plots showed evidence of a normal distribution for play frequency and preferences across gender and age categories.

6.5.4   Summary of Sample and Game Play Behavior

The demographic data obtained within this sample was subjected to extensive analyses, as was undertaken in Studies 1 and 2 (see Appendix K for a full overview of the demographic analyses). The play patterns and preferences exhibited by the current sample largely support previous findings. In general, this sample falls in between the first two samples in terms of play frequency, with 58.8% of the participants reporting engaging in video game play at least once a week (as compared to 50% in the first sample and 65% in the second). Male game players were again found to engage in more frequent video game play and across a greater variety of genre categories than female players (Ghuman & Griffiths, 2012; Griffiths et al., 2004; Griffiths & Hunt, 1998; Williams et al., 2008; Yee, 2006). Overall, RPG, FPS, and puzzle games were the most actively played genres of game. Gender differences were found within each genre, with the exception of sim and party games. This is surprising, as the previous investigations had found that females prefer these genres more than males. However, it is difficult to draw conclusions across gender, as the current sample reflects a more active male game playing population and a less active female game playing population than the previous studies. Similar to previous findings, age effects were largely absent, suggesting that play frequency and genre preferences remain stable over time. Regarding game modality, males and females retained a preference for single-player over multiplayer play, regardless of genre.

As the current sample is a large and diverse adult population, with a considerable distribution of participants across age and gender categories, the play patterns uncovered here are likely representative of play behaviors across the (Caucasian) adult game playing community. Given the sample's characteristics, it seems appropriate for exploring associations between attachment, social skills, and video game involvement.

6.6   RESULTS

6.6.1   Attachment and Emotional Motivations for Play

To evaluate the associations between attachment and emotional motivations for play, partial correlations (controlling for gender and age) were analyzed within the different game playing communities (see Table 6.6).

Table 6.6 Partial correlations (controlling for age and gender) between emotional motivations for play and insecure attachment across game playing groups

	All Participants (N = 514)		Active Online and Offline (n = 145)		Offline Only (n = 102)		Online Only (n = 62)	
	Anxious	Avoidant	Anxious	Avoidant	Anxious	Avoidant	Anxious	Avoidant
Motivation Comfort	.249***	.130*	.238**	.053	.201*	.074	.313*	.328*
Entertainment	.022	.026	-.059	-.002	.031	.083	-.362**	-.107

***p < .001, **p < .01, *p < .05

As predicted, attachment avoidance showed a significant, positive relationship with playing for social comfort (H_8). These effects were magnified among online-exclusive players, where attachment avoidance and anxiety showed a positive association with playing for social comfort and a negative association with playing for entertainment. However, the inverse relationships between playing for entertainment and attachment only reached significance among the anxiously attached, disputing H_9, which predicted that a significant, negative correlation between playing for entertainment and attachment avoidance would emerge.

6.6.2   Attachment, Social Skills, and Video Game Involvement

6.6.2.1   Between-Group Analyses

Broad differences in attachment were assessed between online players and non-online players with MANOVA analyses. Participants were categorized by their current play patterns, and players who reported engaging in online-exclusive video game play were compared to the general sample (i.e., all other participants). If social compensation phenomena underlie the motivation to engage in OVG play through attachment, online-exclusive game players should exhibit a higher degree of insecure attachment as compared to those who do not exclusively engage in OVG play. When controlling for gender and age, no significant differences were found between online-exclusive players ($n = 61$) and non-online-exclusive players ($n = 447$) for anxious or avoidant attachment (F's $< .61$, p's $< .05$), suggesting an absence of broad differences in attachment between online-exclusive players and non-online-exclusive players.

As Studies 1 and 2 uncovered no broad differences in SSI outcomes across game playing categories, these analyses were not replicated here.

6.6.2.2   Within-Group Analyses

To determine the statistical association between attachment, SSI subscale scores, and levels of Involvement, Involvement was regressed by both attachment scales and all six of the SSI subscales. As there were significant gender differences within the SSI subscales, and marginally significant effects with the ECR, gender (dummy coded) was entered as a variable in the regression. Age was also included to account for any variability across age groups. Prior to analysis, standardized residuals were calculated in order to identify any outliers with residuals two or more standard deviations away from the mean. Of the 409 Caucasian players who met the age criteria, 23 outliers were identified and removed, leaving 386 participants (this includes participants who reported to be "inactive" players of offline and online games but also report a play frequency greater than "never").

To evaluate the potential differences in the relationship between Involvement and social skills across different game playing communities, analyses were conducted within current play level categories (i.e., actively play online and offline games, actively play offline games only, actively play online games only). It was predicted that the previous findings would replicate and increased video game involvement would show inverse relationships with Social Expressivity (SE) and a positive relationship with Emotional Sensitivity (ES) as measured by the SSI (H_{10}—H_{11}). In line with the findings of Studies 1 and 2, the relationship between ES and Involvement should also be magnified among online-exclusive players. A positive association with attachment avoidance and Involvement within online-exclusive players was also predicted to emerge (H_7). The total amount of variance explained in the final model and beta weights of each individual predictor are shown in Table 6.7.

Among active online and offline players, increased ES and decreased SE outcomes were found to predict increased levels of video game involvement,

Table 6.7 Total R^2 and unstandardized beta weights for individual predictors in the final model: Social skills

		All Participants	Active Online and Offline	Offline Only	Online Only
		($n = 386$)	($n = 136$)	($n = 102$)	($n = 57$)
Step 2					
	Anxious	.069	.133	−.055	−.138
	Avoidant	.012	−.029	−.030	.295
Step 3					
	Anxious	.095	−.050	.144	−.263
	Avoidant	−.063	.083	−.530*	.556*
	EE	−.127	.211	−.845**	1.02
	ES	.634***	.450***	−.131	.506
	EC	−.126	−.240	.160	.266
	SE	−.098	−.477**	−.268	.102
	SS	−.208	.213	−.323	.072
	SC	−.065	.287	.230	−.167
R^2 Change					
	Step 2	.001	.007	.001	.037
	Step 3	.058***	.107**	.113	.093
Total R^2					
	Step 2	.183	.189	.111	.153
	Step 3	.242	.296	.223	.246

***$p < .001$, **$p < .01$, *$p < .05$

Note: This table has been reprinted from *Computer and human behavior*, R. Kowert and J. A. Oldmeadow, Playing for social comfort: Online video game play as a social accommodator for the insecurely attached, online ahead of print. Copyright 2014, with permission from Elsevier.

supporting the predictions of H_{10} and H_{11}. These patterns are reminiscent Study 2's findings, which also found higher outcomes on the ES subscale and lower outcomes on the SE subscale to significantly predict Involvement levels within this subgroup. Additionally, supporting H_7, avoidant attachment emerged as a significant negative predictor of Involvement among offline-exclusive players and a positive predictor among online-exclusive players.

6.6.2.2.1 MEDIATION ANALYSES

To determine if social skills mediate the effects of attachment on Involvement, extensive mediation analyses were undertaken within each gaming subgroup (i.e., all participants, offline and online players, offline only, online only) using PROCESS (Hayes, 2013). No significant effects of mediation between any of the SSI subscales, within any of the subgroups, were found for the relationship between attachment and video game involvement.

A lack of primary relationships between Involvement and attachment in Step 2 of the regression analyses and no evidence of social skills mediating a relationship between Involvement and attachment indicates the unlikelihood that the relationships between social skills and Involvement are underpinned by insecure attachment.

6.7 DISCUSSION

The current study explored the relationships between social skills and video game involvement through the perspective of attachment theory, examining its potential as an underlying impetus behind the relationship between social skills and OVG involvement. As before, significant linear relationships between social skills and video game involvement emerged, confirming that more involved video game players perceive themselves to be emotionally sensitive (ES) with a lower ability to socially engage others in fluid conversation (SE). While the positive relationship between ES and Involvement remained equivalent among online-exclusive players, the effects of SE diminished. No additional relationships between social skills and Involvement were evident.

A lack of direct relationships between attachment and Involvement suggests that attachment does not drive video game play in a substantial way. Considering the lack of mediation effects (see section 6.6.2.2.1) and no broad differences in attachment between online and non-online players (see section 6.6.2.1), the current results indicate that individuals who engage in OVG play are unlikely doing so to compensate for inept social skills underpinned by an insecure attachment. However, significant correlations between attachment and emotional motivations for play and a positive linear relationship between attachment avoidance and Involvement emerging in the final model of the regression do suggest that the motivation to engage in OVG play does seem to be, at least partially, attributable to avoidant attachment.

Traditionally, individuals high in attachment avoidance avoid closeness with others, value their self-sufficiency, and perceive no need for social relationships. Due to the belief they will eventually be disappointed, these individuals largely dismiss and avoid interpersonal relationships, putting them at risk for social isolation (Buote et al., 2009; E. Smith et al., 1999). However, the proliferation of Internet-based social spaces has led to a social revolution, allowing individuals to easily connect with others in a variety of computer-mediated environments. These virtual social spaces are believed to be particularly desirable, and potentially beneficial, for those high in attachment avoidance, as they can accommodate their need to retain autonomy by promoting the development and maintenance of interpersonal relationships without the need for physical proximity, while also helping them overcome their traditional difficulties with self-disclosure through the provision of visual anonymity and the reduced amount of social cues found online (Lea & Spears, 1995; McKenna & Bargh, 2000; Parks & Floyd, 1996; Reis & Shaver, 1988; Suler, 2004). By accommodating for their traditional difficulties with self-disclosure and allowing for the retention of autonomy through physical distance, OVGs seem to be well suited for avoidant individuals to form, and maintain, intimate bonds online that may have been unattainable in traditional contexts. However, as avoidant attachment did not emerge as a significant individual predictor until the final regression model, the relationship between attachment and Involvement seems to be intertwined with social skills outcomes. Thus, avoidant attachment *and* social skills seem to hold a significant role in Involvement within online-exclusive play. The negative correlations between attachment avoidance and the EE, SE, and SC subscales suggest that social difficulties for avoidant individuals may primarily lie with the abilities associated with those subscales. However, as these subscales did not emerge as consistent, significant individual predictors of Involvement among online-exclusive players in previous assessments, their relationship with Involvement may be minimal.

While attachment seems to play a motivational role in OVG involvement, the linear relationships between attachment and Involvement were limited to attachment avoidance. As predicted, this indicates that online gaming spaces may not be particularly suitable, or desirable, for individuals with high attachment anxiety. Unlike avoidant individuals, those high in attachment anxiety tend to hold a preoccupation with relationships (E. Smith et al., 1999) and are in constant pursuit of excessive closeness with others (Buote et al., 2009). This difference is also evidenced in the correlation analyses. Attachment anxiety showed significant, positive correlations with playing for social comfort within offline and online game playing populations. Thus, unlike avoidant individuals, those high in attachment anxiety seem to be seeking social closeness with others from offline and online social contexts. As a wide variety of Internet-based mediated outlets can potentially generate social satisfaction for individuals high in attachment anxiety (Buote et al., 2009; Oldmeadow et al., 2013), it is possible that the particular qualities of OVGs may not be as necessary, or appealing, to anxious individuals, as compared to avoidant individuals, who may need greater social safeguards, such as visual anonymity. Thus, while both anxious and avoidant attachment showed a significant association with playing for social comfort, these environments seem to be particularly suited for, and utilized to a greater extent by, avoidant individuals.

Taken together, the current results suggest that the motivation to engage in OVG play does seem to be, at least partially, attributable to avoidant attachment. Significant links between avoidant attachment, social skills, and Involvement within the subgroup of online-exclusive players suggests that online players seek social comfort within these spaces that, potentially, socially accommodate for the traditional social challenges associated with attachment avoidance. Rather than being a primary source of entertainment, and unlike traditional video game play, which displayed inverse relationships with attachment avoidance, the playful, social spaces of OVGs seem to hold the potential to be socially beneficial, bringing individuals together within a shared, social space and providing social comfort. However, the role of attachment was limited to play motivations, as a lack of direct relationships between attachment and Involvement indicates that attachment does not drive video game play in a substantial way.

6.7.1   Limitations

One limitation of this study was the relatively small sample size across age and gender categories. The overall sample size was smaller than utilized previously in Study 2, which led to disproportionate sample sizes across ages and game play categories. Future research should aim to recruit a greater sample of players across age brackets and gaming categories to more comprehensively evaluate these relationships. Furthermore, while this sample contained the largest group of online-exclusive players, an even larger sample would provide more reliable evaluations into the potential relationships among this subgroup of players.

Not assessing participants' other online preferences also limits the generalizability of the current findings. For instance, the relationship between avoidant attachment and online-exclusive play could be a single element of a broader preference for mediated communication. Online-exclusive players may be less motivated to engage within a playful, social environment, but may simply hold a desire to engage within any visually anonymous, mediated social outlet. Further research is needed to determine if the features of play within online games contribute a key element to their desirability, or if these relationships are solely driven by the ability of OVGs to provide an easily accessible, mediated, and visually anonymous space.

6.7.2   Conclusions

This study evaluated the relationships between insecure attachment, social skills, and video game involvement. These results signify that reliable relationships between social skills and video game involvement do exist, with consistent relationships between SE, ES, and Involvement across all game players, both offline and online. The only unique relationship with social skills exhibited by online-exclusive players is a positive relationship with ES, indicating higher rates of emotional sensitivity than the broader video game playing sample. Significant links between attachment, emotional motivations for play, and online-exclusive play suggest that OVGs' social functionality may extend beyond the ability to accommodate for the particular social profiles of OVG players. The incorporation of visual anonymity and play within an easily accessible Internet-based social space also seems to hold the potential to serve attachment functions for those high in attachment avoidance. Rather than avoiding others, individuals high in attachment avoidance reported being more involved online-exclusive players and utilizing them for their social functionality more so than their primary purpose of entertainment. While significant links between OVG involvement and avoidant attachment suggest that online gaming environments may provide a social outlet that promotes the sense of closeness, belonging, and security that satisfies attachment for those high in attachment avoidance, the desire to obtain social comfort within online gaming environments remains detached from the primary relationships between social skills and Involvement, indicating the unlikelihood that online game players are engaging within these spaces to compensate for social skill difficulties underpinned by an insecure attachment.

Taken together, these results indicate that more involved video game players exhibit different social skill profiles. However, the relationships between social skills and video game involvement are neither limited to the subgroup of online game players nor attributable to an underlying insecure attachment. The relationships between video game involvement and social skill outcomes appear to be driven by social displacement phenomena, as no broad differences in attachment between online-exclusive, and non-online-exclusive, players were found and increased Involvement demonstrated linear relationships with social skill outcomes that were not mediated by attachment. Thus, while the desire to seek social comfort driven by insecure attachment may motivate OVG play, it does not mediate the relationship between social skill outcomes and Involvement. It can be concluded that significant relationships between social skills and video game involvement exist and that players high in avoidant attachment seem to be more drawn to online gaming environments to obtain social comfort, but these two phenomena are not inexorably intertwined.

NOTES

1. As attachment forms in childhood, a positive linear relationship between attachment avoidance and Involvement (H_{7b}) would not suggest social displacement, but rather that increased OVG involvement linearly corresponds with higher levels of avoidant attachment.
2. Online games are considered to be a less mainstream form of mediated communication in terms of their popularity as indicated by use data. A state of the industry report by Spil Games (2013) reported that there are 700 million online game players worldwide. While sizable, it is still 500 million users less than those who use Facebook (1.23 billion users; C. Smith, 2014), which is just one of many social networking websites and chat client providers available today.
3. This measure is discussed in more detail in section 6.4.1.3.
4. While limiting the sample to Caucasian participants was determined a priori, significant differences on the ES ($F = 4.34$, $p < .05$) and EC ($F = 15.03$, $p < .001$) subscales of the SSI and the Anxious ($F = 16.40$, $p < .001$) and Avoidant ($F = 4.69$, $p < .05$) subscales of the ECR were found (while controlling for age and gender). This variation in outcomes supports the theoretical differences in video game culture and social skills across Eastern and Western populations as outlined in section 4.3.1.1 and substantiates their exclusion from further analyses.

REFERENCES

Ainsworth, M.D.S., Blehar, M. C., Wathers, E., & Wall, S. (1978). *Patterns of attachment*. Hillsdale, NJ: Lawrence Erlbaum.

Allen, J., Marsh, P., McFarland, C., McElhaney, K., Land, D., Jodi, K., & Peck, S. (2002). Attachment and autonomy as predictors of the development of social skills and deliquency during midadolescence. *Journal of Consulting and Clinical Psychology, 70*(1), 56–66.

Attwood, T. (2000). Strategies for improving the social integration of children with Asperger syndrome. *Autism, 4,* 85–100.

Baldwin, M. W., & Fehr, B. (1995). On the instability of attachment style ratings. *Personal Relationships, 2,* 247–261.

Barnhill, G. (2011). What is Asperger syndrome? *Intervention in School and Clinic, 36*(5), 259–265.

Bartholomew, K., & Horowitz, L. M. (1991). Attachment styles among young adults. *Journal of Personality and Social Psychology, 61*(2), 226–244.

Bell, N., Avery, A., Jenkins, D., Feld, J., & Schoenrock, C. (1985). Family relationships and social competence during late adolescence. *Journal of Youth and Adolescence, 14,* 109–119.

Benoit, D., & Parker, K. (1994). Stability and transmission of attachment across three generations. *Child Development, 65,* 1444–1456.

Berlin, L. J., Cassidy, J., & Appleyard, K. (2008). The influence of early attachments on other relationships. In J. Cassidy & P. Shaver (Eds.), *Handbook of attachment: Theory, research and clinical applications*. New York and London: Guilford Press.

Bifulco, A., Moran, P., Ball, C., & Bernazzani, O. (2002). Adult attachment style, I: Its relationship to clincial depression. *Social Psychiatry and Psychiatric Epidemiology, 37*(2), 50–59.

Bowlby, J. (1969). *Attachment and loss. Vol. 1: Attachment*. New York: Basic Books.

Bowlby, J. (1973). *Attachment and loss. Vol. 2: Separation: Anger and anxiety*. London: Hogarth.

Bowlby, J. (1979). *The making and breaking of affectional bonds*. London: Tavistock.

Brennan, K. A., Clark, C. L., & Shaver, P. R. (1998). Self-report measure of adult attachment: An integrative overview. In J. A. Simpson & W. S. Rholes (Eds.), Attachment theory and close relationships (pp. 46–76). New York: Guilford Press.

Buote, V., Wood, E., & Pratt, M. (2009). Exploring similarities and differences between online and offline friendships: The role of attachment style. *Computers in Human Behavior, 25,* 560–567.

Bureau, P. R. (2008). *2008 World population data sheet*. Retrieved from http://www.prb.org/Publications/Datasheets/2008/2008wpds.aspx

Butzer, B., & Campbell, L. (2008). Adult attachment, sexual satisfaction, and relationship satisfaction: A study of married couples. *Personal Relationships, 15,* 141–154.

Cassidy, J., Kirsh, S., Scolton, K., & Parke, R. (1996). Attachment and representations of peer relationships. *Developmental Psychology, 32*(5), 892–904.

Church, C., Alisanski, S., & Amanullah, S. (2000). The social, behavioural, and academic experiences of children with Asperger syndrome. *Focus on Autism and Other Development Disabilities, 15*(1), 12–20.

Cole, H., & Griffiths, M. D. (2007). Social interactions in massively multiplayer online role-playing games. *Cyberpsychology and Behavior, 10*(4), 575–583.

Collins, N., & Allard, L. (2004). Cognitive represenations of attachment: The content and function of working models. In M. Brewer & M. Hewstone (Eds.), *Social cognition*. Malden, MA: Blackwell Publishing.

Cooper, M. L., Shaver, P., & Collins, N. (1998). Attachment styles, emotion regulation, and adjustment in adolescence. *Journal of Personality and Social Psychology, 74*(5), 1380–1397.

Deniz, M., Hamarta, E., & Ari, R. (2005). An investigation of social skills and loneliness levels of university students with respect to their attachment styles in a sample of Turkish students. *Social Behaviour and Personality, 33*(1), 19–32.

DiTommaso, E., Brannen-McNulty, C., Ross, L., & Burgess, M. (2003). Attachment styles, social skills and loneliness in young adults. *Personality and Indivdiual Differences, 35*(2), 303–312.

Ducheneaut, N., Yee, N., Nickell, E., & Moore, R. (2006). "Alone together?": Exploring the social dynamics of massively multiplayer online games. In *SIGCHI Conference on Human Factors in Computing Systems*. New York: ACM.

Eng, W., Heimberg, R., Hart, T., Schneier, F., & Liebowitz, M. R. (2001). Attachment in individuals with social anxiety disorder: The relationship among adult attachment styles, social anxiety, and depression. *Emotion, 1*(4), 365–380.

Engles, R., Finkenauer, C., Meeus, W., & Dekovic, M. (2001). Parental attachment and adolescents' emotional adjustment: The associations with social skills and relational competence. *Journal of Counseling Psychology, 48*(4), 428–439.

Fattig, M. (2008). Early indicators: High functioning autism and Aspergers syndrome. *Diabled World*. Retrieved from http://www.disabled-world.com/artman/publish/article_2255.shtml

Feeny, J., & Noller, P. (1990). Attachment style as a predictor of adult romantic relationships. *Journal of Personality and Social Psychology, 58*(2), 281–291.

Field, A. (2009). *Discovering statistics using SPSS*. London: SAGE Publications.

Fombonne, E., & Tidmarsh, L. (2003). Epidemiologic data on Asperger disorder. *Child and Adolecent Psychiatric Clinics of North America, 12*(1), 15–21.

Fraley, R. C. (2002). Attachment stability from infancy to adulthood: Meta-analysis and dynamic modeling of developmental mechanisms. *Personality and Social Psychology Review, 6*(2), 123–151.

Ghuman, D., & Griffiths, M. D. (2012). A cross-genre study of online gaming: Player demographics, motivation for play, and social interactions among players. *International Journal of Cyber Behavior, Psychology, and Learning, 2*(1), 13–29.

Griffiths, M. D., Davies, M., & Chappell, D. (2004). Demographic factors and playing variables in online computer gaming. *Cyberpsychology and Behavior, 7,* 479–487.

Griffiths, M. D., & Hunt, N. (1998). Dependence on computer games by adolescents. *Psychologial Reports, 82,* 475–480.

Gutstein, S., & Whitney, T. (2002). Asperger syndrome and the development of social competence. *Focus on Autism and Other Development Disabilities, 17*(3), 161–171.

Hamann, D., Lineburg, N., & Paul, S. (1998). Teaching effectiveness and social skill development. *Journal of Research in Music Education, 46,* 87–101.

Hamilton, C. (2000). Continuity and discontinuity of attachment from infancy through adolescence. *Child Development, 71,* 690–694.

Hayes, A. F. (2013). *An introduction to mediation, moderation, and conditional process analysis: A regression-based approach.* New York: Guilford Press.

Hazan, C., & Shaver, P. (1987). Romantic love concepulized as an attachment process. *Journal of Personality and Social Psychology, 52*(3), 511–524.

Hazan, C., & Shaver, P. (1990). Love and work: An attachment theoretical perspective. *Journal of Personality and Social Psychology, 59*(2), 270–280.

Hazan, C., & Shaver, P. (1994). Attachment as an organizational framework for research on close relationships. *Psychologial Inquiry, 5*(1), 1–22.

Hsu, S., Wen, M., & Wu, M. (2009). Exploring user experiences as predictors of MMORPG addiction. *Computers and Education, 53*(3), 990–999.

Iacono, C. S., & Weisband, S. (1997). Developing trust in virtual teams. In *Hawaii International Conference on System Sciences.* Hawaii.

Irons, C., & Gilbert, P. (2005). Evolved mechanisms in adolescent anxiety and depression symptoms: The role of the attachment and social rank systems. *Journal of Adolescence, 28*(3), 325–341.

Kim, E., Namkoong, K., Ku, T., & Kim, S. (2008). The relationship between online game addiction and aggression, self-control, and narcissistic personality traits. *European Psychiatry, 23*(3), 212–218.

Klohnen, E. C., & Bera, S. (1998). Behavioral and experiential patterns of avoidantly and securely attached women across adulthood: A 31-year longitudinal study. *Journal of Personality and Social Psychology, 74*(1), 211–223.

Langlois, M. (2011). *Video games and psychotherapy.* Cambridge, MA: Chateau Escargot Publishing.

Lea, M., & Spears, R. (1995). Love at first byte? Building personal relationships over computer networks. In J. T. Wood & S. W. Duck (Eds.), *Understudied relatonships: Off the beaten track* (pp. 197–233). Newbury Park, CA: Sage.

Lee, A., & Hankin, B. (2009). Insecure attachment, dysfunctional attitudes, and low self-esteem predicting prospective symptoms of depression and anxiety during adolescence. *Journal of Clinical Child and Adolescent Psychology, 38*(2), 219–231.

Lo, S., Wang, C., & Fang, W. (2005). Physical interpersonal relationships and social anxiety among online game players. *Cyberpsychology and Behavior, 8*(1), 15–20.

McKenna, K., & Bargh, J. (2000). Plan 9 from cyberspace: The implications of the Internet for personality and social psychology. *Personality and Social Psychology Review, 4*(1), 57–75.

Miell, D. E., & Duck, S. (1986). Strategies in developing friendships. In V. J. Derlega & B. A. Winstead (Eds.), *Friends and social interaction* (pp. 129–143). New York: Springer-Verlag.

Mikulincer, M., & Shaver, P. (2007). *Attachment in adulthood: Structure, dynamics and change.* New York: Guilford Press.

Morahan-Martin, J., & Schumacher, P. (2003). Loneliness and social uses of the Internet. *Computers in Human Behavior, 19,* 659–671.

Moyes, R. (2001). *Incorporating social goals in the classroom: A guide for teachers and parents of children with high-functioning autism and Asperger syndrome.* Philadelphia, PA: Jessica Kingsley Publishers.

Mullen, S. (2009). Adolescents with Aspergers syndrome and self-perceived social competence. Unpublished doctoral dissertation. Philadelphia College of Osteopathic Medicine, Philadelphia, PA.

Myles, B. S., & Adreon, D. (2001). *Asperger syndrome and adolescence*. Shanee Mission, KS: Autism Asperger Publishing.

Nada Raja, S., McGee, R., & Stanton, W. (1992). Perceived attachment to parents and peers and psychological well-being in adolescence. *Journal of Youth and Adolescence, 21*, 471–485.

Oldmeadow, J., Quinn, S., & Kowert, R. (2013). Attachment style, social skills, and Facebook use amongst adults. *Computers in Human Behavior, 29*(3), 1142–1149.

Parks, M. R., & Floyd, K. (1996). Making friends in cyberspace. *Journal of Communication, 46*, 80–97.

Perse, E. (2008). *Media effects and society*. Mahwah, NJ: Lawerence Erlbaum.

Ponder, E. (2009). *Attachment and Internet relationships*. PhD dissertation. Wheaton College, Wheaton, Illinois.

Reis, H.T.T., & Shaver, P. (1988). Intimacy as an interpersonal process. In S. Duck (Ed.), *Handbook of personal relationships* (pp. 367–389). Chichester, UK: Wiley.

Rice, K. G. (1990). Attachment in adolescence: A narrative and meta-analytic review. *Journal of Youth and Adolescence, 19*(5), 511–538.

Rice, K. G., Cunningham, T. J., & Young, M. B. (1997). Attachment to parents, social competence, and emotional well-being. *Journal of Counseling Psychology, 44*(1), 89–101.

Riggio, R. (1989). *Manual for the Social Skills Inventory*. Palo Alto, CA: Consulting Psychologists Press.

Riggio, R., Throckmorton, B., & DePaola, S. (1990). Social skills and self-esteem. *Personality and Indivdiual Differences, 11*(8), 799–804.

Roberts, J., Gotlib, I., & Kassel, J. (1996). Adult attachment security and symptoms of depression: The mediating roles of dysfunctional attitudes and low self-esteem. *Journal of Personality and Social Psychology, 70*(2), 310–320.

Rosengren, K. E. (1974). Uses and graticiations: A paradigm outlined. In J. G. Blumer & E. Katz (Eds.), *The uses of mass communications: Current perspectives on gratifications research* (Vol. 3, pp. 269–286). Beverly Hills, CA: Sage Publications.

Rubin, A.M. (2002). The uses-and-gratifications perspective of media effects. In J. Bryant & D. Zillmann (Eds.), *Media effects: Advances in theory and research* (2nd ed., pp. 525–548). Mahwah, NJ: Lawrence Erlbaum.

Safran, S., Safran, J., & Ellis, K. (2003). Intervention ABCs for children with Asperger syndrome. *Topics in Language Disorders, 23*(2), 154–165.

Schaffer, R. (2007). *Introducing child psychology*. Oxford: Blackwell.

Scharfe, E., & Bartholomew, K. (1994). Reliability and stability of adult attachment patterns. *Personal Relationships, 9*, 51–64.

Schneider, B. H., & Younger, A. J. (1996). Adolescent-parent attachment and adolescents' relations with their peers: A closer look. *Youth and Society, 28*, 95–108.

Schramm, W., Lyle, J., & Parker, E. B. (1961). *Television in the lives of our children*. Stanford, CA: Stanford University Press.

Segrin, C. (1996). The relationship between social skills deficits and psychosocial problems. A test of a vulnerability model. *Communication Research, 23*, 425–450.

Segrin, C. (1998). Interpersonal communication problems associated with depression and loneliness. In P. Andersen & L. Guerrero (Eds.), *Handbook of communication and emotion: Research, theory, applications, and contexts* (pp. 215–242). San Diego, CA: Academic Press.

Segrin, C., & Flora, J. (2000). Poor social skills are a vulnerability factor in the development of psychosocial problems. *Human Commuication Research, 26*(3), 489–514.

Sibley, C., Fischer, R., & Liu, J. (2005). Reliability and validity of the Revised Experiences in Close Relationships (ECR-R) self-report measure of adult romantic attachment. *Personality and Social Psychology Bulletin, 31*(11), 1524–1536.

Smith, C. (2014). How many people use 370 of the top social media, apps and tools? *Digital Market Media Ramblings (DMR)*. Retrieved from http://expandedram blings.com/index.php/resource-how-many-people-use-the-top-social-media/

Smith, E., Murphy, J., & Coats, S. (1999). Attachment to groups: Theory and measurement. *Journal of Personality and Social Psychology, 77*(1), 94–110.

Spil Games. (2013). *State of online gaming report*. Retrieved from http://auth-8 3051f68-ec6c-44e0-afe5-bd8902acff57.cdn.spilcloud.com/v1/archi ves/1384952861.25_State_of_Gaming_2013_US_FINAL.pdf

Sroufe, L. A., & Fleeson, J. (1986). Attachment and the construction of relationships. In W. Hartup & Z. Rubin (Eds.), *Relationships and development* (pp. 51–57). Hillsdale, NJ: Erlbaum.

Steinkuehler, C., & Williams, D. (2006). Where everybody knows your (screen) name: Online games as "third places." *Journal of Computer-Mediated Communication, 11*(4), 885–909.

Suler, J. (2004). The online disinhibition effect. *Cyberpsychology and Behavior, 7*(3), 321–326.

Tatum, D. (2000). Psychologial disorder in adolescents and adults with Asperger syndrome. *Autism, 4*(1), 47–62.

Thompson, R. (2010). Attachment and life history: A rejoinder. *Child Development Perspectives, 4*(2), 106–108.

TMachine.org. (2008). *More than 1 billion people play online games in 2008*. Retrieved from http://t-machine.org/index.php/2008/11/18/more-than-1-billion-people-play-online-games-in-2008/

Urban, J., Carlson, E., Egeland, B., & Sroufe, L. (1991). Patterns of indivdual adaption across childhood. *Development and Psychopathology, 3*, 445–460.

Walther, J. (1996). Computer-mediated communication: Impersonal, interpersonal, and hyperpersonal interaction. *Communication Research, 23*(1), 3–43.

Waters, E., Merrick, S., Treboux, D., Crowell, J., & Albersheim, L. (2000). Attachment security infancy and early adulthood: A twenty-year longitudinal study. *Child Development, 71*(3), 684–689.

Wei, M., Russell, D. W., Mallinckrodt, B., & Vogel, D. (2007). The Experiences in Close Relationship scale (ECR)—Short form: Reliability, validity, and factor structure. *Journal of Personality Assessment, 88*(2), 187–204.

Wellman, B., & Wortley, S. (1990). Different strokes for different folks: Community ties and social support. *American Journal of Sociology, 96*(3), 558–588.

Williams, D. (2006). Groups and goblins: The social and civic impact of online games. *Journal of Broadcasting and Electronic Media, 50*, 651–681.

Williams, D., Martins, N., Consalvo, M., & Ivory, J. (2009). The virtual census: Representations of gender, race and age in video games. *New Media & Society, 11*(5), 815–834.

Williams, D., Yee, N., & Caplan, S. (2008). Who plays, how much, and why? Debunking the stereotypical gamer profile. *Journal of Computer-Mediated Communication Monographs, 13*(4), 993–1018.

Wiseman, H., Mayseless, O., & Sharabany, R. (2006). Why are they lonely? Perceived quality of early relationships with parents, attachment, personality predispositions and loneliness in first-year university students. *Personality and Indivdiual Differences, 40*(2), 237–248.

Yee, N. (2002). Befriending ogres and wood-elves—Understanding relationship formation in MMORPGs. *Nickyee*. Retrieved from http://www.nickyee.com/hub/relationships/home.html

Yee, N. (2006). The demographics, motivations, and derived experiences of users of massively-multi-user online graphical environments. *Teleoperators and Virtual Environments, 15*(3), 309–329.

7 Research Findings and Implications

The work contained within this monograph aimed to evaluate the relationship between social skills and OVG involvement among adult players to uncover if and how OVG involvement supports or undermines the development and maintenance of traditional social skills. This chapter will discuss the primary findings from the empirical work contained within this monograph and outline the theoretical and practical implications of these findings. It will begin with an overview of the demographic assessments. Next, an examination of the findings related to social goals, social skills, attachment, and video game involvement will be presented. The social utility of OVGs and the potential social gains and losses will also be discussed. This chapter will conclude with a review of the strengths and limitations of the current work.

7.1 RESEARCH AIMS AND MAIN FINDINGS

7.1.1 Demographic Assessment

Previous demographic work has largely neglected the video gaming population as a whole by being limited to more specialist gaming groups, such as MMORPG players (Cole & Griffiths, 2007; Griffiths, Davies, & Chappell, 2004; Kolo & Baur, 2004; Shen & Williams, 2010; Williams, Ducheneaut, Xiong, Yee, & Nickell, 2006; Williams, Yee, & Caplan, 2008; Yee, 2006, 2007) or addicted populations (Kim et al., 2008; Wan & Chiou, 2006). In order to broaden the understanding of the demographic characteristics of the video game playing community, the current research evaluated a wide variety of demographic variables across gender and age categories within a broader video game playing sample. To ensure the recruitment of a broad sample, participants were recruited from multiple avenues: online advertisements, Amazon's Mechanical Turk, and the electronic booking system of the University of York's Department of Psychology. Online advertisements on video game–related websites targeted the more highly involved players, whereas the participant pool obtained from the University of York and MTurk aimed to recruit a broader spectrum of video game players, ranging from the casual to the more involved. Additionally, participant recruitment targeted an adult game playing population to ensure evaluations were independent of any developmental influences on social competence.

A summary of the demographic findings across all three studies is presented in the following ($N = 1526$), and the theoretical and practical implications that can be drawn from these outcomes are discussed. It is important to note that the findings discussed here are only applicable to the samples in which they were sourced. As the samples enlisted within this monograph were not representative samples (i.e., not drawn from the general population), these findings should not be considered typical of all game players but rather game players within university and online-sourced populations. A discussion of the sample bias is discussed further in section 7.2.2.3.

7.1.1.1   *Theoretical Implications*

7.1.1.1.1   NORMATIVENESS

The results of the demographic assessments undertaken within this sample indicate the relative normativeness of video game play within university and online-sourced samples and counter the common perception of online gaming as an activity only enjoyed by a niche group of individuals. On average, 89.03% of all participants reported playing video games at some point, and 77.96% of those participants reported experience with OVG play. A majority of participants (58.13%) reported engaging in video game play at least once a week. Males were found to play a greater variety of video game genres and reported more frequent video game play (between 1–10 hours per week) than females (between once a month and once a week). Similar gender differences were found for OVG play frequency, with males reporting an average of once per week to 1–5 hours a week of online play and females reporting an average of once a month. The more frequent players (10 hours a week or more) constituted only one-fifth (20.56%) of the sample. It is notable that this rate of media consumption is substantially less than what has been found for other forms of popular media (for example, a 2012 report by the Broadcasters Alliance Research Board found that the average UK resident reported watching 31.96 hours a week of TV). Therefore, rather than being a niche activity predominantly enjoyed by young teenage males, video game play (both off- and online) appears to be a common leisure activity engaged in on a regular (and not typically obsessive) basis across gender and age categories within university and online-sourced samples.

7.1.1.1.2   HETEROGENEITY OF VIDEO GAME PLAY

While the frequency evaluations illustrate the relative normativeness of video game play, the assessment of video game preferences demonstrates video games' growth and versatility. Video games are no longer specialist activities that are engaged in within dedicated arcade parlors. In fact, twice as many participants reported playing video games on a computer than a dedicated games console. Furthermore, video game players reported enjoying a variety of games, with more than three-quarters of all participants reporting regularly playing more than one game genre/modality combination.

While the vast majority of participants reported playing video games on a computer (72.78%), the use of dedicated video game consoles remains popular. Sony's consoles (e.g., PlayStation 2, PlayStation 3, etc.) were the most popular, with 36.43% of participants reporting active use, followed by Nintendo (e.g., SNES, GameCube, Wii, etc.) with 33.56% of participants, and Microsoft (e.g., Xbox, Xbox 360) with 30.26% of participants. In addition, approximately one-third (31.70%) of all participants reported playing video games on their smartphones. Most individuals reported playing between one and six different genres of video games (66.19%), with the most popular genres being puzzle, party, FPS, and RPG. Male players reported a preference for FPS and RPGs, while females' genre preferences were indicative of more casual game play, with sim, party, and puzzle games consistently emerging as their most frequently played genres. Genre preferences reported in the "other" category varied widely, but the most commonly reported genres were platformers (e.g., *Mario Brothers* series), action-adventure games (e.g., the *Uncharted* series), and Sandbox games (e.g., *Minecraft*).

7.1.1.1.3 SINGLE-PLAYER VERSUS MULTIPLAYER INVOLVEMENT

While online multiplayer video games are often perceived to be more involving than offline single-player games, engaging within a multiplayer modality did not guarantee higher levels of Involvement. FPS and puzzle games were the only genres to show consistent variation in Involvement levels across modalities, with players of the multiplayer modalities showing significantly higher levels of Involvement than their single-player counterparts. The strongest differences found between modalities were within the puzzle genre. However, this divergence in Involvement levels may have less to do with the games themselves and more to do with the intrinsic qualities of those who choose to play these kinds of video games. Single-player puzzle games are highly popular and widely available, as they often come standard on home computers (Kuittinen, Kultima, Niemelä, & Paavilainen, 2007). Due to their accessibility, even the most sporadic gamer is likely to engage in these kinds of games. However, multiplayer puzzle games are a more recent phenomenon, are less popular, and are less accessible than their single-player counterparts. As such, multiplayer puzzle games are likely to be played only by more devoted video game players. Future researchers should remain mindful of these findings and reconsider the assumption that multiplayer games are more 'involving' than their single-player counterparts.

7.1.1.2 *Practical Implications*

7.1.1.2.1 POPULATION FOCUS

In consideration of the results discussed here, researchers should reconsider the use of MMORPG players as the standard sample for OVG research.

Since the beginning, MMORPGs have been the primary population utilized in academic assessments of OVG engagement. While not inherently problematic, researchers have consistently generalized the findings from within these smaller communities to OVG players as a whole. This is troublesome, as MMORPG players are a unique subgroup that differs from the broader online game playing community in a variety of ways.

For example, only a minority of participants in the current sample of online players were found to engage in more than 10 hours a week of game play, while reports of MMORPG players engaging in 20 or more hours per week of active game play are commonplace (Ghuman & Griffiths, 2012; Griffiths et al., 2004; Williams et al., 2008; Yee, 2006). This inordinate rate of play has contributed to numerous cases of MMORPG players suffering physical and psychological consequences due to extended game play sessions (Associated Press, 2007; BBC News, 2005; Kohn, 2002) and has led to MMORPG communities being targeted for studies on problematic and addicted use of OVGs (Kim, Namkoong, Ku, & Kim, 2008; Lemmens, Valkenburg, & Peter, 2009; Liu & Peng, 2009; Wan & Chiou, 2007). Differences between MMORPG players and the online gaming community as a whole are also evident on the cultural level, as MMORPG players are perceived to be more obsessed, reclusive, and socially inept than other video game playing groups (i.e., arcade, console, or online players) (Kowert & Oldmeadow, 2012). While the focus on this population for addiction studies is somewhat reasonable, it is not prudent to generalize these findings to the broader OVG playing community.

Thus, while MMORPG players may be an easily accessible and recruitable community of OVG players, they should not be considered representative of the broader OVG playing population. Future research should reconsider the focus on MMORPG communities when aiming to draw conclusions about OVG players more generally.

7.1.1.3 Demographic Findings: Summary
The current demographic assessment illustrates the breadth and diversity of video game play, both offline and online. While the findings of this demographic assessment largely corroborate previous findings, some new patterns were identified. Corroborating previous research (e.g., Entertainment Software Association, 2012; Ghuman & Griffiths, 2012; Williams et al., 2008), male players demonstrated higher levels of Involvement than female players by reporting greater play frequency and variety, as well as a stronger identity with the social group of gamers. While males demonstrated higher levels of Involvement than females, the vast majority of female participants reported a history of video game play, both offline and online. Females' general preference for casual games (i.e., sim, party, puzzle) likely explains their lower rates of play, as these games typically require less time commitment. Males displayed a greater frequency of play across the remaining genres; however, FPSs and RPGs emerged as the most preferred. In general, there

were few differences in Involvement levels across genres and modalities. This is interesting as it counters the belief that multiplayer RPGs (specifically, MMORPGs) are more involving for their users than other game genre/modality combinations.

Taken together, these results demonstrate that video game play is a common activity among the current sample, with a majority of participants reporting weekly engagement with this medium. Across studies, over 95% of the participants reported a history of video game play, reiterating the popularity of this activity among university and online-sourced samples and the role it is playing in their lives as a form of entertainment.

7.1.2   Social Competence and Online Video Game Involvement

The following section will review the main findings of the work contained within this monograph and discuss them in relation to the proposed hypotheses. Theoretical and practical implications will also be discussed.

7.1.2.1   *H_1: More involved video game players will rate offline social goals as less important to them, and less likely to be achieved, than less involved video game players.*

7.1.2.1.1   SUMMARY OF FINDINGS

Previous research has suggested that the perception of game players' social ineptitude may be related to a difference in social goals, not social skills (Ng & Wiemer-Hastings, 2005). That is, more involved video game players may have equal social abilities, but be less interested in offline social goals and/or perceive themselves as less able to attain offline social goals, than less involved players. To examine this possibility, broad differences in the perceived importance of, and likelihood to achieve, offline and online social goals were examined between high- and low-involved players.

Contrary to predictions, substantial differences in social goals were not found. While low-involved players did rate offline social goals as more important than highly involved players, the mean differences between groups were minimal, indicating the unlikelihood that these differences represent broad divergences in the everyday importance placed upon offline social goals. Furthermore, high- and low-involved players rated offline social goals as equally achievable, as well as significantly more important and achievable than online social goals.

Significant linear relationships between social goals and video game involvement did emerge across game playing groups, indicating that increased Involvement corresponds with social goal outcomes. Specifically, increased Involvement was found to correspond with an increase in the perceived likelihood of achieving online social goals and a decline in the interest in, and potential to achieve, offline social goals.

7.1.2.1.2 THEORETICAL IMPLICATIONS

The lack of substantial mean differences between groups largely disputes the claims put forth by Ng and Wiemer-Hastings (2005) and indicates that more involved players do not have substantially less interest in, or perceived capability of achieving, social goals in face-to-face contexts than less involved players. Regardless of one's level of Involvement, players reported the desire to socialize offline and perceive themselves as having the appropriate abilities to do so. However, linear relationships between social goals and Involvement indicate that as Involvement increases, players report less interest in, and exhibit less confidence for their ability to successfully attain, offline social goals. Combined with an increase in the perceived likelihood of achieving online social goals, these findings seem to represent a shift in social priorities and perceived abilities from offline to online socialization as Involvement increases. To explore this further, the linear relationships between Involvement and social goals were analyzed within online-exclusive players. The results of this analysis are discussed in section 7.1.2.2.1.

7.1.2.2 *H₂: Online video game players will rate offline social goals as less important to them, and less likely to be achieved, than the broader video game playing population.*

7.1.2.2.1 SUMMARY OF FINDINGS

As OVG play is a highly social activity that provides a greater array of social affordances than offline video game play, differences in players' interest and perceived likelihood to achieve offline and online social goals were predicted to be magnified among this subgroup of players. Contrary to predictions, mean differences were not found between online and non-online game players for social goal outcomes.

However, linear relationships between social goals and video game involvement were found to be magnified among online players, indicating that increased Involvement, particularly online, corresponds with social goal outcomes. Higher levels of Involvement were found to correspond with an increase in the perceived likelihood of achieving online social goals and a decrease in the interest in, and potential to achieve, offline social goals.

7.1.2.2.2 THEORETICAL IMPLICATIONS

Uncovering no substantial differences in social goals between online game players and non-online game players disputes the hypotheses put forth by Ng and Wiemer-Hastings (2005) and suggests that the underlying perception of social incompetence for OVG players is not underpinned by broad differences in social goals. However, the magnified linear relationships between social goals and Involvement for the subgroup of online game players suggests that as online players become more involved, they may experience a decline of interest in, and confidence for, their ability to successfully attain offline social goals.

The inverse relationships between Involvement, offline social interest, and the perceived likelihood to achieve offline social goals, found among the subgroup of online game players, provides preliminary support for social displacement theorists, who contend that players may begin to displace their offline contacts for online ones as they become more involved in online video game play (Cole & Griffiths, 2007; Hussain & Griffiths, 2009; Lo, Wang, & Fang, 2005; Morahan-Martin & Schumacher, 2003; Shen & Williams, 2010). This exchange of offline for online contacts is believed to impede one's ability to maintain real-world interpersonal relationships and is feared to contribute to more long-term consequences, such as a deterioration of social skills (Cole & Griffiths, 2007; Hussain & Griffiths, 2009; Lo et al., 2005; Morahan-Martin & Schumacher, 2003; Shen & Williams, 2010). The links between Involvement and social goals uncovered here provide initial support for these contentions and suggest that online players may become socially disengaged due to increased Involvement (e.g., decrease in offline interest) and, consequently, may experience tangible social consequences (e.g., decrease in offline, and increase in online, likelihood). However, it is important to note that these analyses are representative of an inverse relationship between these variables, not causal mechanisms. As such, these findings only represent a variation in players' social interest and perceived social ability that corresponds with increased Involvement, rather than the actual exchange of offline for online contacts or tangible declines in socialization.

7.1.2.3   *H₃: An inverse relationship between Social Control (SC) and video game involvement will emerge.*

7.1.2.3.1   SUMMARY OF FINDINGS

Social Control refers to one's ability to regulate his or her social self-presentation. Individuals with well-developed social control skills are adept, tactful, and self-confident in any kind of social situation (Riggio, 1989). Due to the provision of visual anonymity and asynchronous communication, a lack of non-verbal cues, and the ability to actively manipulate one's physical presentation, OVGs allow substantially greater control over one's social self-presentation than is permitted by face-to-face communication (Walther, 1996). This greater sense of control over one's impression formation can be highly desirable for those who lack effective self-presentational skills (Caplan, 2003; McKenna & Bargh, 1999) as it can compensate for the sense of social anxiety typically associated with a lack of Social Control (Leary & Kowalski, 1995; Segrin & Kinney, 1995). Consequently, the mediated social spaces found in OVGs may come to be perceived as less threatening than traditional socialization and, as a result, may become utilized to a greater extent. Reflecting this desirability, previous research has identified significant and consistent links between low SC and social Internet use (Caplan, 2005; Korgaonkar & Wolin, 1999; Utz, 2000; Walther, 1996), as well as

OVG involvement specifically (Liu & Peng, 2009). As such, significant relationships between SC and OVG involvement were predicted to emerge within the current evaluations. However, no significant links between these two variables were found.

While it has been hypothesized that the links between SC and Involvement reflect individuals' greater involvement within online games due to their ability to accommodate their social self-presentation, a lack of significant relationships between these variables in the current assessments suggests this relationship is not as straightforward. A closer examination of the previous research reveals that the inverse links between SC, social Internet use (Caplan, 2005; Korgaonkar & Wolin, 1999; Utz, 2000; Walther, 1996), and OVG involvement (Liu & Peng, 2009) have only been uncovered and discussed in relation to excessive and problematic use and/or addicted populations. As such, it is possible that the links between SC and Involvement may not be direct, but rather indicators of a broader concern. That is, lower SC among addicted and/or problematic users of OVGs could be less reflective of a weakened social self-presentation and more indicative of a broader self-regulatory deficiency.

Self-regulation forms the basis for purposeful social action through the successful application of self-monitoring (i.e., the observation of one's own actions to acquire information about the impact of the behavior on the self, others, and the environment), self-evaluation (i.e., comparing the self-observations of one's behavior against personal or societal norms and standards), and self-reactive processes (i.e., behavioral or psychological reward derived from successfully accomplishing an activity that met the desired standards) (Bandura, 1986, 1991). Diminished self-control leads to deficient self-regulation (Bandura, 1999), which has been identified as an indicator of Internet addiction (Caplan, 2005; Chak & Leung, 2004; LaRose, Mastro, & Eastin, 2001; Young, 1996, 2004). For instance, Chak and Leung (2004) uncovered an inverse relationship between locus of control and Internet addiction, but not general Internet use, indicating that people are less likely to be addicted to the Internet when they perceive themselves as being able to effectively self-regulate their behavior. The self-regulatory process of SC is also a key element of Caplan's (2005) model of problematic Internet use, as he linked low SC to an inability to control one's impulse to use the Internet. Similar links between problematic and addicted use of OVGs and SC have also been identified among OVG playing populations (Liu & Peng, 2009).

As significant relationships between SC and OVG involvement were not found to emerge in the current evaluations and have only been previously uncovered among excessive, problematic, and addicted populations, it is possible that the association between SC and OVG use is more related to deficient self-regulation than social presentation. This does not rule out the possibility that SC is linked to OVG involvement; it simply suggests that these relationships are not direct. Further research is needed to explore these links, particularly among addicted and problematic online game playing populations.

7.1.2.4 H_4: An inverse relationship between Social Expressivity (SE) and video game involvement will emerge.

7.1.2.4.1   SUMMARY OF FINDINGS

Social Expressivity refers to one's ability to engage another in social conversation and display verbal fluency (Riggio, 1989, 2005). Video game play may be a particularly desirable activity for those low in SE, as active engagement promotes socialization while reducing the pressure to initiate and guide the social interactions (de Kort & Ijsselsteijn, 2008; Gajadhar, de Kort, & IJsselsteijn, 2008; Ijsselsteijn et al., 2008; Sjöblom, 2008). Online video games provide an extra level of accommodation, as the provision of asynchronous communication could further accommodate for any limitations in verbal fluency. As previous research has uncovered consistent, inverse relationships between SE and OVG play (e.g., Lemmens, Valkenburg, & Peter, 2011), inverse links between these two variables were hypothesized to replicate in the current analyses.

This hypothesis was not fully supported. Across all three studies, significant, inverse relationships between SE and video game involvement were found within the broad video game playing population; however, they did not show unique or enhanced effects within online-exclusive players. Additionally, no broad differences in SE were found across gaming groups.

7.1.2.4.2   THEORETICAL IMPLICATIONS

While previous research has uncovered significant inverse relationships between SE and video game involvement among the online game playing community (Lemmens et al., 2011), the results contained within this monograph suggest that this relationship applies to the broader community of video game players, both offline and online. Additionally, contrary to previous claims (e.g., Lemmens et al., 2011), this relationship does not seem to be driven by social compensation mechanisms. If players were engaging in OVG play to compensate for a lack of the skills associated with SE, mean differences between game playing groups should have been evident, with OVG players exhibiting lower SE outcomes than non-online players. Instead, linear relationships emerged between SE and Involvement. Uncovering a linear association between SE and Involvement demonstrates that social skill outcomes vary with Involvement and provides support for the contention that increased video game involvement may stimulate the deterioration of effective social skills through displacement mechanisms (Cole & Griffiths, 2007; Hussain & Griffiths, 2009; Lo et al., 2005; Morahan-Martin & Schumacher, 2003; Shen & Williams, 2010). While causality cannot be determined, the inverse pattern of this relationship could be indicative of a decline in players' ability to engage and guide others in social conversation as Involvement increases.

The impact of social displacement on SE may be particularly strong due to the fact that video game play largely accommodates for the skills associated with SE. When engaged in video game play, either offline or online, the pressure to initiate and guide conversation is substantially reduced, as communication becomes intertwined, mediated, and paced, by the activity itself (Sjöblom, 2008). Gaining social success within these environments could encourage increased involvement to the detriment of other social activities and, in the case of online gaming, promote the further exchange of offline for online contacts. As the skills associated with SE are not required for effective socialization in these contexts, prolonged displacement of offline social contacts and increased interaction within this mediated social space could thwart the development of this particular skill. However, if this is the case, one could expect to see similar relationships between SE and Involvement among participants within other kinds of shared, mediated activities. Further research is needed to examine this possibility and determine if the link between SE and Involvement is unique to the use of video game involvement.

7.1.2.5 H_5: A positive relationship between Emotional Sensitivity (ES) and video game involvement will emerge.

7.1.2.5.1 SUMMARY OF FINDINGS

Emotional Sensitivity refers to one's ability to interpret the emotional, and non-verbal, cues of others (Riggio, 1989). However, high ES can also indicate a social self-consciousness characterized by a hypersensitivity to others' communicative messages (Riggio, 1989). This can behaviorally manifest itself in ways similar to shyness (Riggio, 1987), through social hesitancy in spontaneous communication, a reluctance to engage in social interactions, and/or ineffective socialization (Chak & Leung, 2004; Zimbardo, 1997).

The Internet-based, mediated social spaces of OVGs can offer an alternative social environment that can accommodate for social difficulties associated with high ES as the distinguishing features of these playful, social spaces can reduce social inhibitions (Caplan, 2002; Chak & Leung, 2004; Liu & Peng, 2009; Peng & Liu, 2010; Roberts, Smith, & Pollock, 2000; Suler, 2004; Yuen & Lavin, 2004) and remove the behavioral manifestations of shyness as an obstacle to effective communication (Scealy, Phillips, & Stevenson, 2002). While links between ES and OVG involvement have not been extensively evaluated (e.g., Kowert, Domahidi, & Quandt, 2014), previous research has found shyness to hold significant relationships with social uses of the Internet (Caplan, 2002; Chak & Leung, 2004; Roberts et al., 2000; Yuen & Lavin, 2004) as well as problematic and addicted use of online video games (Liu & Peng, 2009; Peng & Liu, 2010). Therefore, it was predicted that significant, positive links between ES and Involvement would emerge within the current evaluations.

This hypothesis was partially supported, as significant, positive linear relationships between ES and video game involvement emerged across all three studies and were magnified among online-exclusive players. However, no broad differences in ES were found across game playing groups.

7.1.2.5.2   THEORETICAL IMPLICATIONS

The emergence of significant linear relationships between ES and Involvement, but lack of broad differences in ES between groups, could indicate that as players become more involved in video game play, particularly online, they experience an increase in Emotional Sensitivity. While the effects of social displacement are often conceptualized as a "loss" in ability (Cole & Griffiths, 2007; Hussain & Griffiths, 2009; Lo et al., 2005; Morahan-Martin & Schumacher, 2003; Shen & Williams, 2010), an increase in ES may also represent a deterioration of effective 'offline' social skills for game players by indicating a hypersensitivity to the emotional cues of others. This hypersensitivity can lead to social discomfort in interpersonal situations, including social self-consciousness or avoidance (Chak & Leung, 2004; Zimbardo, 1997) and social hesitancy (Riggio & Carney, 2003; Riggio, Throckmorton, & DePaola, 1990; Riggio, 1989), all of which can inhibit social participation. This may be the case particularly for online players, as the strongest links between ES and Involvement emerged within this subgroup.

However, based on these results alone, it is unclear whether this is the case. The development of a hypersensitivity to non-verbal cues is one possibility given the relative lack of non-verbal cues in mediated spaces and the established links between ES, shyness, and social self-consciousness (Riggio, 1989). However, the links between Involvement and ES could also represent the development of a greater aptitude for the skills associated with ES. Further research is needed to determine if this is the case.

It is also unclear whether the positive associations between ES and Involvement are representative of the development of a hypersensitivity to offline, non-verbal cues underpinned by differences in *social skills* or a late-developing shyness disposition (Bruch & Cheek, 1995; Cheek & Melchior, 1990; Kerr, 2000; Miller, 1995) (this limitation is discussed further in section 7.2.2.7.3). Further research is needed to understand the mechanisms behind this social change and the extent to which it influences effective socialization.

7.1.2.6   *Attachment Avoidance, Playing for Social Comfort, and Online Video Game Involvement (H₇—H₉)*

7.1.2.6.1   SUMMARY OF FINDINGS

Analyses uncovered no broad differences in attachment between online and non-online players, no direct linear relationships between attachment and Involvement, and no mediation effects of social skills on attachment and Involvement. Taken together, these results indicate that the relationships between social skills and OVG involvement are not driven by an underlying social compensatory motivation relating to insecure attachment.

However, links between attachment and emotional motivations for play did emerge, and, in the final step of the regression analyses, a positive, linear relationship between attachment avoidance and Involvement within online-exclusive players was found. An inverse relationship between attachment avoidance and Involvement within offline-exclusive players was also uncovered. Taken together, this suggests that individuals who exhibit high attachment avoidance are more drawn to online, rather than offline, video game play. However, as no other associations were found between attachment and Involvement, the influence of attachment seems limited to play motivations.

7.1.2.6.2   THEORETICAL IMPLICATIONS

The absence of direct relationships between attachment and Involvement and lack of evidence to suggest that social skills mediate the relationships between attachment and Involvement indicate that insecure attachment does not drive video game play in any substantial way. An insecure attachment does not seem to underpin the relationships between social skills and Involvement, nor is it inexorably intertwined with Involvement itself. As such, insecure attachment should be dismissed as a potential compensatory antecedent underlying the links between video game involvement and social skill outcomes.

However, significant links between attachment and emotional motivations for play and the emergence of attachment as a significant predictor of Involvement among online players in the final step of the regression model does indicate that the motivation to engage in OVG play can be, at least partially, attributable to avoidant attachment. The emergence of a positive correlation between attachment avoidance and playing for social comfort indicates that those who display greater attachment avoidance are more likely to play online games when feeling stressed, anxious, sad, and lonely. This is in contrast to 'playing for entertainment' (i.e., playing when feeling happy or excited), which displayed a negative correlation with attachment avoidance among online-exclusive players. As the same patterns were not found for players of offline and online games or offline-exclusive players, the relationship between attachment avoidance and playing for social comfort seems to be unique to online-exclusive play.

By allowing the retention of autonomy through physical distance, accommodating for their traditional difficulties with self-disclosure, and incorporating play, OVGs seem to be particularly suited to serve attachment functions for the highly avoidant. Rather than being a primary source of entertainment, the playful, social spaces of OVGs seem to hold the potential to be socially beneficial, as avoidant individuals report engaging within these spaces when feeling particularly socially disengaged (i.e., stressed, anxious, sad, lonely). These spaces seem to provide an environment where those high in attachment avoidance can serve attachment needs by obtaining a level of social comfort that has likely been inaccessible in traditional contexts.

Links between social comfort and attachment anxiety were also found. However, attachment anxiety showed positive correlations with playing for social comfort within offline and OVG playing populations. Thus, unlike avoidant individuals, those high in attachment anxiety seem to be seeking social closeness with others in online and offline contexts. Therefore, while both anxious and avoidant attachment showed significant associations with playing for social comfort, individuals high in attachment avoidance seem to be specifically seeking OVG environments for their social functionality.

7.1.2.6.3 PRACTICAL IMPLICATIONS

While insecure attachment was not found to underlie the relationships between OVG involvement and social skill outcomes, significant associations with emotional motivations for play suggests that the motivation to engage in online-specific play may be, at least partially, attributable to avoidant attachment. Individuals high in attachment avoidance reported playing OVGs for social comfort (i.e., playing when feeling stressed, anxious, sad, lonely), rather than entertainment (i.e., playing when happy or excited), but exhibited no overall differences in Involvement. This indicates that individuals high in attachment avoidance demonstrate no differences in their overall involvement in video game play but are motivated to play OVGs for reasons that differ from those low in attachment avoidance (i.e., for social comfort).

Traditionally, individuals high in attachment avoidance avoid closeness with others, value their self-sufficiency, and perceive no need for social relationships. Due to the belief they will eventually be disappointed, these individuals largely dismiss and avoid interpersonal relationships, putting them at risk for social isolation (Buote, Wood, & Pratt, 2009; Smith, Murphy, & Coats, 1999). However, the current results suggest that individuals high in attachment avoidance are specifically seeking OVG environments for their provision of a social outlet. Online games may be a particularly desirable social outlet for those high in attachment avoidance as they promote the development and maintenance of interpersonal relationships without a need for physical proximity and accommodate for the traditional social difficulties associated with avoidant attachment (e.g., self-disclosure) through visual anonymity and the reduced amount of social cues found online (Lea & Spears, 1995; McKenna & Bargh, 2000; Parks & Floyd, 1996; Reis & Shaver, 1988; Suler, 2004). Online video also incorporate elements of play, which may allow OVGs to serve attachment functions in beneficial ways that differ from other mediated outlets that center on socialization alone.

For example, unlike chat rooms, OVG play is both instrumental and social, with its primary purpose and strongest motivator of game play being to achieve in-game objectives (Cole & Griffiths, 2007; Williams et al., 2008; Yee, 2007). As these goals are often more easily accomplished with the assistance of others, players often form collectives and work together. The shared, playful activities experienced by co-players create intimate bonds between them, more so than socialization itself (Hill, 1988; Holman & Jacquart, 1988; Orthner, 1975), and promote the formation of close and long-standing friendship bonds between a player and the other members of their online community not traditionally found in other mediated channels (Cole & Griffiths, 2007; Hsu, Wen, & Wu, 2009; Iacono & Weisband, 1997; Williams, 2006; Yee, 2002). Because friendship bonds between co-players are essentially 'emotionally jumpstarted' through a rapid series of stressful, trust-building situations (e.g., killing a difficult enemy), individuals can choose to befriend those who have already demonstrated trustworthiness through their course of action during the many spontaneous crises that occur in-game and require quick decision making (Yee, 2002). This could be particularly beneficial for those high in attachment avoidance, as they would be able to identify others as trustworthy, prior to befriending them, substantially reducing the fear and likelihood of social disappointment.

However, as avoidant individuals value their self-sufficiency and autonomy, they may prefer to complete the in-game objectives without the company or assistance of others. Even if this were the case, the social utility of online games would not be diminished. Even when a player completes the instrumental goals alone, they are participating "alone together" (Ducheneaut, Yee, Nickell, & Moore, 2006; Turkle, 2011). To use an analogy put forth by Ducheneaut and colleagues (2006), engaging within OVGs is like reading a book in a popular café. While one can choose to interact with the others within the space, the sense of being in a social environment can be attractive enough for individuals to conduct independent activities there. This element of social presence, within the context of an achievement-based environment, allows for independent pursuits within a shared space that is inhabited by others. Thus, even without direct socialization with other players, individuals are engaged within a social environment where one's co-players maintain a constant presence and source of company and entertainment (Ducheneaut et al., 2006; Steinkuehler & Williams, 2006). This is in stark contrast to more traditional mediated spaces, such as chat rooms, where the primary purpose, and sole function, of the space is to directly socialize with others. While social presence may be higher within these mediated spaces, without direct interaction an individual is not involved in the social atmosphere. In this sense, OVGs may be socially advantageous to other Internet-based mediated outlets for those high in attachment avoidance. Future research is needed to examine these possibilities and establish OVGs' potential to prevent social isolation for those high in attachment avoidance.

7.1.2.7 *Additional Findings: Social Skills*
Additional relationships between social skills and Involvement were not predicted to emerge. However, due to the lack of comprehensive evaluations

between social skills and video game involvement, uncovering additional relationships was not necessarily surprising. The regression analyses presented in section 4.4.2 indicated significant relationships between EE, EC, and Involvement among the broader video game playing population. Significant positive relationships between Involvement and these subscales suggest that greater involvement is associated with increased emotional expressivity and control. Among online-exclusive players, the direction of the relationships between EE, EC, and Involvement reversed, suggesting that more involved online-exclusive players become less emotionally expressive and controlled than the broader video game playing sample. However, these particular patterns were not uncovered in previous or subsequent analyses. Additionally, previous research has not identified a consistent link between these skills and video game play. As such, it is not prudent to draw broad conclusions from these findings.

7.1.2.8   *Social Competence and Online Video Game Involvement: Summary*

The results from the empirical inquiries included within this monograph indicated that there are not extensive associations between social skills and OVG involvement. While consistent relationships did emerge between SE, ES, and Involvement, the only consistent, unique relationship between social skills and video game involvement among online players was limited to the ES subscale. Thus, while OVGs have been theoretically linked to a wide variety of social outcomes (e.g., low SE, low SC, etc.), the current results suggest that OVG involvement may only be uniquely associated with an increase in emotional sensitivity.

The emergence of linear relationships between social outcomes and Involvement, and the lack of mean differences in social outcomes between high- and low-involved players or online-exclusive and non-online-exclusive players, also indicates the unlikelihood that players engage in video game play, or online-specific play, to compensate for a lack of social skills that existed prior to video game involvement. Rather, the evidence suggests that video game players may be experiencing social changes that correspond with increased Involvement, as higher levels of Involvement were found to be associated with a greater hypersensitivity to non-verbal cues and a weakened ability to socially engage others. However, the pattern of relationships uncovered here does not dismiss the potential role of social compensation altogether, as the interplay of social displacement and compensation is particularly likely (this is discussed in more detail in chapter 8). Therefore, the results presented within this monograph should not be interpreted as a dismissal of social compensation processes that may initiate video game play but rather an indication that social compensation phenomena were not evident on the social skills level.

Taken together, it can be concluded that the online game playing community is not a population of reclusive, socially inept individuals who have turned to online video gaming environments for social refuge. It can also be concluded that increased OVG involvement does not inevitably lead to worse social outcomes as more involved online players did not demonstrate the all-encompassing, maladaptive social skills that are anecdotally attributed to them (Griffiths, Davies, & Chappell, 2003; Kowert, Griffiths, & Oldmeadow, 2012; Kowert & Oldmeadow, 2012; Williams et al., 2008).

7.2 STRENGTHS AND LIMITATIONS

The results presented within this monograph indicate that there are significant links between video game involvement and social outcomes that are likely representative of social displacement phenomena. However, these findings need to be considered in relation to the relative strengths and limitations of the studies contained within this monograph. These are discussed in more detail in the following.

7.2.1 Strengths

The work contained within this monograph provides the first known attempt to reconcile the inconsistencies in the assessment of video game involvement and social competence among video game players. To address the inconsistencies in the conceptualization of video game involvement (see section 3.3.3) and move beyond assessments that rely on a single component, a variable called 'Involvement' was developed to represent the degree to which participants are involved in video game play as a form of activity. Involvement scores were generated as a composite of participants' reported weekly play frequency, game play variety, and social identity. The integration of behavioral (i.e., play frequency and variety) and psychological (i.e., social identity) measures provided a more systematic assessment of video game involvement than has been employed previously and allowed for the evaluation of players across a broad spectrum.

Inconsistencies in the quantification of social competence have also plagued the literature. While social competence can, and has been, conceptualized in a multitude of ways, the empirical investigations contained within this monograph primarily employed the social skills approach to measuring social competence. This approach operationalizes social competence as having, or not having, certain social skills (Rose-Kransor, 1997). The social skills approach was chosen because it forms the base of social competence models (e.g., Cavell, 1990; DuBois & Felner, 1996; Rose-Kransor, 1997) by supplying the foundation for the other facets of social competence to build upon. This approach is also the most frequently employed within the social competence literature (Rose-Kransor, 1997) and has shown significant relationships with performance based assessments (Baron & Markman, 2003; Riggio, Watring, & Throckmorton, 1993), suggesting that it is a valid methodology to assess social skill and social performance. The Social Skills Inventory (SSI; Riggio, 1989) was chosen as the measure of social skills as it is a highly reliable, validated assessment that evaluates a wide range of social abilities. A broad, unambiguous measure such as this permitted a more accurate, and comprehensive, evaluation of the social profile of video game players than has been enlisted previously (see Table 3.1) and allowed for a more precise determination of the social abilities that hold a relationship with OVG play.

The work contained within this monograph also enlisted a broad, adult video game playing sample. This is a divergence from previous research in this area, as sample selection has largely been limited to more specialist game playing groups (such as MMORPG players). The recruitment of a broader game playing sample was advantageous, as the findings discussed within this monograph can be considered representative of video game players from a range of genres, both off- and online.

By accommodating for the inconsistencies in the conceptualization of Involvement, by quantifying social competence, and by recruiting a broad video game playing sample, the work contained within this monograph has generated a more accurate and complete assessment of the relationships between social skills and video game involvement than has been previously undertaken.

7.2.2   Limitations

Although the research presented in this monograph has made a number of important contributions to the previous literature, it also has a number of limitations. While they have been discussed previously (see sections 4.5.1, 5.5.2, and 6.7.1), this section will provide an overview of the most critical limitations.

7.2.2.1   *Magnitude of Effects*

While consistent links were found between ES, SE, and Involvement, the relationships between these variables were relatively small in magnitude, indicating that the influence of Involvement on social competence is limited. This supports previous research that has found media effects to be relatively minimal (Ferguson & Kilburn, 2010; Ferguson, 2007; Klapper, 1960; McGuire, 1986), with the main effect of media being behavior reinforcement (Perse, 2008), rather than change. To fully understand the relationships between social outcomes and Involvement uncovered here, additional consideration needs to be given to the potential influences apart from the media use itself. One potential underlying mechanism (i.e., insecure attachment) was explored within this monograph; however, the potential for the relationships between social outcome variables and Involvement to be driven by a third variable, such as personality characteristics (e.g., introversion) and/ or psychosocial dispositions (e.g., loneliness, depression, social anxiety), cannot be dismissed. Additional research is needed to examine the potential interplay between these variables and the relationships between social competence and video game involvement.

7.2.2.2 Consistency of Effects

Across studies, there were some inconsistencies in the relationships between Involvement and social skill outcomes. In particular, Study 2 (chapter 5) revealed links between EE, EC, and Involvement across the broader video game playing population that were not evident in any prior or subsequent analyses. It is unclear why this is the case; however, this variation may have emerged due to differences in sampling across studies. In Study 2 the majority of participants were recruited from MTurk. It is possible that individuals who choose to complete tasks through this forum are somehow socially different from those who do not. However, as the relationships between EE, EC, and Involvement did not emerge in any other analysis, and as they have not been theoretically linked to video game Involvement, they were not explored further and should not be considered to represent reliable relationships between social skills and video game involvement.

7.2.2.3 Sample Bias

Due to differences in the perception of video game players, and differences in the quantification of social competence, the current inquiries were limited to Western, Caucasian participants. As such, the findings discussed within this monograph are limited to this sample only. Additional research is needed to examine the potential differences in the relationship between video game involvement and social outcomes across cultures. Furthermore, although large, broad samples of video game players were acquired, the limited number of online-exclusive players restricts the generalizability of the findings. While significant effects were found, future research is needed to evaluate these associations across a larger sample of online-exclusive players.

Additionally, the samples enlisted within this monograph were opportunity samples of university students and online-sourced players and not representative samples drawn from the population. As participants were largely sourced online through forums targeted toward the game playing community and Amazon's MTurk, it is likely that the current sample is less characteristic of game players generally and more representative of online-savvy, and potentially more involved, game players. Additional research is needed to replicate the findings uncovered within this monograph within a representative sample to determine if the patterns remain among the general game playing population.

7.2.2.4 Genre-Specific Analyses

While the research questions examined within this monograph were not genre specific, it is possible that the relationships between social goals, social skills, attachment, and OVG involvement differ between players who predominantly engage in different gaming environments. For example, previous research has largely focused on the relationship between MMORPG play and social outcomes as MMORPGs are believed to have a unique ability to promote sociability between users (Barnett, Coulson, & Foreman, 2009; Cole & Griffiths, 2007; Liu & Peng, 2009; Smyth, 2007). As cooperation between users is often crucial to game play (Chen, 2009; Ducheneaut & Moore, 2005; Jakobsson & Taylor, 2003; Moore, Ducheneaut, & Nickell, 2007; Taylor, 2003, 2006), the social environment of MMORPGs differs from other genres, such as multiplayer FPS games where game play is more about competition than cooperation and the social environment is characterized by competitiveness, trash talking, and gloating (Zubek & Khoo, 2002). These differences in social environments could differentially affect the relationships between social outcomes and OVG involvement. For example, it is possible that the relationships between attachment avoidance and playing for social comfort among online-exclusive players could be limited to MMORPG players, as these gaming environments are more focused on cooperation and, thus, may be more suitable for social comfort than FPS environments, which are based on competition. Due to the small pool of online-exclusive players, a post hoc exploration of the relationships between social goals, social skills, attachment, and Involvement across game genres was not possible. Future research should aim to recruit a larger pool of online-exclusive players, particularly those who predominantly participate in different genres, in order to determine if the relationships between social outcomes and OVG involvement vary between players of particular genres.

7.2.2.5   Self-Report Measures

While the primary measures enlisted within this study (i.e., SSI and Experiences in Close Relationships [ECR]) have been shown to have high external validity, self-report and objective measures of behavior can sometimes lead to different validity correlations (Armitage & Conner, 2001). For example, Rapee and Lim (1992) found that individuals with high social phobia were more likely to report lower social ability on a subjective measure of ability while their objective performance on a social task was equivalent to nonphobic participants. Thus, while individuals' self-perceptions can be strong predictors of behavior, their perceptions are not always accurate. Future researchers should consider enlisting more objective measures (e.g., performance evaluation of social competence) when evaluating the relationships between social outcomes and video game involvement to determine if the relationships discussed here are more related to self-perception differences than objective relationships between these variables.

7.2.2.6   Cross-Sectional Design

The current research was also limited by its cross-sectional design. A longitudinal design would have been advantageous as it would have permitted the documentation of variation in social outcomes and Involvement over time. This would have provided a more accurate examination of the potential social changes due to displacement and its influence on social outcomes and Involvement. Future researchers should consider enlisting such a design to gain a greater understanding of the effects of video game involvement on social outcomes over time.

7.2.2.7 *Additional Measures*

7.2.2.7.1 SOCIAL INTERNET USE

In addition to OVGs, there are a variety of Internet-based social services that can provide alternative social outlets where individuals engage with others free from the rules and pressures of traditional, face-to-face socialization (e.g., chat rooms, online dating, etc.). As the current research did not consider the frequency of use, or preference for, other Internet-based social services, it cannot be concluded whether the relationships between social skills and OVG involvement are unique to OVG play or a single element of a broader preference for mediated communication. That is, the current findings could be less representative of social displacement due to players' desire to engage within a playful, social environment and more reflective of displacement due to engagement within *any* mediated social outlet. Further research is needed to determine if the features of OVGs contribute a key element to their desirability and their relationships with social skills or if these relationships are solely driven by their ability to provide an easily accessible, mediated, social space.

7.2.2.7.2 PROBLEMATIC PLAY

The work contained within this monograph is among the first to move beyond the focus on problematic play and evaluate social skills among the broad online game playing population. However, the inclusion of a problematic play assessment would have allowed for an evaluation of the relationships between attachment, social skills, and Involvement across problematic and non-problematic game playing samples. This would have been particularly advantageous when evaluating the links between SC and Involvement, as it could have been enlisted to determine if the relationships between these variables are specifically related to problematic play outcomes. Future research should consider evaluating the similarities and differences within, and between, problematic play populations and the broader game playing population.

7.2.2.7.3 SHYNESS AND SOCIAL ANXIETY

While high levels of ES are associated with shyness (Riggio, 1987), ES is just one potential behavioral manifestation of a shyness disposition. Social avoidance driven by social anxiety/social self-consciousness (Holt, Heimberg, & Hope, 1992; Riggio, 1989; Zimbardo, Pilkonis, & Norwood, 1974) can also be associated with high ES. Whereas 'shyness' may be an apt description of those who are mildly to moderately socially phobic, the term 'social phobia' refers to the upper end of the continuum. As up to 40% of the population diagnosed with social phobia describe themselves as 'shy' and not socially phobic (Zimbardo et al., 1974), it is difficult to distinguish between the two (Holt et al., 1992). Future research should examine the relationships between ES, shyness, and social anxiety to determine if the heightened emotional sensitivity exhibited by OVG players can be attributed to a manifestation of the psychosocial components of mild to moderate shyness or social anxiety, which then become exacerbated as Involvement increases, or are best attributed to the social skills associated with emotional sensitivity.

7.2.2.7.4   PSYCHOSOCIAL MEASURES

The primary aim of the current work was to examine the relationship between social goals, social skills, and video game involvement. As such, psychosocial dispositions, such as loneliness, depression, and social anxiety, were not assessed. However, as these dispositions have been shown to hold significant relationships with social skill outcomes (DiTommaso, Brannen-McNulty, Ross, & Burgess, 2003; Leary & Kowalski, 1995; Riggio et al., 1990; Segrin & Flora, 2000; Segrin, 1996, 1998; Tse & Bond, 2004), the inclusion of psychosocial measures would have permitted an examination of the potential for these dispositions to mediate the relationships between social skills and Involvement. An analysis such as this would have generated a greater understanding of the relationships between social skills and Involvement as well as the interplay between social compensation and displacement mechanisms on social outcomes for video game players. Future research should consider the inclusion of such measures when examining the relationships between social competence and video game involvement.

7.3   CONCLUSION

The work contained within this monograph aimed to clarify the veracity of previously drawn conclusions by comprehensively evaluating social skill differences among adult video game players to uncover if, and how, OVG involvement may support, or undermine, the development and maintenance of traditional social skills. To this end, three survey studies evaluating the relationships between social goals, social skills, and video game involvement were conducted. In an attempt to reconcile the inconsistencies within the literature, a social skills approach to conceptualizing social competence was adopted and a new measure of video game involvement that comprised of both behavioral (i.e., play frequency and variety) and psychological (i.e., social identity) measures was constructed. Targeted statistical analyses were also employed to examine the role of social compensation and displacement phenomena as the underlying mechanisms behind the relationships between social outcomes and video game involvement. An extensive demographic analysis of the sample was also undertaken.

In light of the strengths and limitations of the work contained within this monograph, it can be concluded that there are significant relationships between video game involvement and social outcomes, some of which are unique to the subgroup of OVG players. Greater Involvement in online-specific play was found to be associated with higher ES (which could suggest the development of social hypersensitivities) and less interest in, and perception of ability for, offline socialization. Greater involvement in video game play, both off- and online, also exhibited a linear, inverse relationship with SE. This indicates that lower SE corresponds with higher levels of Involvement and suggests that the ability to successfully engage and guide social conversation diminishes as Involvement increases. While the linear pattern of these relationships implicates displacement phenomena as underlying the links between social outcomes and Involvement, it remains unclear whether these associations may be underpinned by a third, compensatory, variable.

Taken together, the emergence of linear relationships between video game involvement, social goals, and social skills suggests that video game play may be a socially displacing activity. Variation in social outcomes was found to correspond with levels of Involvement, with more involved players reporting less interest in offline socialization, demonstrating a lower perceived ability to effectively socialize in offline contexts, and displaying tangible variability in social skills. However, the general lack of relationships between Involvement and SSI subscales discredits the contention that increased OVG involvement coincides with *severe* negative social consequences and largely disputes the all-encompassing, maladaptive social skills that are anecdotally attributed to OVG players (Griffiths et al., 2003; Kowert et al., 2012; Kowert & Oldmeadow, 2012; Williams et al., 2008).

REFERENCES

Armitage, C. J., & Conner, M. (2001). Efficacy of the theory of planned behaviour: A meta-analytic review. *British Journal of Social Psychology/British Psychological Society*, 40, 471–499. doi:10.1348/014466601164939

Associated Press. (2007). Chinese man drops dead after three-day gaming binge. *Fox News*. Retrieved from http://www.foxnews.com/story/0,2933,297059,00.html?sPage=fnc/scitech/videogaming

Bandura, A. (1986). *Social foundations of thought and action: A social cognitive theory*. Englewood Cliffs, NJ: Prentice-Hall.

Bandura, A. (1991). Social cogntiive theory of self-regulation. *Organizational Behavior and Human Decision Processes*, 50, 248–297.

Bandura, A. (1999). A sociocognitive analysis of substance abuse: An agentic perspective. *Psychological Science*. doi:10.1111/1467–9280.00138

Barnett, J., Coulson, M., & Foreman, N. (2009). *The WoW! factor: Reduced levels of anger after violent on-line play*. London: Middlesex University.

Baron, R., & Markman, G. (2003). Beyond social capital: The role of entrepreneurs' social competence in their financial success. *Journal of Business Venturing, 18*(1), 41–60.

BBC News. (2005). South Korean dies after games session. *BBC News*. Retrieved from http://news.bbc.co.uk/1/hi/technology/4137782.stm

Broadcasters Alliance Research Board. (2012). *BARB Bulletin, 30*(2), 1–6.

Bruch, M. A., & Cheek, J. M. (1995). Developmental factors in childhood and adolescent shyness. In R. Heimberg, M. R. Liebowitz, D. A. Hope, & F. Schneier (Eds.), *Social phobia: Diagnosis, assessment, and treatment* (pp. 163–182). New York: Guilford Press.

Buote, V., Wood, E., & Pratt, M. (2009). Exploring similarities and differences between online and offline friendships: The role of attachment style. *Computers in Human Behavior, 25*, 560–567.

Caplan, S. (2002). Problematic Internet use and psychosocial well being: Development of a theory-based cognitive-behavioral measurement instrument. *Computers in Human Behavior, 18*, 553–575.

Caplan, S. (2003). Preference for online social interaction: A theory of problematic Internet use and psychosocial well-being. *Communication Research, 30*, 625–648.

Caplan, S. (2005). A social skill account of problematic Internet use. *Journal of Communication, 55*, 721–736.

Cavell, T. A. (1990). Social adjustment, social performance, and social skills: A tri-component model of social competence. *Journal of Clinical Child Psychology, 19*, 111–122.

Chak, K., & Leung, L. (2004). Shyness and locus of control as predictors of Internet addiction and Internet use. *Cyberpsychology and Behavior, 7*(5), 559–570.

Cheek, J. M., & Melchior, L. A. (1990). Shyness, self-esteem, and self-consciousness. In H. Litenberg (Ed.), *Handbook of social and evaluation anxiety* (pp. 47–82). New York: Plenum Press.

Chen, M. (2009). Communication, coordination, and camaraderie in *World of Warcraft*. *Games and Culture, 4*(1), 47–73.

Cole, H., & Griffiths, M. D. (2007). Social interactions in massively multiplayer online role-playing games. *Cyberpsychology and Behavior, 10*(4), 575–583.

de Kort, Y.A.W., & Ijsselsteijn, W. A. (2008). People, places, and play: Player experience in a socio-spatial context. *Computers in Entertainment, 6*(2), 18.

DiTommaso, E., Brannen-McNulty, C., Ross, L., & Burgess, M. (2003). Attachment styles, social skills and loneliness in young adults. *Personality and Indivdiual Differences, 35*(2), 303–312.

DuBois, D. L., & Felner, R. D. (1996). The quadripartite model of social competence: Theory and applications to clinical intervention. In M. A. Reinecke (Ed.), *Cognitive therapy with children and adolescents: A casebook for clinical practice*. New York: Guilford Press.

Ducheneaut, N., & Moore, R. (2005). More than just "XP": Learning social skills in massively multiplayer online games. *Interactive Technology and Smart Education, 2*(2), 89–100.

Ducheneaut, N., Yee, N., Nickell, E., & Moore, R. (2006). "Alone together?": Exploring the social dynamics of massively multiplayer online games. In *SIGCHI Conference on Human Factors in Computing Systems*. New York: ACM.

Entertainment Software Association. (2012). *Game player data*. Retrieved from http://www.theesa.com/facts/gameplayer.asp

Ferguson, C. J. (2007). The good, the bad and the ugly: A meta-analytic review of positive and negative effects of violent video games. *Psychiatric Quarterly, 78*, 309–316.

Ferguson, C. J., & Kilburn, J. (2010). Much ado about nothing: The misestimation and overinterpretation of violent video game effects in eastern and western nations: comment on Anderson et al. (2010). *Psychological Bulletin, 136*, 174–178; discussion 182–187. doi:10.1037/a0018566

Gajadhar, B., de Kort, Y., & Ijsselsteijn, W. (2008). Influence of social setting on player experience of digital games. In *CHI'08 extended abstracts on human factors in computing systems* (pp. 3099–3104). New York: ACM.

Ghuman, D., & Griffiths, M. D. (2012). A cross-genre study of online gaming: Player demographics, motivation for play, and social interactions among players. *International Journal of Cyber Behavior, Psychology, and Learning, 2*(1), 13–29.

Griffiths, M. D., Davies, M., & Chappell, D. (2003). Breaking the stereotype: The case of online gaming. *Cyberpsychology and Behavior, 6*(1), 81–91.

Griffiths, M. D., Davies, M., & Chappell, D. (2004). Demographic factors and playing variables in online computer gaming. *Cyberpsychology and Behavior, 7*, 479–487.

Hill, M. S. (1988). Marital stability and spouces' shared time: A multidisciplinary hypothesis. *Journal of Family Issues, 9*(4), 427–451.

Holman, T. B., & Jacquart, M. (1988). Leisure-activity patterns and marital satisfaction: A further test. *Journal of Marriage and the Family,* (50), 69–77.

Holt, C. S., Heimberg, R., & Hope, D. A. (1992). Avoidant personality disorder and the generalised subtype of social phobia. *Journal of Abnormal Psychology, 101*, 318–325.

Hsu, S., Wen, M., & Wu, M. (2009). Exploring user experiences as predictors of MMORPG addiction. *Computers and Education, 53*(3), 990–999.

Hussain, Z., & Griffiths, M. (2009). The attitudes, feelings, and experiences of online gamers: A qualitative analysis. *Cyberpsychology and Behavior, 12*(6), 747–753.

Iacono, C. S., & Weisband, S. (1997). Developing trust in virtual teams. In *Hawaii International Conference on System Sciences*. Hawaii.

Ijsselsteijn, W. A., Hoogen, W., Klimmt, C., de Kort, Y.A.W., Lindley, C., Mathiak, K., . . . Vorderer, P. (2008). Measuring the experience of digital game enjoyment. In *Proceedings of Measuring Behavior* (pp. 88–89). Maastricht, Netherlands.

Jakobsson, M., & Taylor, T. L. (2003). *The Sopranos* meets *EverQuest*: Social networking in massively multiplayer online games. In *Proceedings of the 2003 Digital Arts and Culture (DAC) conference, Melbourne, Australia* (pp. 81–90).

Kerr, M. (2000). Childhood and adolescent shyness in long-term perspective: Does it matter? In R. Crozier (Ed.), *Shyness* (pp. 64–87). New York: Routledge.

Kim, E., Namkoong, K., Ku, T., & Kim, S. (2008). The relationship between online game addiction and aggression, self-control, and narcissistic personality traits. *European Psychiatry, 23*(3), 212–218.

Klapper, J. T. (1960). *The effects of mass communication*. New York: Free Press.

Kohn, D. (2002). Addicted: Suicide over *Everquest*? *CBS News*. Retrieved from http://www.cbsnews.com/stories/2002/10/17/48hours/main525965.shtml

Kolo, C., & Baur, T. (2004). Living a virtual life: Social dynamics of online gaming. *International Journal of Computer Game Research, 4*(1), 1–31.

Korgaonkar, P., & Wolin, L. (1999). A mulitvariate analysis of Web usage. *Journal of Advertising Research*, 56–68.

Kowert, R., Domahidi, E., & Quandt, T. (2014). The relationship between online video game involvement and gaming-related friendships among emotionally sensitive individuals. *Cyberpsychology, Behavior, and Social Networking, 17*(7), 447–453. doi:10.1089/cyber.2013.0656

Kowert, R., Griffiths, M. D., & Oldmeadow, J. A. (2012). Geek or chic? Emerging stereotypes of online gamers. *Bulletin of Science, Technology & Society, 32*(6), 471–479. doi:10.1177/0270467612469078

Kowert, R., & Oldmeadow, J. A. (2012). The stereotype of online gamers: New characterization or recycled prototype. In *Nordic DiGRA: Games in Culture and Society conference proceedings*. Tampere, Finland: DiGRA.

Kuittinen, J., Kultima, A., Niemelä, J., & Paavilainen, J. (2007). Casual games discussion. In *Proceedings of the 2007 conference on Future Play* (pp. 105–112). New York: ACM.

LaRose, R., Mastro, D., & Eastin, M. (2001). Understanding Internet usage. *Social Science Computer Review, 19*(4), 395–413.

Lea, M., & Spears, R. (1995). Love at first byte? Building personal relationships over computer networks. In J. T. Wood & S. W. Duck (Eds.), *Understudied relationships: Off the beaten track* (pp. 197–233). Newbury Park, CA: Sage.

Leary, M., & Kowalski, R. (1995). *Social anxiety*. New York: Guilford Press.

Lemmens, J., Valkenburg, P., & Peter, J. (2009). Development and validation of a game addiction scale for adolescents. *Media Psychology, 12*(1), 77–95.

Lemmens, J., Valkenburg, P., & Peter, J. (2011). Psychological causes and consequences of pathological gaming. *Computers in Human Behavior, 27*(1), 144–152.

Liu, M., & Peng, W. (2009). Cognitive and psychological predictors of the negative outcomes associated with playing MMOGs (massively multiplayer online games). *Computers in Human Behavior, 25*(6), 1306–1311.

Lo, S., Wang, C., & Fang, W. (2005). Physical interpersonal relationships and social anxiety among online game players. *Cyberpsychology and Behavior, 8*(1), 15–20.

McGuire, W. J. (1986). The myth of massive media impact: Savagings and salvagings. In G. Comstock (Ed.), *Public communication and behaviour* (Vol. 1, pp. 173–257). San Diego, CA: Academic Press.

McKenna, K., & Bargh, J. (1999). Causes and consequences of social interaction on the Internet: A conceptual framework. *Media Psychology, 1*(3), 249–269.

McKenna, K., & Bargh, J. (2000). Plan 9 from cyberspace: The implications of the Internet for personality and social psychology. *Personality and Social Psychology Review, 4*(1), 57–75.

Miller, R. (1995). On the nature of embarrassability: Shyness, social evaluation, and social skill. *Journal of Personality, 63*(2), 315–339.

Moore, R., Ducheneaut, N., & Nickell, E. (2007). Doing virtually nothing: Awareness and accountability in massively multiplayer online worlds. *Computer Supported Cooperative Work, 16*(3), 265–305.

Morahan-Martin, J., & Schumacher, P. (2003). Loneliness and social uses of the Internet. *Computers in Human Behavior, 19*, 659–671.

Ng, B., & Wiemer-Hastings, P. (2005). Addiction to the Internet and online gaming. *Cyberpsychology and Behavior, 8*(2), 110–113.

Orthner, D. K. (1975). Leisure activity patterns and marital satisfaction over the marital career. *Journal of Marriage and the Family*, (37), 91–101.

Parks, M. R., & Floyd, K. (1996). Making friends in cyberspace. *Journal of Communication, 46*, 80–97.

Peng, W., & Liu, M. (2010). Online gaming depdendency: A preliminary study in China. *Cyberpsychology and Behavior, 13*(3), 329–333.

Perse, E. (2008). *Media effects and society*. Mahwah, NJ: Lawrence Erlbaum.

Rapee, R. M., & Lim, L. (1992). Discrepancy between self-and observer ratings of performance in social phobics. *Journal of Abnormal Psychology, 101*, 728–731. doi:10.1037/0021–843X.101.4.728

Reis, H.T.T., & Shaver, P. (1988). Intimacy as an interpersonal process. In S. Duck (Ed.), *Handbook of personal relationships* (pp. 367–389). Chichester, UK: Wiley.

Riggio, R. (1987). *The charisma quotient: What it is, how to get it, how to use it.* New York: Dodd Mead.

Riggio, R. (1989). *Manual for the Social Skills Inventory*. Palo Alto, CA: Consulting Psychologists Press.

Riggio, R. (2005). The Social Skills Inventory (SSI): Measuring nonverbal and social skills. In V. Manusov (Ed.), *The sourcebook of nonverbal measures: Going beyond words* (pp. 25–33). Mahwah, NJ: Lawrence Erlbaum.

Riggio, R., & Carney, D. C. (2003). *Manual for the Social Skills Inventory* (2nd ed). Mountain View, CA: Mind Garden.

Riggio, R., Throckmorton, B., & DePaola, S. (1990). Social skills and self-esteem. *Personality and Indivdiual Differences*, 11(8), 799–804.

Riggio, R., Watring, K., & Throckmorton, B. (1993). Social skills, support, and psychosocial adjustment. *Personality and Individual Differences*, 15(3), 275–280.

Roberts, L. D., Smith, L., & Pollock, C. (2000). "U r a lot bolder on the net": Shyness and Internet use. In *Shyness, development, consolidation, and change* (pp. 121–135). New York: Routledge.

Rose-Kransor, L. (1997). Nature of social competence: A theoretical review. *Social Developmental Psychology*, 6(1), 111–135.

Scealy, M., Phillips, J., & Stevenson, R. (2002). Shyness and anxiety as predictors of patterns of Internet usage. *Cyberpsychology and Behavior*, 5(6), 507–515.

Segrin, C. (1996). The relationship between social skills deficits and psychosocial problems. A test of a vulnerability model. *Communication Research*, 23, 425–450.

Segrin, C. (1998). Interpersonal communication problems associated with depression and loneliness. In P. Andersen & L. Guerrero (Eds.), *Handbook of communication and emotion: Research, theory, applications, and contexts* (pp. 215–242). San Diego, CA: Academic Press.

Segrin, C., & Flora, J. (2000). Poor social skills are a vulnerability factor in the development of psychosocial problems. *Human Commuication Research*, 26(3), 489–514.

Segrin, C., & Kinney, T. (1995). Social skills deficits among the socially anxious: Loneliness and rejection from others. *Motivation and Emotion*, (19), 1–24.

Shen, C., & Williams, D. (2010). Unpacking time online: Connecting Internet and massively multiplayer online game use with psychological well-being. *Communication Research*, 20(10), 1–27.

Sjöblom, B. (2008). Language and perception in co-located gaming. Paper presented at the Language, Culture, Mind III conference, Odense, Denmark.

Smith, E., Murphy, J., & Coats, S. (1999). Attachment to groups: Theory and measurement. *Journal of Personality and Social Psychology*, 77(1), 94–110.

Smyth, J. (2007). Beyond self-selection in video game play. *Cyberpsychology and Behavior*, 10(5), 717–721.

Steinkuehler, C., & Williams, D. (2006). Where everybody knows your (screen) name: Online games as "third places." *Journal of Computer-Mediated Communication*, 11(4), 885–909.

Suler, J. (2004). The online disinhibition effect. *Cyberpsychology and Behavior*, 7(3), 321–326.

Taylor, T. L. (2003). Multiple pleasures: Women and online gaming. *Convergence: The International Journal of Research into New Media Technologies*, 9(1), 21–46.

Taylor, T. L. (2006). *Play between worlds: Exploring online game culture*. Cambridge, MA: MIT Press.

Tse, W., & Bond, A. (2004). The impact of depression on social skills: A review. *Journal of Nervous and Mental Disease*, 192(4), 260–268.

Turkle, S. (2011). *Alone together: Why we expect more from technology and less from each other*. New York: Basic Books.

Utz, S. (2000). Social information processing in MUDs: The development of friendships in virtual worlds. *Journal of Online Behavior*, 1(1).

Walther, J. (1996). Computer-mediated communication: Impersonal, interpersonal, and hyperpersonal interaction. *Communication Research*, 23(1), 3–43.

Wan, C., & Chiou, W. (2006). Why are adolescents addicted to online gaming? An interview study in Taiwan. *Cyberpsychology and Behavior*, 9(6), 762–766.

Wan, C., & Chiou, W. (2007). The motivations of adolescents who are addicted to online games: A cognitive perspective. *Adolescence*, 42(165), 179–197.

Williams, D. (2006). Groups and goblins: The social and civic impact of online games. *Journal of Broadcasting and Electronic Media, 50*, 651–681.

Williams, D., Ducheneaut, N., Xiong, L., Yee, N., & Nickell, E. (2006). From tree house to barracks. *Games and Culture, 1*(4), 338–361.

Williams, D., Yee, N., & Caplan, S. (2008). Who plays, how much, and why? Debunking the stereotypical gamer profile. *Journal of Computer-Mediated Communication Monographs, 13*(4), 993–1018.

Yee, N. (2002). Befriending ogres and wood-elves—Understanding relationship formation in MMORPGs. *Nickyee.* Retrieved from http://www.nickyee.com/hub/relationships/home.html

Yee, N. (2006). The demographics, motivations, and derived experiences of users of massively-multi-user online graphical environments. *Teleoperators and Virtual Environments, 15*(3), 309–329.

Yee, N. (2007). Motivations of play in online games. *Journal of CyberPsychology and Behavior, 9*(6), 772–775.

Young, K. (1996). Internet addiction: The emergence of a new clinical disorder. *Cyberpsychology and Behavior, 1*, 237–244.

Young, K. (2004). Internet addiction: A new clinical phenomenon and its consequences. *American Behavioral Scientist, 48*(4), 402–415.

Yuen, C. N., & Lavin, M. J. (2004). Internet dependence in the collegiate population: The role of shyness. *Cyberpsychology and Behavior, 7*(4), 379–383.

Zimbardo, P. (1997). *Shyness: What it is, what to do about it.* Reading, MA: Addison-Wesley.

Zimbardo, P., Pilkonis, P. A., & Norwood, R. (1974). *The silent prison of shyness.* Stanford, CA: Stanford University Press.

Zubek, R., & Khoo, A. (2002). *Making the human care: On building engaging bots* (pp. 1–5). AAAI Technical Report, Northeastern University Computer Science. Retrieved from http://www.aaai.org/Papers/Symposia/Spring/2002/SS-02-01/SS 02-01-020.pdf

8 Sociability and Online Video Games
What We Know Now

While OVG involvement has long been assumed to have a direct negative impact on an individual's sociability, researchers have been unable to demonstrate consistent links between OVG play and social outcomes or identify what theoretical mechanisms may underlie such relationships. Overcoming the limitations of previous work, the research outlined within this monograph aimed to clarify the relationships between OVG involvement and sociability by evaluating if and how OVG involvement is related to social goals and social skills. The current chapter will synthesize the findings of this research within the context of the previous work in this area to develop a comprehensive overview and understanding of the relationships between OVG involvement and sociability.

This chapter will begin with a discussion of how the findings contained within this monograph contribute to the long-discussed 'causal versus consequential' debate relating to OVG involvement and social outcomes. While the linear relationships between OVG involvement and social outcomes found in chapters 4–6 suggest poorer social outcomes are a consequence of engagement through displacement effects, the links between insecure attachment and social motivations for play presented in chapter 6 suggest the presence of social compensation motivations for use, at least for the insecurely attached. At first glance these findings seem contradictory; however, they may actually be some of the first evidence to support of a 'Cycle Model of Use' whereby social compensation motivations and displacement effects interact together rather than exist as independent processes. This possibility is discussed in more detail in section 8.1.1.

This chapter will also outline several suggestions for future research in this area of study. While the research discussed within this monograph provides insight into the relationships between video game involvement and social outcomes, a number of additional inquiries are needed to account for the limitations of the current research (see section 7.2.2). The current research has also inspired a range of new avenues for future work, such as a further examination of the social impact of mediated socialization across mediums (e.g., online gaming, social networking, chat rooms, etc.). This will also be discussed.

The chapter will conclude with a discussion of the implications that the current findings have for the millions of OVG players worldwide. While anecdotal claims of social ineptitude among OVG players continue to spark concern, the empirical data contained within this monograph does not support the magnitude of these fears or the stereotypical portrayal of OVG players as a community of socially inept individuals. As such, it is argued that the anecdotal characterization of the socially inept OVG player should be rejected.

8.1   SOCIAL DISPLACEMENT OR SOCIAL COMPENSATION: WHAT DOES THE DATA SAY?

When discussing the social impact of OVG play, researchers have typically supported one of two theoretical positions: social displacement or social compensation. Proponents of the social displacement perspective contend that the range of social affordances provided by online games (e.g., visual anonymity, asynchronicity, etc.) are "socially liberating" and free users from the rules and pressures of traditional socialization and allow them to feel socially "safer, more efficacious, more confident, and more comfortable" (Caplan, 2003, p. 629). However, due to the "inelasticity of time" (Nie & Hillygus, 2001, p. 420), this newfound freedom in the online world leads to increased time invested in online relationships at the expense of face-to-face interactions (Caplan, Williams, & Yee, 2009; Chiu, Lee, & Huang, 2004; Kraut et al., 1998; Morahan-Martin & Schumacher, 2003; Nie & Erbring, 2002; Williams, 2006). Thus, increased time spent online is believed to contribute to the exchange, *or displacement*, of offline social contacts for online ones (Bessière, Kiesler, Kraut, & Boneva, 2004; Blais, Craig, Pepler, & Connolly, 2008; Davis, 2001; Kraut et al., 1998).

The exchange of offline for online contacts is believed to be socially problematic as rather than replacing one's offline friends with a virtual substitute, users are supplanting valuable sources of social and emotional support for less intimate and more diffuse online relationships that are less 'socially valuable' in terms of their ability to provide social and emotional support (Galston, 2000; Slouka, 1995; Williams, 2007). In support of these claims, researchers have found significant relationships between OVG play and declines in time invested in offline communication (Hussain & Griffiths, 2009; Shen & Williams, 2010; Smyth, 2007; Williams, 2006) as well as poorer relationship quality for offline friends (Cole & Griffiths, 2007; Kim, Namkoong, Ku, & Kim, 2008; Lo, Wang, & Fang, 2005; Shen & Williams, 2010). However, as the work in this area has primarily been cross-sectional in nature, definitive conclusions as to whether OVG engagement directly leads to displacement effects cannot be drawn.

Conversely, proponents of the social compensation hypothesis argue that the highly accommodating social spaces of online video games (e.g., through the provision of visual anonymity, asynchronicity of communication, lack of non-verbal cues, etc.) are particularly desirable to individuals who have experienced difficulties in forming interpersonal relationships in traditional contexts (e.g., those with low social skills, high social anxiety, etc.). Thus, rather than online video game involvement directly contributing to poorer social outcomes, proponents of this hypothesis believe that individuals with low social resources or social opportunity are simply more motivated to engage in these spaces. In support of these claims, researchers have found that more involved OVG players display higher rates of the symptoms associated with loneliness, depression, and social anxiety (Caplan et al., 2009; Kim et al., 2008; Lemmens, Valkenburg, & Peter, 2011; Lo et al., 2005; Shen & Williams, 2010; Williams, Yee, & Caplan, 2008). However, as with the research put forth by social displacement advocates, a lack of longitudinal research has made it difficult to determine if low social resources motivate OVG use (i.e., social compensation) or develop and/or become exacerbated through use (i.e., social displacement).

In fact, it is generally difficult to draw definitive conclusions from the wealth of research in this area as the majority of it could easily be interpreted as support for either hypothesis, despite the fact that researchers often contend that their particular research findings clearly support either a social displacement or a compensation perspective. In an attempt to address this particular confound, targeted statistical analyses were used throughout the analyses in this monograph to determine whether the relationships between OVG involvement and social outcomes are more indicative of social compensation motivations or social displacement effects. First, social compensation motivations were evaluated with between-group analyses. Uncovering mean differences in social outcomes between groups would be indicative of broad social dissimilarities between those who choose to engage in video game play, either to a greater extent than other players (i.e., high-/low-involved players) or in online-specific play (i.e., online/non-online players), and could suggest that these differences may have been apparent prior to video game involvement. However, throughout the monograph, no mean differences were found across game playing groups for social goals (chapter 4) or social skills (chapter 4 and 5), indicating a lack of evidence for social compensation phenomena.

To examine the presence of displacement phenomena, within-group analyses were conducted whereby the linear relationships between social outcomes and video game involvement were assessed and compared across gaming groups (i.e., all participants, active players of offline and online games, offline-exclusive players, online-exclusive players, history/no history of online video game play). Uncovering a linear correspondence between increased Involvement and social outcomes would be suggestive of social displacement phenomena, as it would indicate social outcomes vary among game players in ways that linearly correspond with increased levels of video game involvement. Supporting the contentions of the social displacement hypothesis, analyses uncovered evidence of significant linear relationships between social outcomes and video game involvement across all three studies (chapters 4–6), with social goals and social skills demonstrating significant linear relationships with Involvement.

However, before drawing definitive conclusions as to the presence, or absence, of social displacement and compensation phenomena, consideration must also be given to influences apart from media use itself as various personal attributes of the game players themselves could also be influencing these relationships. To this end, the relationships between social skills and video game involvement were examined through the lens of attachment theory (chapter 6). Attachment was chosen as the construct of choice due to its intrinsic relationship with various social outcomes as well as because attachment forms in childhood (Ainsworth, Blehar, Wathers, & Wall, 1978; Bowlby, 1969, 1973, 1979), which is likely prior to video game exposure. Thus, significant links between attachment, OVG involvement, and social outcomes would signify that social differences among game players are, at least partially, attributable to an underlying construct that existed *prior* to video game exposure even in the absence of a longitudinal research design. However, contrary to predictions, broad differences in attachment were not found between game playing groups, and attachment was not found to mediate the relationships between social skills and video game involvement (see chapter 6).

Uncovering linear relationships between social skills and Involvement, rather than mean differences, implicates the presence of displacement mechanisms underlying the relationships between social skills and video game involvement. The patterns of the relationships between social goal outcomes and Involvement (i.e., increased Involvement corresponding with decreases in the importance and likelihood of attaining offline social goals and an increase in the likelihood of attaining online social goals) also support a displacement perspective and suggest that online gaming communities thrive at the expense of offline relationships and activities (Cole & Griffiths, 2007; Hussain & Griffiths, 2009). A lack of relationships between insecure attachment, social outcomes, and OVG involvement further solidified these conclusions. Taken together, these findings of the research contained within this monograph implicate the role of social displacement phenomena in underlying the relationships between social goals, social skills, and video game involvement.[1]

However, rather than dismissing social compensation motivations and implicating social displacement as the lone underlying mechanism, one must also consider the possibility that social compensation and displacement phenomena are working together. In fact, the interplay of social displacement and compensation effects in a Cycle Model of Use is quite likely. As aforementioned, the wealth of previous research in this area seems to provide support for both perspectives, despite researchers typically taking a strong stance for one hypothesis over the other. Even within the series of studies outlined within this monograph, evidence for both social displacement (i.e., inverse relationships between social skills and video game involvement) and social compensation (i.e., players high in avoidant attachment reported being motivated to play OVGs to obtain social comfort) was found. While it is not novel to suggest that social compensation motivations and social displacement effects are somehow intertwined, no one has yet to formally propose a model of use that integrates these two theoretical constructs. The first known formal outline of a Cycle Model of Use is presented in the following.

8.1.1   Cycle Model of Use

Rather than social compensation and displacement mechanisms independently underlying the inverse relationships between social outcomes and video game involvement, it is possible that elements of both theoretical constructs are working together in a Cycle Model of Use.[2] As can be seen in Figure 8.1, the Cycle Model of Use contains two components. The first component represents social compensation motivations. This is where the cyclical process originates, as the initial use of online games is, at least partially, believed to be motivated by low social resources. As a socially accommodating space, OVGs are believed to be highly desirable alternative social spaces for who are insecurely attached (see chapter 6), lonely, depressed, socially anxious, or socially unskilled, those who have limited access to peer groups, or those who are in any other way hindered from gaining social success in traditional face-to-face contexts.

Due to low social success or opportunity in traditional contexts, initial engagement within this medium would likely produce short-term social benefits, such as access to new social circles or greater social success due to the range social accommodations these environments provide. However, over time, users may experience a deterioration of their real-world friendships through the displacement of offline for online contacts. This is the second component of the model. While individuals would gain an increased sense of online community, due to the *"inelasticity of time"* (Nie, 2001, p. 420), this is believed to come at the expense of one's offline contacts and social community (Hussain & Griffiths, 2009; Smyth, 2007; Williams, 2006). Prolonged engagement within OVGs and the subsequent detachment from offline contacts could then contribute to a deterioration of offline friendships and further discourage individuals from further investing in face-to-face relationships. Over time, this could exacerbate the user's already low social resources and underwrite the 'cycle' element of the model, whereby the player continues to disregard his or her offline social commitments and communities in lieu of online ones and suffers increasingly severe social consequences.

The individual components of the Cycle Model of Use have been widely discussed in previous research. For example, low social resources, such as ineffective social skills (Griffiths, 2010; Kowert, Domahidi, & Quandt,

Figure 8.1   Cycle Model of Use

2014; Lemmens et al., 2011; Liu & Peng, 2009), have long been implicated as motivating one's initial engagement within online gaming environments (Caplan et al., 2009; Kim et al., 2008; Lemmens et al., 2011; Lo et al., 2005; Shen & Williams, 2010; Williams et al., 2008). Researchers have also suggested that through use one's low social resources may become exacerbated through displacement mechanisms (Caplan et al., 2009; Kim et al., 2008; Lemmens et al., 2011; Lo et al., 2005; Shen & Williams, 2010; Williams et al., 2008), which may lead to tangible social declines. However, a lack of longitudinal work has limited researchers' ability to validate this model. The work of Lemmens and colleagues (2011) provides some preliminary support, as they found loneliness to be both a cause (i.e., motivator) and a consequence of problematic video game play among adolescents. Thus, adolescent players who turn to OVGs to alleviate feelings of loneliness seem to experience an exacerbation of these feelings, potentially due to the exchange of their offline friends, as they are valuable sources of emotional and social support (Galston, 2000; Slouka, 1995; Williams, 2007). The work of Kowert and colleagues (under review) also evaluated the psychosocial causes and consequences of OVG use over time. However, their investigation was conducted among a representative sample of adult players. Unlike Lemmens and colleagues (2011), they found no evidence for a cyclical model of use. This does not negate the validity of the model, but rather suggests that that a Cycle Model of Use may only be valid for particular social resources or for particular populations. For example, Lemmens et al. (2011) found evidence for a cycle among lonely, adolescent, problematic game players. Thus, it is possible that the cyclical pattern is limited to particular outcomes (i.e., loneliness) among particularly vulnerable groups (i.e., problematic players, adolescents). Additional research is needed to evaluate these relationships among different populations of game players in order to generate a greater understanding of the causal and consequential relationships between OVG involvement and social outcomes as well as the mechanisms that underlie them.

8.2   FUTURE DIRECTIONS

While the research discussed within this monograph provides insight into the relationships between video game involvement and social outcomes, it has also sparked a range of new avenues for future research in this area. Several possible directions for future research are presented in the following. While some of the suggestions build directly upon the findings discussed within this monograph, others outline potential new research questions pertaining to the broader relationships between social outcomes, social Internet use, and computer-mediated communication.

8.2.1   Social Displacement

It has been argued that the work contained within this monograph provides evidence in support of social displacement effects underpinning the relationships between video game involvement and social outcomes. However, before one can conclude causality, research must be conducted examine the fluctuation of offline and online social contacts and social competence outcomes over a period of time. Future researchers should enlist longitudinal designs and evaluate friendship networks alongside social outcome measures (e.g., social goals, social skills, social capital, etc.) to demonstrate how social networks and social outcomes may change in conjunction with video game involvement. Longitudinal research such as this would also allow for a further validation of the proposed Cycle Model of Use. These outcomes could also be assessed and compared across various mediated outlets to uncover any patterns unique to the social, playful spaces of OVGs as their unique characteristics have sparked particular concern (this is discussed in more detail in section 8.2.2).

Future research should also consider additional mediators when examining the links between OVG involvement and social outcomes. While age, gender, and attachment were accounted for in the current research, play motivations and players' perceptions of a game's realism may also significantly affect the ways in which OVG involvement influences social outcomes. For example, recent work by Kaczmarek and Drazkowski (2014) examined the impact of OVG play on perceptions of offline and online social support among MMORPG escapists—players who engage in OVG explicitly to avoid real-world problems. The results indicated that playing for escapism was negatively related to offline social support and well-being.

However, MMORPG escapists who perceived the gaming environment to be realistic, in terms of being a 'direct reality,' were more likely to report receiving support from other players in ways that helped them cope with everyday problems independent of the effects of their pre-existing offline support. Thus, while the results of this work initially indicated inverse links between playing for escapism and social outcomes, the negative impact of escapist play on offline social support diminished, and reports of online social support magnified, once perceptions of realism were considered. While these results need to be interpreted with caution, as this study focused solely on MMORPG players motivated by escapism, it does suggest there are a range of factors that may mediate the relationship between OVG play and social outcomes.

8.2.2   Social Internet Use

While a substantial amount of research has evaluated social Internet use and OVGs, there is no known research evaluating the similarities and differences between the two. While all Internet-based social services provide alternative social outlets where individuals can engage with others free from the rules and pressures of traditional, face-to-face socialization, all mediated spaces are not created equal. That is, it is possible that some spaces may contribute to more severe displacement effects or be better able to socially accommodate particular users than others. For instance, revealing positive links between OVG play and avoidant attachment and inverse links between offline video game play and avoidant attachment in chapter 6 suggests that OVGs may be socially functional for those high in attachment avoidance. These significant links may be partially due to the fact that OVGs are able to provide a strong, social community even in the absence of direct socialization (Ducheneaut, Yee, Nickell, & Moore, 2006; Steinkuehler & Williams, 2006). This is unlike some other Internet-based social spaces, such as chat rooms, where the primary purpose and sole function of the space is to directly socialize with others. Thus, the particular qualities of online games may generate a social environment that is better suited to generate social support networks for individuals high in attachment avoidance than chat rooms.

Uncovering the key features of different mediated environments would not only be valuable for researchers who are interested in how and why certain individuals choose to engage in particular mediated social spaces, but also for clinicians who want to enlist the use of mediated environments in treatment programs for socially isolated or inhibited individuals. Qualitative research may be particularly advantageous to determine what key social features of mediated spaces appeal to users.

8.2.3   Attachment Functions

Uncovering significant links between avoidant attachment, playing for social comfort, and video game involvement among online-exclusive players suggests that OVGs may be well suited to serve vital attachment functions. However, further research is required to investigate the ways in which online games may serve attachment functions for individuals high in avoidant attachment. Understanding the particular elements that contribute to OVGs' functionality to serve attachment functions would help further the understanding of the social uses and effects of prolonged involvement within online games and determine whether or not the unique elements of online games extend beyond the advantages of simply interacting within a visually anonymous environment. For example, future research could investigate the element of play contained within OVGs and its role in serving attachment functions for avoidant individuals, as the sense of playfulness greatly contributes to the sense of affiliation and belonging and promotes long-standing, intimate bonds not typically found in other mediated outlets (Cole & Griffiths, 2007; Hsu et al., 2009; Iacono & Weisband, 1997; Williams, 2006; Yee, 2002).

Research is also needed to evaluate the potential social benefits of prolonged involvement over time to determine if the utilization of OVGs for social comfort leads to positive outcomes, like improved moods or social confidence, for those with an avoidant attachment or if it leads to intensified feelings of social isolation as suggested by the Cycle Model of Use (see Figure 8.1). Longitudinal research would be particularly advantageous and would allow researchers to examine the ways that the relationships between attachment, social skills, and Involvement evolve over time.

8.2.4   Social Augmentation

As OVGs seem to hold the potential to serve attachment functions and provide social comfort for players, it is possible that for some, the social environment of OVGs may supplement one's social relationships by providing an additional outlet for social interaction (Katz & Rice, 2002; Kraut et al., 2002; Wellman, 2004). For example, for individuals high in attachment avoidance, OVGs may not only lead to an expansion of one's social circle but may also provide the user's primary social outlet. That is, it is possible that OVGs are portals for the first social experiences in which highly avoidant individuals feel at ease and are able to overcome their difficulties in self-disclosure and intimacy without fear of repercussions. Previous research has found visually anonymous, mediated socialization to be particularly beneficial for avoidant individuals, as they report a greater likelihood to disclose personal information to their online contacts (Buote et al., 2009) and a greater comfort with self-disclosure and intimacy in their semi-anonymous, online relationships than their offline counterparts (Ponder, 2009). As self-disclosure is an integral component of developing intimacy (Miell & Duck, 1986; Reis & Shaver, 1988), and an inability to self-disclose has been a fundamental hindrance to the formation of intimate friendship bonds among avoidant individuals, contributing to their potential social isolation (Buote et al., 2009; Smith et al., 1999), the provision of a visually anonymous, social space may be well suited to serve attachment needs for these individuals. Thus, rather than OVG involvement promoting an online community at the expense of one's offline social contacts, OVGs could be socially augmenting by providing a primary friendship group where avoidant individuals can freely engage. Further research is needed to explore the potential augmenting role OVGs may play for those high in attachment avoidance.

8.2.5   Social Skill Development

Additional research is also needed to fully examine the scope of the relationship between social skills and OVG involvement. Some researchers have suggested that OVGs are ideal spaces for social learning, as they provide the ability for players to observe, rehearse, and practice a range of social strategies (Ducheneaut & Moore, 2005; Steinkuehler & Williams, 2006). Indeed, some researchers have found significant, positive links between video game play and specific aspects of sociability, such as pro-social behaviors and cooperation. For example, Ewoldsen and colleagues (2012) found that individuals who played video games cooperatively with others demonstrated an increase in cooperative behaviors out of the game context (Ewoldsen et al., 2012). Gentile and colleagues (2009) noted similar patterns with pro-social games and pro-social behaviors, such as helping. Numerous studies have also found links between civic engagement and video game play. For example, Lenhart et al. (2008) found that adolescents who played games with civic experiences (such as an MMORPG) were more likely to be engaged in social and civic activities in their everyday lives. An increase in civic engagement could translate to an improvement for a range of social skills over time, such as the ability to organize groups and leadership skills.

The possibility for video game play to contribute to long-term increases in sociability has recently been discussed in an overview paper by Granic, Lobel, and Engles (2014) in *American Psychologist*. The researchers note a lack of research that has examined the potential *positive and negative* social impact of video game play and address the need for more research evaluating the conditions under which these effects are most likely to be manifested. As aforementioned, longitudinal research is desperately needed in this area to address these concerns and generate a clear understanding of the implications, either positive or negative, of video game play on everyday social functioning.

8.3   CONCLUDING THOUGHTS

The work contained within this monograph provides the most comprehensive assessment into the relationships between social goals, social skills, and OVG involvement to date. In addition to assessing these relationships through a series of studies, a new proposed measure of video game involvement was put forth that incorporates behavioral and psychological components of being a 'gamer.' Various suggestions for future research were also proposed in an effort to further the work in this area and clarify the nature and scope of the relationships between OVG play and sociability.

While the current research neither provides support for the magnitude of the fears as to the social impact of OVG play nor reinforces the stereotypical portrayal of OVG players as a community of socially inept individuals, significant inverse links between video game play and social outcomes were uncovered. As such, one cannot conclude that there are no grounds for concern, but rather that an individual's desire to socialize (i.e., social goals) and ability to do so (i.e., social skills) do seem to fluctuate with his or her level of video game involvement; however, this relationship is related to an individual's general level of video game involvement and is not unique to OVG play. As such, it is possible that these relationships have less to do with video games and more to do with prolonged engagement within an activity that supports and compensates a user socially. Through prolonged interaction within such a medium, one may not only displace some offline contacts (i.e., those whom they do not play with) but also may lose valuable time that would typically be spent learning, adopting, and practicing a range of social skills and strategies. While the work contained within this monograph provides evidence to suggest that video game play may be but one of these potentially displacing and socially compensating activities, future research is needed to assess if these relationships are unique to video game play, other forms of media, or other forms of mediated socialization.

Taken together, it can be concluded that online game players are not a community of socially inept individuals. In fact, significant relationships between social goals and video game play were not found to be unique to this community but rather evident among the broader group of video game players. To further understand these relationships, researchers are encouraged to adopt longitudinal research, provide more comprehensive assessments of video game involvement, and account for the potential *positive and negative* ways in which OVGs may be associated with players' social competence and confidence.

NOTES

1. It must be noted that these conclusions are theoretical, as the analyses were cross-sectional and the exchange of offline for online contacts, or social displacement, was not directly measured over time. Furthermore, these findings do not completely dismiss the potential for social compensation processes to initiate video game play. Rather, they indicate that social compensation phenomena are not likely to be found at the social skills level and cannot be attributed to an underlying insecure attachment.
2. This model is proposed to explain OVG involvement, rather than social video game use in general, as social offline players do not experience a displacement of offline for online contacts due to use.

REFERENCES

Ainsworth, M.D.S., Blehar, M. C., Wathers, E., & Wall, S. (1978). *Patterns of attachment*. Hillsdale, NJ: Lawrence Erlbaum.

Bessière, K., Kiesler, S., Kraut, R., & Boneva, B. (2004). Longitudinal effects of Internet uses on depressive affect: A social resources approach. Unpublished manuscript, Carnegie Mellon University, Philadelphia, PA.

Blais, J., Craig, W. M., Pepler, D., & Connolly, J. (2008). Adolescents online: The importance of Internet activity choices on salient relationships. *Journal of Youth and Adolescence, 37*, 522–536. doi:10.1007/s10964–007–9262–7

Bowlby, J. (1969). *Attachment and loss. Vol. 1: Attachment*. New York: Basic Books.

Bowlby, J. (1973). *Attachment and loss. Vol. 2: Separation: Anger and Anxiety*. London: Hogarth.

Bowlby, J. (1979). *The making and breaking of affectional bonds*. London: Tavistock.

Buote, V., Wood, E., & Pratt, M. (2009). Exploring similarities and differences between online and offline friendships: The role of attachment style. *Computers in Human Behavior, 25*, 560–567.

Caplan, S. (2003). Preference for online social interaction: A theory of problematic Internet use and psychosocial well-being. *Communication Research, 30*, 625–648.

Caplan, S., Williams, D., & Yee, N. (2009). Problematic Internet use and psychosocial well-being among MMO players. *Computers in Human Behavior, 25*(6), 1312–1319. doi:10.1016/j.chb.2009.06.006

Chiu, S., Lee, J., & Huang, D. (2004). Video game addiction in children and teenagers in Taiwan. *Cyberpsychology and Behavior, 7*(5), 571–581.

Cole, H., & Griffiths, M. D. (2007). Social interactions in massively multiplayer online role-playing games. *Cyberpsychology and Behavior, 10*(4), 575–583. doi:10.1089/cpb.2007.9988

Davis, R. A. (2001). A cognitive behavioral model of pathologial Internet use. *Computers in Human Behavior, 17*(2), 187–195.

Ducheneaut, N., & Moore, R. (2005). More than just "XP": Learning social skills in massively multiplayer online games. *Interactive Technology and Smart Education, 2*(2), 89–100.

Ducheneaut, N., Yee, N., Nickell, E., & Moore, R. (2006). "Alone together?": Exploring the social dynamics of massively multiplayer online games. Presented at the SIGCHI conference on human factors in computing systems, New York, New York.

Entertainment Software Association. (2012). *Game player data*. Retrieved from http://www.theesa.com/facts/gameplayer.asp

Ewoldsen, D. R., Eno, C. A., Okdie, B. M., Velez, J. A., Guadagno, R. E., & DeCoster, J. (2012). Effect of playing violent video games cooperatively or competitively on subsequent cooperative behavior. *Cyberpsychology, Behavior, and Social Networking, 15*(5), 277–280. doi:10.1089/cyber.2011.0308

Galston, W. A. (2000). Does the Internet strengthen community? *National Civic Review, 89*(3), 193–202.

Gentile, D. A., Anderson, C. A., Yukawa, S., Ihori, N., Saleem, M., Ming, L. K., . . . Sakamoto, A. (2009). The effects of prosocial video games on prosocial behaviors: International evidence from correlational, longitudinal, and experimental studies. *Personality and Social Psychology Bulletin, 35*, 752–763. doi:10.1177/0146167209333045

Granic, I., Lobel, A., & Engels, R.C.M.E. (2014). The benefits of playing video games. *American Psychologist, 69*, 66–78. doi:10.1037/a0034857

Griffiths, M. D. (2010). Computer game playing and social skills: A pilot study. *Aloma, 27*, 301–310.

Hussain, Z., & Griffiths, M. (2009). The attitudes, feelings, and experiences of online gamers: A qualitative analysis. *Cyberpsychology and Behavior*, 12(6), 747–753.

Hsu, S., Wen, M., & Wu, M. (2009). Exploring user experiences as predictors of MMORPG addiction. *Computers and Education*, 53(3), 990–999.

Iacono, C. S., & Weisband, S. (1997, January). Developing trust in virtual teams. In *Proceedings of the Thirtieth Hawaii International Conference on System Sciences*, 2, 412–420.

Kaczmarek, L. D., & Drazkowski, D. (2014). MMORPG escapism predicts decreased well-being: Examination of gaming time, game realism beliefs, and online social support for offline problems. *Cyberpsychology, Behavior, and Social Networking*, 17(5), 298–302.

Katz, J. E., & Rice, R. E. (2002). Social consequences of Internet use: Access, involvement, and interaction. Cambridge, MA: MIT Press.

Kim, E., Namkoong, K., Ku, T., & Kim, S. (2008). The relationship between online game addiction and aggression, self-control, and narcissistic personality traits. *European Psychiatry*, 23(3), 212–218. doi:10.1016/j.eurpsy.2007.10.010

Kowert, R., Domahidi, E., & Quandt, T. (2014). The relationship between online video game involvement and gaming-related friendships among emotionally sensitive individuals. *Cyberpsychology, Behavior, and Social Networking*, 17(7), 447–453. doi:10.1089/cyber.2013.0656

Kowert, R., Vogelgesang, J., Festl., R., & Quandt, T. (under review). Psychosocial causes and consequences of online video game involvement.

Kraut, R., Kiesler, S., Boneva, B., Cummings, J., Helgeson, V., & Crawford, A. (2002). Internet paradox revisited. *Journal of Social Issues*, 58(1), 49–74.

Kraut, R., Patterson, M., Lundmark, V., Kiesler, S., Mukopadhyay, T., & Scherlis, W. (1998). Internet paradox: A social technology that reduces social involvement and psychological well-being? *American Psychologist*, 53(9), 1017–1031.

Lemmens, J., Valkenburg, P., & Peter, J. (2011). Psychological causes and consequences of pathological gaming. *Computers in Human Behavior*, 27(1), 144–152. doi:10.1016/j.chb.2010.07.015

Lenhart, A., Kahne, J., Middaugh, E., Macgill, A., Evans, C., & Vitak, J. (2008). *Teens, video games and civics*. Pew Internet and American Life Project. Retrieved from http://www.pewinternet.org/Reports/2008/Teens-Video-Games-and-Civics.aspx

Liu, M., & Peng, W. (2009). Cognitive and psychological predictors of the negative outcomes associated with playing MMOGs (massively multiplayer online games). *Computers in Human Behavior*, 25(6), 1306–1311. doi:10.1016/j.chb.2009.06.002

Lo, S., Wang, C., & Fang, W. (2005). Physical interpersonal relationships and social anxiety among online game players. *Cyberpsychology and Behavior*, 8(1), 15–20. doi:10.1089/cpb.2005.8.15

Miell, D. E., & Duck, S. (1986). Strategies in developing friendships. In V. Derlega & B. A. Winstead (Eds.), *Friends and social interaction* (pp. 129–143). New York: Springer-Verlag.

Morahan-Martin, J., & Schumacher, P. (2003). Loneliness and social uses of the Internet. *Computers in Human Behavior*, 19, 659–671.

Nie, N., & Erbring, L. (2002). Internet and mass media: A preliminary report. *IT & Society*, 1(2), 134–141.

Nie, N., & Hillygus, S. (2001). Eduation and democratic citizenship. In D. Ravitch & J. Viteritti (Eds.), *Making good citizens: Education and civial society*. New Haven, CT: Yale University Press.

Ponder, E. (2009). *Attachment and Internet relationships*. PhD dissertation. Wheaton College, Wheaton, Illinois.

Reis, H. T., & Shaver, P. (1988). Intimacy as an interpersonal process. In S. Duck (Ed.), *Handbook of personal relationships* (pp. 367–389). Chichester, UK: Wiley.

Shen, C., & Williams, D. (2010). Unpacking time online: Connecting Internet and massively multiplayer online game use with psychological well-being. *Communication Research, 20*(10), 1–27. doi:10.1177/0093650210377196

Slouka, M. (1995). *War of the worlds: Cyberspace and the high-tech assault on reality.* New York: Basic Books.

Smith, E. R., Murphy, J., & Coats, S. (1999). Attachment to groups: Theory and management. *Journal of Personality and Social Psychology, 77*(1), 94–110.

Smyth, J. (2007). Beyond self-selection in video game play. *Cyberpsychology and Behavior, 10*(5), 717–721.

Steinkuehler, C., & Williams, D. (2006). Where everybody knows your (screen) name: Online games as "third places." *Journal of Computer-Mediated Communication, 11*(4), 885–909.

Wellman, B. (2004). Connecting communities: On and offline. *Contexts, 3*(4), 22–28.

Williams, D. (2006). Groups and goblins: The social and civic impact of online games. *Journal of Broadcasting and Electronic Media, 50,* 651–681. doi:10.1207/s15506878jobem5004_5

Williams, D. (2007). The impact of time online: Social capital and cyberbalkanization. *Cyberpsychology and Behavior, 10*(3), 398–406.

Williams, D., Yee, N., & Caplan, S. (2008). Who plays, how much, and why? Debunking the stereotypical gamer profile. *Journal of Computer-Mediated Communication Monographs, 13*(4), 993–1018. doi:10.1111/j.1083–6101.2008.00428.x

Yee, N. (2002). Befriending ogres and wood-elves—Understanding relationship formation in MMORPGs. *Nickyee.* Retrieved from http://www.nickyee.com/hub/relationships/home.html

Appendices

Appendix A
Ford's (1982) Adapted Offline Social and Non-Social Goals

Social Goals

- Getting along with my parents
  - Changed to: Getting along with my family
- Having a lot of close friends
- Being romantically involved with someone
- Helping other people with their problems
- Getting involved with other people in activities outside of school
  - Changed to: Getting involved with other people in activities outside of school/work

Non-Social Goals

- Getting good grades in school
  - Changed to: Getting good grades in school/performing well at work
- Earning a lot of money
- Having or getting a steady job
  - Changed to: Having or getting an enjoyable job
- Learning new skills and knowledge
- Having lots of free time to pursue my own interests

Appendix B
Online Social and Non-Social Goals

Social Goals

- Getting along with my guild
- Having a lot of close friends in game
- Being romantically involved with someone in game
- Helping others in game
- Being involved in lots of activities with different groups

Non-Social Goals

- Optimizing character performance (e.g., theorycrafting)
- Earning a lot of in-game money
- In-game accomplishments (e.g., raid progression, PVP achievements, etc.)
- Learning new strategies
- Having time to pursue your own interests in-game

Individuals who reported no experience with MMO-type games were presented with the following supplementary instructions:

"*Imagine that you were playing an MMO, such as* World of Warcraft. *MMOs are unique environments in that you are connected with other players in real time, the environment exists and evolves even when an individual is not playing, and these games have no clear ending. The majority of game play in MMOs involves completing a series of challenges, or quests. To facilitate the aiding of other characters, as well as one's own, players often form collectives with one another, commonly called guilds. Being a member of a guild is useful in that it provides a convenient way to group up with other players to complete common goals. Below is a list of 10 virtual-world goals. In this context, a goal is defined as something you would actively work to attain.*"

Appendix C
SSI Subscale Descriptions

The subscales are as follows (Riggio, 1989):

Emotional Expressivity (EE): Emotional Expressivity measures the skill with which individuals communicate non-verbally, particularly in sending emotional messages, but it also includes the non-verbal expression of attitudes, dominance, and interpersonal orientation. In addition, this scale reflects the ability to accurately express felt emotional states. Persons who are highly expressive emotionally are animated and emotionally charged and are able to arouse or inspire others from their ability to transmit feelings. Example item: "*I am able to liven up a dull party.*"

Emotional Sensitivity (ES): Emotional Sensitivity measures skill in receiving and interpreting the non-verbal communications of others. Individuals who are emotionally sensitive attend to and accurately interpret the subtle emotional cues of others. Those who are highly sensitive emotionally may be susceptible to becoming emotionally aroused by others, empathically experiencing their emotional states. Example item: "*I sometimes cry at sad movies.*"

Emotional Control (EC): Emotional Control measures ability to control and regulate emotional and non-verbal displays. Emotional Control includes the ability to convey particular emotions on cue and to hide behind an assumed 'mask'—laughing appropriately at a joke or putting on a cheerful face to cover sorrow. Persons whose scores are very high on this scale may tend to control against the display of felt emotions. Example item: "*I am easily able to make myself look happy one minute and sad the next.*"

Social Expressivity (SE): Social Expressivity assesses skill in verbal expression and the ability to engage others in social discourse. High scores on this scale are associated with verbal fluency in individuals who appear outgoing and gregarious and who are skilled in initiating and guiding conversations on just about any subject. In extremes, and particularly when scores on Social Control are low, socially expressive persons may speak spontaneously without monitoring the content of what they are saying. Example item: "*I always mingle at parties.*"

Social Sensitivity (SS): Social Sensitivity assesses ability to interpret the verbal communication of others. It also assesses an individual's sensitivity to and understanding of the norms governing appropriate social behavior. Persons who are socially sensitive are attentive to social behavior and are conscious and aware of the appropriateness of their own actions. Extremely high scores on this scale, in conjunction with moderate to low scores on Social Expressivity and Social Control, may indicate self-consciousness that may inhibit participation in social interaction. Example item: "*Sometimes I think that I take things other people say to me too personally.*"

Social Control (SC): Social Control assesses skill in role-playing and social self-presentation. Persons whose Social Control skills are well developed are generally adept, tactful, and self-confident in social situations and can fit in comfortably in just about any kind of social situation. Social Control is also important in guiding the direction and content of communication in social interaction. Example item: "*I am usually very good at leading group discussions.*"

Appendix D
Principal Axis SSI Factor Loadings

Table D-1 Principal axis analysis of the SSI factor loadings using item sets and a six-factor solution

SSI Item Sets	Factor 1	Factor 2	Factor 3	Factor 4	Factor 5	Factor 6
EE 1	.147	.023	.157	−.276	.180	**.740**
EE 2	.317	.040	.151	−.075	.248	**.588**
EE 3	.125	.103	.409	−.297	.259	**.366**
ES 1	.181	.183	**.668**	.055	.291	.047
ES 2	.145	.136	**.775**	.007	.090	.127
ES 3	.182	.267	**.727**	−.036	.116	.146
EC 1	.085	−.094	.058	**.800**	.050	−.098
EC 2	.195	−.283	−.092	**.737**	−.105	.020
EC 3	.025	−.119	.008	**.769**	.088	−.237
SE 1	.282	.112	.179	−.007	**.758**	.184
SE 2	.420	.067	.298	.029	**.728**	.262
SE 3	.488	.020	.252	.070	**.554**	.270
SS 1	−.051	**.879**	.152	−.087	.142	.047
SS 2	−.159	**.720**	.181	−.202	−.074	.027
SS 3	−.166	**.747**	.212	−.210	.070	.019
SC 1	**.823**	−.168	.190	.113	.250	.178
SC 2	**.685**	−.148	.148	.149	.186	.138
SC 3	**.633**	−.269	.264	.086	.388	.153

Appendix E
List of Game Genres/Modalities

List of Game Genres and Modalities Presented in Study 1:

- Single-Player First-Person Shooter (e.g., *Call of Duty*)
- Multiplayer First-Person Shooter (e.g., *Unreal Tournament*)
- Single-Player Role-Playing Game (e.g., the *Final Fantasy* series)
- Multiplayer Role-Playing Game (e.g., *World of Warcraft*)
- Single-Player Simulation Game (e.g., *The Sims*)
- Single-/Multiplayer Sports Game (e.g., *FIFA*)
- Single-/Multiplayer Party Game (e.g., *Rock Band*)
- Other

List of Game Genres and Modalities Presented in Studies 2 and 3:

- Single-Player First-Person Shooter (e.g., *Call of Duty*)
- Multiplayer First-Person Shooter (e.g., *Unreal Tournament*)
- Single-Player Role-Playing Game (e.g., the *Final Fantasy* series)
- Multiplayer Role-Playing Game (e.g., *World of Warcraft*)
- Single-Player Simulation Game (e.g., *The Sims*)
- Multiplayer Simulation Game (e.g., multiplayer mode in *Microsoft Flight Simulator*)
- Single-Player Real-Time Strategy (e.g., single-player campaign in *Starcraft*)
- Multiplayer Real-Time Strategy (e.g., multiplayer campaign in *Starcraft*)
- Single-Player Turn-Based Strategy (e.g., *Civilization*)
- Multiplayer Turn-Based Strategy (e.g., multiplayer mode in *Total War*)
- Single-Player Puzzle Game (e.g., *Tetris*)
- Multiplayer Puzzle Game (e.g., co-op in *Portal 2*)
- Single-/Multiplayer Party Game (e.g., *Rock Band*)
- Single-/Multiplayer Sports Game (e.g., *FIFA*)
- Other

Appendix F
Demographic Analyses from Study 2

Time spent playing across gender and age groups: A MANOVA analysis of gender, age, and game play revealed a significant effect of gender, $F(1, 527) = 61.42$, $p < .001$, but not age ($p = .83$, ns), for overall game play. Males ($M = 4.45$, $SD = 1.86$) reported engaging in more overall game play more than females ($M = 2.85$, $SD = 1.92$). In terms of the scale, males averaged between 1–10 hours a week of game play, whereas females averaged between once a month and once a week (see Figure F-1). No significant interaction between gender and age was found ($p = .68$, ns).

Online play frequency: A significant effect of gender ($F(1, 527) = 31.12$, $p < .001$), but not age ($p = .92$), was also found for online play frequency, with males ($M = 3.15$, $SD = 2.22$) engaging in more online game play than females ($M = 1.92$, $SD = 1.87$). In terms of the scale, males' online play frequency averaged between once a week and 1–5 hours a week, whereas females' play frequency ranged between less than once a month to about once a month (see Figure F-2). A significant interaction between gender and age was not found ($p = .21$, ns).

Types of games played: Participants were asked to indicate which genre of games, and in which modalities, they were currently playing by selecting from a list of 15 options (see appendix E). The total number of selected game types was summed to create game variety totals for each participant. As seen in Figure F-3, game playing participants appear to enjoy a variety of games and do not typically limit themselves to one genre or modality. Most participants (60.89%) reported playing between 1 and 4 types of games, 30.54% reported between 5 and 9 types of games, and 4.47% reported playing more than 10 types of games. Of those participants who reported playing only one type of game, the largest percentage reported playing single-player puzzle games (34.8%). No participants reported playing all 15 different types of games.

Modality and genre preferences: Genre preferences, across modality (e.g., single- or multiplayer), are shown in Figure F-4. As sports, party, and other games could not be differentiated by modality, they are presented within the modality in which they are most likely to be experienced (e.g., multi-player modality for party games). Games reported in the "other" category widely varied, but the most commonly reported genre was action-adventure.

Besides puzzle games (e.g., *Tetris*), the most popular game genres were first-person shooters (FPS) and role-playing games (RPG).

Participants reported a preference for single-player games when able to choose across modalities, particularly for puzzle and simulation games.

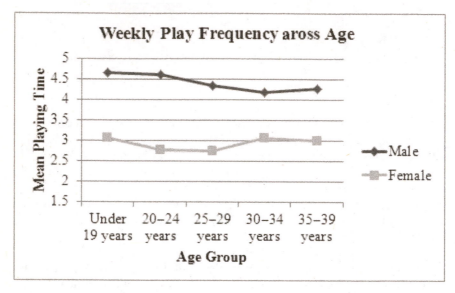

Figure F-1   Mean frequency of overall game play across gender and age (N = 537)

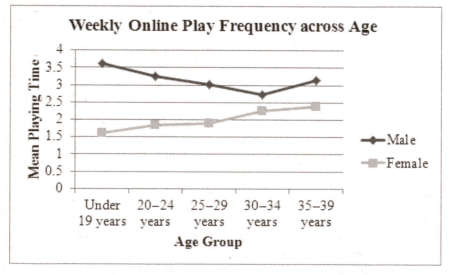

Figure F-2   Mean frequency of online game play across gender and age (N = 537)

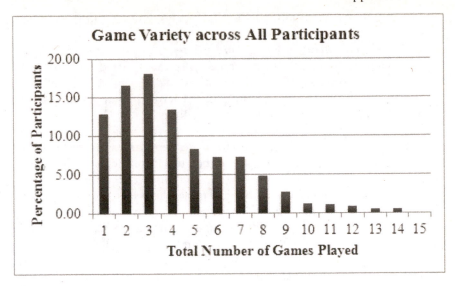

Figure F-3   Frequency of game variety among the sample (*N* = 537)

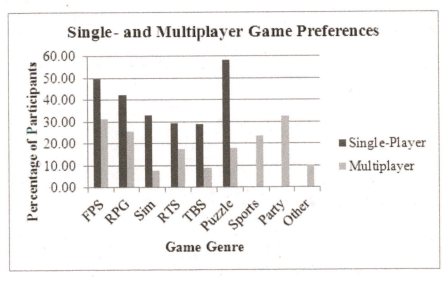

Figure F-4   Single- and multiplayer game genre preferences among the sample (*N* = 537)

However, those who play with others are likely to also to play at least occasionally in single-player mode, whereas those who play in single-player mode may not necessarily also play with others (through either an Internet connection or co-located gaming). Therefore, the percentage of individuals reporting to play in single-player modalities may be slightly overestimated and not representative of individuals who solely play without the presence of others.

Modality preferences across age and gender: To evaluate modality preferences independent of genre, the game types that were differentiable by single- or multiplayer modalities were summed to create modality-preference scores. Genres that could not be distinguished across modalities (i.e., sports, party, and other) were excluded from this analysis.

Repeated measures ANOVA analyses uncovered a significant effect of gender, $F(1, 527) = 23.48$, $p < .001$, with males reporting a greater incidence of play for single- and multiplayer games than female participants. No significant main effect of age ($p = .33$, *ns*), or interactions, was found.

Within subjects, Mauchly's test indicated that the assumption of sphericity had been violated; therefore, the following numbers have been adjusted using the Greenhouse-Geisser correction. A significant main effect of modality within males, $F(1, 285) = 129.54$, $p < .001$, and females, $F(1, 242) = 232.55$, $p < .001$, confirmed that single-player modalities are played to a greater extent than multiplayer, regardless of gender (see Figure F-5).

Genre preferences across age and gender: To examine genre preferences across age and gender, a repeated measures ANOVA was conducted. In order to evaluate genre preferences for all eight genres, the six game genres that spanned modality (FPS, RPG, sim, real-time strategy [RTS], turn-based strategy [TBS], and puzzle) were collapsed, and averaged, prior to analysis, to produce a score that would represent a participant's genre preference regardless of modality.

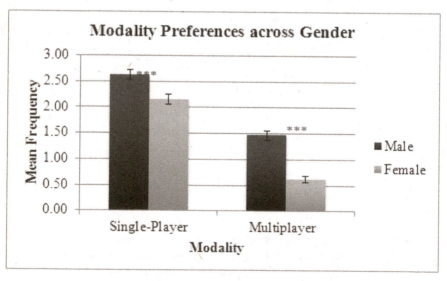

Figure F-5   Modality preferences across gender collapsed across game types (error bars represent standard error) ($N = 537$) ***$p < .001$

A significant main effect of gender, $F(1, 527) = 15.19$, $p < .001$, and a marginally significant effect of age ($F=2.33$, $p=.06$), was found. Pairwise comparisons revealed that across gender, males reported a greater preference for FPS, RPG, RTS, TBS, and sports games (F's > 6.5, p's $< .01$), while females showed a preference for sim and party games (F's > 12, p's $< .001$). No gender differences were found within the puzzle genre (see Figure F-6).

Within subjects, Mauchly's test indicated that the assumption of sphericity had been violated ($p < .001$). Therefore, the following values have been adjusted using the Greenhouse-Geisser corrections. A significant main effect of genre, $F(5.95, 3132.89) = 25.63$, $p < .001$, was uncovered. Across all participants, FPS and puzzle games were reported as the most actively played genres of game, followed by RPGs. Sim, RTS, TBS, and sports games were played with the least frequency, with no significant differences between them.

A significant interaction between game genre and gender, $F(5.95, 3132.89) = 27.72$, $p < .001$, was also found, while the interactions between gender and age ($p = .71$, *ns*) and game genre, age group, and gender ($p = .49$, *ns*) did not reach significance.

To examine the nature of the gender interactions, analyses were conducted within gender categories. Within male participants, Mauchly's test indicated that the assumption of sphericity had been violated ($p < .001$); therefore, the following values have been adjusted using the Greenhouse-Geisser corrections. A significant main effect of genre, $F(5.86, 1668.62) = 24.87$, $p < .001$, but not age ($p = .09$, *ns*), was found. No interaction between genre and age was evident ($p = .35$, ns). Pairwise comparisons confirmed that FPS games are preferred above all other genres (p's $< .001$). RPG, puzzle, and sports

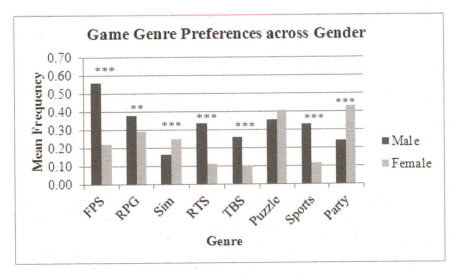

Figure F-6   Genre preferences across gender (collapsed across game types) ($N = 537$) **p < .01, ***p < .001

games were the second most preferred (p's < .05) among male participants, whereas simulation games were the least preferred.

Within female participants, Mauchly's test again indicated that sphericity assumptions had been violated (p <. 001); therefore, the figures reported here have been corrected using the Greenhouse-Geisser correction. A significant main effect of genre, $F(5.19, 1256.13) = 29.89$, p < .001, but not age (p = .34, *ns*), was found for female participants. No significant interaction between genre and age was found (p = .77, *ns*). Pairwise comparisons confirmed females' preference for puzzle and party games (p's < .001), with RPG and sim genres emerging as second favorites (p's < .05). RTS, TBS, and sports games were least favored among women.

Appendix G
Abridged SSI Factor Loadings

Table G-1 Factor loadings for abridged SSI

Subscale	Item Number	Factor Loading
Emotional Expressivity		
	25	.684
	37	.579
	55	.698
	73	.316
Emotional Sensitivity		
	26	.742
	32	.647
	38	.797
	50	.745
Emotional Control		
	21	.619
	39	.654
	45	.721
	69	.663
Social Expressivity		
	16	.706
	28	.777

(Continued)

Subscale	Item Number	Factor Loading
	58	.808
	70	.786
Social Sensitivity		
	65	.733
	71	.685
	83	.804
	89	.851
Social Control		
	12	.620
	30	.434
	42	.676
	78	.588

Appendix H
Abridged SSI

Emotional Expressivity

- I usually feel uncomfortable touching other people*
- Sometimes I have trouble making my friends and family realize how angry or upset I am with them
- I often touch my friends when talking to them
- I rarely show my feelings or emotions

Emotional Sensitivity

- I can easily tell what a person's character is by watching his or her interactions with others
- I always seem to know what peoples' true feelings are no matter how hard they try to conceal them
- I can accurately tell what a person's character is upon first meeting him or her
- I can instantly spot a 'phony' the minute I meet him or her

Emotional Control

- I am not very skilled in controlling my emotions*
- It is very hard for me to control my emotions*
- I am very good at maintaining a calm exterior even if I am upset
- I am rarely able to hide a strong emotion*

Social Expressivity

- I love to socialize
- I always mingle at parties
- At parties I enjoy talking to a lot of different people
- I enjoy going to large parties and meeting new people

Social Sensitivity

- I am very sensitive of criticism
- It is very important that other people like me
- I'm generally concerned about the impression I'm making on others
- I am often concerned with what others are thinking of me

Social Control

- When I'm with a group of friends I am often the spokesperson for the group
- I am usually very good at leading group discussions
- I am often chosen to be the leader of a group
- I find it very difficult to speak in front of a large group of people*

*Indicates a reverse scored item

Appendix I
Experiences in Close Relationships Scale

Experiences in Close Relationships (ECR) scale (Brennan, Clark, & Shaver, 1998)

Ratings from each question are summed to provide outcome scores. Odd-numbered questions measure attachment avoidance, while even-numbered questions measure attachment anxiety.

1. I prefer not to show a partner how I feel deep down.
2. I worry about being abandoned.
3. I am very comfortable being close to romantic partners.*
4. I worry a lot about my relationships.
5. Just when my partner starts to get close to me I find myself pulling away.
6. I worry that romantic partners won't care about me as much as I care about them.
7. I get uncomfortable when a romantic partner wants to be very close.
8. I worry a fair amount about losing my partner.
9. I don't feel comfortable about opening up to romantic partners.
10. I often wish that my partner's feelings for me were as strong as my feelings for him/her.
11. I want to get close to my partner, but I keep pulling back.
12. I often want to merge completely with romantic partners, and this sometimes scares them away.
13. I am nervous when partners get too close to me.
14. I worry about being alone.
15. I feel comfortable sharing my private thoughts and feelings with my partner.*
16. My desire to be very close sometimes scares people away.
17. I try to avoid getting too close to my partner.
18. I need a lot of reassurance that I am loved by my partner.
19. I find it relatively easy to get close to my partner.*
20. Sometimes I feel that I force my partners to show more feeling, more commitment.*
21. I find it difficult to allow myself to depend on romantic partners.

22. I do not often worry about being abandonded.*
23. I prefer not to be too close to romantic partners.
24. If I can't get my partner to show interest in me, I get upset or angry.
25. I tell my partner just about everything.*
26. I find that my partner(s) don't want to get as close as I could like.
27. I usually discuss my problems and concerns with my partner.*
28. When I'm not involved in a relationship, I feel somewhat anxious and insecure.
29. I feel comfortable when depending on romantic partners.*
30. I get frustrated when my partner is not around as much as I would like.
31. I don't mind asking romantic partners for comfort, advice, or help.*
32. I get frustrated if romantic partners are not available when I need them.
33. It helps to turn to my romantic partner in times of need.*
34. When romantic partners disapprove of me, I feel really bad about myself.
35. I turn to my partner for many things, comfort and reassurance.*
36. I resent it when my partner spends time away from me.

*Indicates a reverse scored item

Appendix J
Emotional Motivations for Play Factor Loadings

Table J-1 Factor loadings for all factors and factor items ($N = 409$)

	Playing for Comfort	Playing for Entertainment
Stressed	.775	–.208
Anxious	.787	–.268
Sad	.771	–.331
Lonely	.652	–.309
Happy	.673	.610
Sad	.673	.621

Appendix K
Demographic Analyses from Study 3

Time spent playing across gender and age: A MANOVA analysis of gender, age, and game play among active game players revealed a significant effect of gender, $F(1, 399) = 38.88$, $p < .001$, but not age ($p = .11$) for overall game play. Males ($M = 5.61$, $SD = 1.83$) reported engaging in more overall game play more than females ($M = 4.22$, $SD = 1.92$). In terms of the scale, males averaged between 1–10 hours a week of game play whereas females played between once a week to 5 hours a week (see Figure K-1). No significant interactions between gender and age were found ($p = .74$, *ns*).

Online play frequency: A significant effect of gender, $F(1, 399) = 25.67$, $p < .001$, but not age ($p = .08$, *ns*) was also found for online play time, with males ($M = 4.61$, $SD = 2.17$) engaging in more online game play than females ($M = 3.17$, $SD = 2.11$). In terms of the scale, males averaged between once a week and 1–5 hours a week, whereas females' play frequency averaged between about once a month to once a week (see Figure K-2). Similar patterns between overall and online play are supported by their high correlation, $r = .756$, $p < .001$. A significant interaction between gender and age was not found ($p = .79$, *ns*).

Types of games played: Participants were asked to indicate which genre of games, and in which modalities, they were currently playing by selecting from a list of 15 options (see appendix E). The total number of selected game types was summed to create game variety totals for each participant. As seen in Figure K-3, game playing participants appear to enjoy a variety of games and do not typically limit themselves to one genre or modality. Most participants (48.6%) reported playing between 1 and 7 types of games, 8.2% reported playing between 8 and 10 types of games, and 3.2% of participants reported playing more than 10 types of games. No participants reported playing more than 13 types of games. Of those who reported playing only one type of game, the largest percentage reported playing multiplayer role-playing games (29.4%). 40.1% (206 participants) of the sample did not report being an active player of any of the 15 types of games; however, this includes the 119 inactive players within the sample. Of the remaining 87 participants who chose none of the provided game types, 17.6% reported playing an "other" game genre, the most common of which was sandbox games (e.g., *Minecraft*).

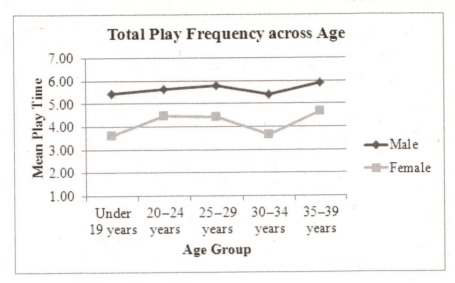

Figure K-1   Mean frequency of overall game play across gender and age (*n* = 409)

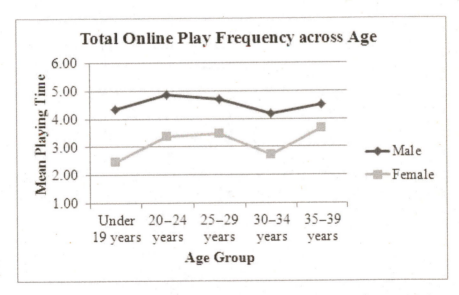

Figure K-2   Mean frequency of online game play across gender and age (*n* = 409)

Modality and genre preferences: Genre preferences, across modality (e.g., single- or multiplayer), are shown in Figure K-4. As sports, party, and other games could not be differentiated by modality, they are presented within the modality in which they are most likely to be experienced (e.g., multiplayer modality for party games). Games reported in the "other" category widely varied, but the most commonly reported genre was platformers (e.g., *Mario*

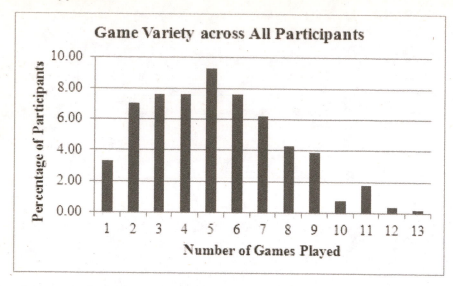

Figure K-3   Frequency of game variety among the sample (*N* = 514)

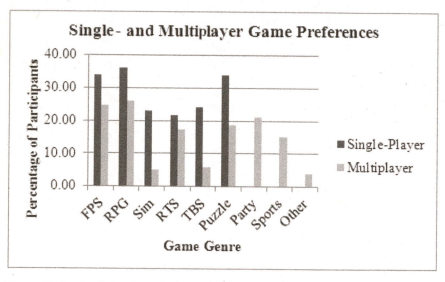

Figure K-4   Single- and multiplayer game genre preferences among the sample (*N* = 514)

Brothers series). Besides puzzle games (e.g., *Tetris*), the most popular game genres were first-person shooters (FPS) and role-playing games (RPG).

Participants reported a preference for single-player games when able to choose across modalities, particularly for puzzle and simulation games. However, those who play with others are likely to also to play at least occasionally in single-player mode, whereas those who play in single-player mode may not necessarily also play with others (through either an Internet connection or co-located gaming). Therefore, the percentage of individuals reporting to play in single-player modalities may be slightly overestimated and not representative of individuals who solely play without the presence of others.

Modality preferences across age and gender: To evaluate modality preferences independent of genre, the game types that were differentiable by single- or multiplayer modalities were summed to create modality-preference scores. Genres that could not be distinguished across modalities (i.e., sports, party, and other) were excluded from this analysis.

Repeated measures ANOVA analyses uncovered a significant effect of gender, $F(1, 504) = 31.92$, $p < .001$, indicating that males report playing more single- and multiplayer games than female participants (see Figure K-5). No main effect of age ($p = .62$) was found; however, a significant interaction between age and gender emerged, $F(4, 504) = 2.65$, $p < .05$. While males show a greater preference for multiplayer modalities than females, this preference decreases over time, reaching levels below their female counterparts by the age of 35.

Within subjects, only a significant effect of modality ($F(1, 504) = 86.70$, $p < .001$) was found, confirming that within genre, single-player modalities are played to a greater extent than multiplayer.

Genre preferences across age and gender: To examine genre preferences across age and gender, a repeated measures ANOVA was conducted. In order

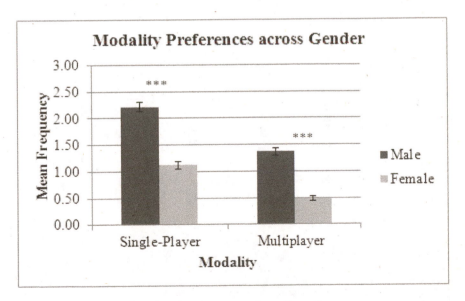

Figure K-5 Modality preferences across gender collapsed across game types (error bars represent standard error) ($N = 514$) ***$p < .001$

to evaluate genre preferences for all eight genres, the six game genres that spanned modality (FPS, RPG, sim, RTS, TBS, and puzzle) were collapsed, and averaged, prior to analysis, to produce a score that would represent a participant's genre preference regardless of modality.

A significant main effect of gender, $F(1, 504) = 33.77$, $p < .001$, but not age ($p = .66$, ns), was found. An interaction between gender and age, $F(4, 504) = 2.65$, $p < .05$, also emerged. Multivariate ANOVA analyses revealed this interaction to be evident only within the FPS genre ($p < .01$). For FPSs, males show an overall preference; however, this gradually decreases over time.

Within subjects, Mauchly's test indicated that the assumption of sphericity had been violated ($p < .001$). Therefore, the following values have been adjusted using the Greenhouse-Geisser corrections. A significant main effect of genre, $F(5.69, 2872.31) = 32.00$, $p < .001$, was found. Overall, RPG was the most preferred genre, followed by FPS and puzzle games. No significant differences were found for sim, RTS, and TBS games, while sports and party games were the two genres with the lowest frequency of all eight categories.

A significant interaction between genre and gender ($F = 10.64$, $p < .001$), and genre and age ($F = 1.98$, $p < .01$), was also found. Pairwise comparisons revealed gender differences within most genres, with males reporting a greater preference for FPS, RPG, RTS, TBS, and sports games (F's > 27, p's $< .001$). No gender differences were found for sim, puzzle, or party games (see Figure K-6). Interaction effects between age and genre showed no consistent patterns.

To further examine the nature of the gender interactions, analyses were conducted within gender categories. Within male participants, Mauchly's

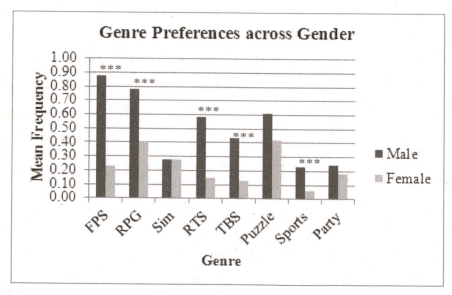

Figure K-6 Genre preferences across gender (collapsed across game types) ($N = 514$). ***$p < .001$

test indicated that the assumption of sphericity had been violated ($p < .001$); therefore, the following values have been adjusted using the Greenhouse-Geisser corrections. A significant main effect of genre, $F(5.66, 1591.02) = 24.370$, $p < .001$, but not age ($p = .28$, *ns*), and a significant interaction between game genre and age ($F = 2.38$, $p < .01$), was found. Pairwise comparisons revealed that among males, FPS and RPGs are preferred above all other genres, with RTS, TBS, and puzzle games being the second most preferred (p's $< .05$). Sim, sports, and party games were the least preferred among male participants. The interaction between genre and age can be seen within the FPS and RPG genres, as the overall preference for FPSs within the younger age groups (18 to 24) shifts to a preference for RPGs above all other genres between the ages of 25 and 29.

Within females, Mauchly's test again indicated that sphericity assumptions had been violated ($p < .001$); therefore, the figures reported here have been corrected using the Greenhouse-Geisser correction. A significant main effect of genre, $F(5.14, 1146.18) = 16.54$, $p < .001$, but not age ($p = .08$, *ns*), was found. No significant interactions between genre and age were found ($p = .58$, ns). Pairwise comparisons indicated a preference for RPG and puzzle games among women, with sim and FPS falling second. The sports genre was the least favorite among female participants.

REFERENCES

Brennan, K.A., Clark, C.L., & Shaver, P.R. (1998). Self-report measure of adult attachment: An integrative overview. In J.A. Simpson & W.S. Rholes (Eds.), *Attachment theory and close relationships* (pp. 46–76). New York: Guilford Press.

Ford, M. (1982). Social cognition and social competence in adolescence. *Developmental Psychology*, 18(3), 323–340. doi:10.1037/0012-1649.18.3.323

Riggio, R. (1989). *Manual for the Social Skills Inventory.* Palo Alto, CA: Consulting Psychologists Press.

Index